or

vood:

...movies—not sequels, prequels, or reboots—Lynda Obst explains why the movies we all loved growing up don't get made anymore. With her sharp wit, she gives an inside account of how the industry has changed but also offers hope that Hollywood will meet the challenges of the digital age and the global marketplace. If you love movies, this is a must read."

—Arianna Huffington

"A useful primer if you haven't quite figured out why so many blockbusters take place in China these days."

—*Forbes*

"A witty and frequently incisive look at a business that is attracting an ever more globalized and diverse audience by manufacturing increasingly homogenized content that can be sequelized, rebooted and monetized across a dizzying array of platforms."

—*The Wrap*

"Obst . . . casts a sharp eye over recent developments in Tinseltown. Depth of detail and shrewd illustrative examples make this a must-read for anyone interested in the movie business."

—*Kirkus Reviews*

"Obst's *Sleepless in Hollywood* [is] nothing if not informative and instructional about present-day Hollywood and perhaps even revelatory."

—Jeff Simon, *Buffalo News*

"Written in warm, conversational prose, Obst's tales from the movie front together offer an engrossing look at the state of the entertainment industry today."

—*Booklist*

"A wonderful textbook full of mysteries, loss and longing. I just couldn't stop reading it, even though I have never had movie-making impulses."

—Liz Smith, *Huffington Post*

ALSO BY LYNDA OBST

Hello, He Lied

LYNDA OBST

SLEEPLESS IN
HOLLYWOOD

Tales from the NEW ABNORMAL
in the Movie Business

Simon & Schuster Paperbacks
New York   London   Toronto   Sydney   New Delhi

Simon & Schuster Paperbacks
A Division of Simon & Schuster, Inc.
1230 Avenue of the Americas
New York, NY 10020

First Simon & Schuster trade paperback edition June 2014

SIMON & SCHUSTER PAPERBACKS and colophon are registered trademarks
of Simon & Schuster, Inc.

For information about special discounts for bulk purchases,
please contact Simon & Schuster Special Sales at
1-866-506-1949 or business@simonandschuster.com.

The Simon & Schuster Speakers Bureau can bring authors
to your live event. For more information or to book an event,
contact the Simon & Schuster Speakers Bureau at
1-866-248-3049 or visit our website at www.simonspeakers.com.

Designed by Akasha Archer

Manufactured in the United States of America

10 9 8 7 6 5 4 3 2 1

The Library of Congress has cataloged the hardcover edition as follows:

Obst, Lynda.
    Sleepless in Hollywood : tales from the new abnormal in the movie business /
Lynda Obst. — 1st ed.
        p.   cm.
    1. Motion picture industry—United States.   I. Title.
    PN1993.5.U6O29   2013
    384'.8'0973—dc23   201251638

ISBN 978-1-4767-2774-5
ISBN 978-1-4767-2775-2 (pbk)
ISBN 978-1-4767-2776-9 (ebook)

To Oly, who keeps me in the game with his wisdom, humor and tenacity, and is still the best trench-mate around.

To Sunny, Marlowe and Julie, who make Tuesday night my favorite night, so I remember what all the tenacity is for.

And to Nora, who died the day I finished. Now I have to plod on without her. I still try to imagine her telling me what to do and hear her fixing my sentences. Though, as ever, when I get it wrong it's not her fault.

CONTENTS

INTRODUCTION • xv

SCENE 1 • 1
THE NEW ABNORMAL

SCENE 2 • 34
THE GREAT CONTRACTION

SCENE 3 • 51
HAVE YOUR POPCORN WITH SOME CHOPSTICKS

SCENE 4 • 79
CREATING PREAWARENESS

SCENE 5 • 108
FROM PARAMOUNT TO PARANOIA

SCENE 6 • 162
THE CATASTROPHE: THE WRITERS' STRIKE OF 2007–8

SCENE 7 • 196
THE DIASPORA: THE GOLDEN AGE OF TELEVISION

SCENE 8 • 240
DOES THE FUTURE HAVE A FUTURE?

EPILOGUE • 265
2014: THE NEWS OF OUR DEATH HAS BEEN
GREATLY EXAGGERATED

ACKNOWLEDGMENTS • 273

SOURCES • 275

PHOTO CREDITS • 277

INDEX • 279

SLEEPLESS IN
HOLLYWOOD

INTRODUCTION

I first arrived in L.A. from New York in the early 1980s, a trained reporter, unhappily untethered from the *New York Times*. All my friends were still in New York City, along with everything else familiar to me. Hollywood was a strange new habitat where people appeared to lie for a living, thus the title of my memoir of surviving that shock, *Hello, He Lied*. By the time I started this book, all that was old hat.

By the mid-2000s, after sixteen movies and a nice share of hits and (luckily) fewer flops, my colleagues and I were undergoing something much weirder than lying. It had become harder and harder to get movies made, and I'd been steadily making movies for years. This wasn't just me or my studio, though we were certainly part of the story—there was something systemic going on that was changing what we could make. It seemed that whatever it was, it suddenly wasn't what I was selling and what I'd been successfully making. It was more than frustrating. It was catastrophic, and for many more people than just me. I had to figure it out.

My life and my work became part of the book. I started asking questions of every smart person I knew. Unlike a reporter, because I work and dine and live here (and intend to continue both eating and working here), my sources are my colleagues and friends, past and current—people I know well. I can't be as exhaustive as a reporter can be and speak to the multitudes of excellent sources whom I don't know, and might someday work with.

But my sources, some of the most important executives in

town—studio heads, marketing heads and the like—the players who turn the levers of this business and set its course, are relaxed, intimate and funny in their interviews for the same reason, and in these pages, you can get to know these people as I do. You can see them at this moment of transition, trying to create and open the movies they came into the business to make as the economic model of the industry shifts beneath them.

It took me a long time to write this book, mostly because it took me a long time to figure it out. At many moments when I thought I'd "gotten it," it was like Heraclitus's river: Just as I came to understand something, it changed, or as I wrote about it, it changed, or I captured the change, and then it changed again. And of course, living and working through "the most interesting of times," the Chinese curse warns you, slows you down. I tell the story as I suffered through it, survived it (hopefully), thought I cracked it and then began to see the light at the end of the tunnel.

LYNDA OBST—FILMOGRAPHY

1983 *Flashdance* (associate producer, as Lynda Rosen Obst)

1987 *Adventures in Babysitting* (producer)

1988 *Heartbreak Hotel* (producer)

1991 *The Fisher King* (producer)

1992 *This Is My Life* (producer)

1993 *Sleepless in Seattle* (executive producer)

1994 *Bad Girls* (executive producer)

1996 *One Fine Day* (producer)

1997 *Contact* (executive producer)

1998 *Hope Floats* (producer)

1998 *The Siege* (producer)

1999 *The '60s* (TV miniseries) (executive producer)

2001 *Someone Like You . . .* (producer)

2002 *Abandon* (producer)

2003 *How to Lose a Guy in 10 Days* (producer)

2009 *The Invention of Lying* (producer)

2010–13 *Hot in Cleveland* (TV series) (executive producer—66 episodes)

2012 *The Soul Man* (TV series) (executive producer—6 episodes)

2013 *Helix* (TV series) (executive producer—13 episodes) (shooting August, airing November 2013)

*No person who is enthusiastic about his work
has anything to fear from life.*

—Samuel Goldwyn

SCENE ONE

THE NEW ABNORMAL

I can trace the moment when I noticed that what seemed like normal was changing—that the ways we'd always done things since time immemorial (at least in the three decades since I came to Hollywood) were beginning to become obsolete. It was the death of what I now call the "Old Abnormal" and the birth of the "New."

I call them the Old Abnormal and the New Abnormal because Hollywood, let's face it, is never *actually* normal. Think of how bizarre the people are, for starters. Famous hairdressers, notable Israeli gunrunners, Russian gangsters, mothers who score on their daughters' successfully leaked sex-tape escapades, and Harvard grads who chase hip-hop stars and Laker Girls make a unique kind of melting pot. It boasts smart people galore with and without prestigious diplomas, and loves a craven con man with a new angle, a new pot of gold or a new look. It's an equal-opportunity exploiter of talent.

No wonder it draws such dysfunction: Lying is a critical job skill; poker is as good a starter course as film school. How else would you know that the line "Sandra Bullock wants to do this" really means "It's on her agent's desk," and "Three studios are bidding on this script" means "Everyone's passed but one buyer who hasn't answered yet." The language has a sublanguage, and there is no libretto. It's just plain Abnormal, and always has been.

I saw that some key aspects of the abnormal Hollywood I'd

come to love, or at least enjoy heartily, were changing into something new, but of course I didn't know what. It was when the long-stable Sherry Lansing/Jon Dolgen administration of Paramount, where I was working in 2001, began to teeter a bit as I was making *How to Lose a Guy in 10 Days,* a romantic comedy starring Kate Hudson and Matthew McConaughey about two players playing each other and losing the game but unwittingly winning love.

Forty-eight at the time, Sherry Lansing was tall and effortlessly glamorous, one of the few women in Hollywood whose face and body had never seen a needle or a knife. The first chairwoman of a major studio, she shattered a glass ceiling in 1992 that hasn't been mended since. Mentored by men and a mentor to women, she is that rare combination of a man's woman and a woman's woman at the same time.

Dolgen and Lansing were a great duo: She was class, he was crass. While Dolgen's screaming could be heard throughout the administration building, no one would ever get bad news in Sherry's office. (She had employees for that.) Dolgen's belligerence was as famous as Sherry's graciousness. The whole thing worked for them for a long time.

Sherry had been a big supporter of my little romantic comedy—she loved the script I'd developed with her team, and that helped me get it into production. But much to my surprise, it turned out that Paramount wasn't even paying for the movie. My real financier was a lovely guy named Winnie, who ran a German tax shelter. I found this out on the set when Winnie introduced himself to me and told me that Paramount had sold off their domestic and international box office rights to him to fund the relatively low cost of the movie ($40 million). Paramount kept only the DVD rights. But that, I understood, was how they often put together their movies, selling off the ancillary rights to keep their production costs down. This is called risk aversion. It either meant they thought the movie had no upside other than its DVD value, or that it was the only way Sherry could get the movie made at the time.

As the rest of the country veered from red alerts to orange alerts in the aftermath of 9/11—*Variety* headline: "Showbiz Rocked by Reel Life!"—I was absorbed in simpler problems, like casting a guy for Kate Hudson to lose in ten days. As rocked as we may have been—and we were rocked—the show must go on. I was going into production. But in the boardrooms and executive suites of Viacom, which owns Paramount, everything was getting very unsettled in a consequential way.

The year 2001, as we began the movie, turned out to be a profoundly transitional one, not just for America (and the world, in the wake of 9/11), but for the movie business as well. Looking back, it would seem that Paramount had been looking through the wrong end of the telescope, in keeping only the DVD rights in its sights and ignoring the world. It was the year of the first *Harry Potter* and the first *Shrek,* and the audiences were getting their first exposure to the brave new world of breakthrough special effects in CGI and animation. But the historical fiscal conservatism of Paramount meant they were ignoring most of the new special-effects-oriented scripts, created for this startling technology, starting to hit the town.

Paramount had a philosophy under Sherry Lansing and Jon Dolgen, and for a long time it had worked: Sherry chose pictures by following her gut, and then would make them for the lowest possible budget (and lower). She'd made *Forrest Gump* (giving Tom Hanks and director Robert Zemeckis a big piece of the profits in success, but little in up-front fees). She green-lighted Mel Gibson's Scottish epic and Oscar winner *Braveheart*. When Fox went way over budget on *Titanic* and needed a partner to finish the film, Sherry was able to say yes by buying domestic rights (U.S. and Canada) based on an overnight read. But it wasn't working anymore.

I felt plenty of tension on the studio lot from a string of recent flops* and bad word on the street. *Paramount's not buying anything! They're underbidding! Not bidding! Who's getting fired? What the hell are they making?* How to Lose a *what?* Everyone was smoking and speculating on the quad as always, but the joy of putting *How To Lose a Guy* together inured me to any drama behind the scenes.

But as our team made *How to Lose a Guy in 10 Days,* the fate of Paramount and Hollywood was beginning to undergo—I don't think it would be exaggerating to say—cataclysmic change. The studio that I had joined after six comfy, productive years at Fox was about to experience an enormous realignment due to both interior and exterior convulsions. Some studios had an easier time during the transition, because they were more prepared for the transformed landscape that lay ahead. Disney, for example, had revenue from its theme parks and cable and broadcast networks like ESPN and ABC, so it was variegated as a conglomerate and not dependent on its movie income. Fox was reaping profits from its wide international presence. As a global media company, it was aware early of the power of the global market and made the most of its international penetration in movies and in TV via its satellite network Star TV and its broadcast networks. Warner Bros. had its moneymaker, HBO, but had problems at the time as a result of its takeover by AOL (the squid eating the whale). The more a studio depended on the domestic movie business for its income, the harder the turn would be.

I think none had a hairpinier turn to make than Paramount, as they lost many and hustled many more overboard. Yet the New Abnormal that followed the convulsions has no better representative than the Paramount that emerged: Pictures are now chosen for reasons, we will see, based not on gut as in Sherry's day—or David

---

* *Vanilla Sky, Texas Rangers, Domestic Disturbance, Zoolander, Hardball, Rat Race, Lara Croft: Tomb Raider, Along Came a Spider, Down to Earth.*

O. Selznick's, for that matter—but on whether they are properties that can be marketed into international franchises. With *Iron Man, Mission: Impossible, Transformers,* and *Star Trek* all among its key international franchises, Paramount emerged from this long fray as a key player in the New Abnormal. And it all began to happen soon after Mr. Dolgen, the board at Viacom, and the rest of us were swept up in gale forces that weren't unlike the tornado that took Dorothy into Munchkinland. For us in the movie business, we landed not in little Munchkinland, for sure, but in giant Franchise-land. The New Abnormal.

In the past ten years or so, the studios have tried to patent a formula for surefire hits, and their product is filling your multiplex. They are what the industry calls "tentpoles": sequels, prequels, reboots. Origin stories with a brand-new cast like *The Amazing Spider-Man,* with Andrew Garfield and Emma Stone, and *X-Men: First Class,* in which James McAvoy plays the young Charles Xavier from the original *X-Men;* or brand-name multimillion-dollar megashots built on familiar properties like comic books (*The Avengers,* the *Dark Knight* trilogy, *Spider-Man, Thor, Captain America, Green Lantern*), or best-selling novels (à la *The Hunger Games, Harry Potter* or *Twilight,* and now *Fifty Shades of Grey*); remakes (*Planet of the Apes, The Thing*); fairy tales (*Alice in Wonderland* and its spawn, *Snow White and the Huntsman* and the failed twin *Mirror Mirror*); and video games (*Assassin's Creed, Call of Duty, World of Warcraft*). Handheld games born as iPhone apps like *Angry Birds* are now becoming properties-cum-movies, as are board games based on books (like *Jumanji*), or just plain games (like Hasbro's Battleship); and, of course, toys (Transformers, G.I. Joe). (Hasbro is a movie company as well as a toy company now.) These properties are meant to work with or without a star and have a built-in audience in the United States and overseas. They are developed inside the studios' development factories, designed by committee for surefire success.

A tentpole movie was once merely the stanchion that held the yearly studio circus calendar together: Big Christmas Movie. Big Easter Holiday Break Movie. Big Summer Movie. Each studio built what it called its "slate"—its compilation of yearly pictures— around these seasons because the greatest attendance was garnered during these distribution periods: Kids were out of school; families went to movies together; teens went in gaggles to malls. Business drove business drove business. If one theater was full, you would go to another, then return the next day for the movie you'd planned to see. Blockbusters and family movies were designed to position each studio to win each of these seasonal races like a studio Olympiad, and, like the Missile Defense System under Reagan, they had no cost-containment quotient. Win at all costs.

Around ten years ago, there was only one, at most two, tentpole from each studio each distribution season. But then things started to change. Inexorably, in the transition to the business model of the New Abnormal, the studios have grown their slates into a diet of pure tentpoles, with almost nothing in between. We producers fight for the precious diminishing space you could justifiably call the "in-between."

So the question is, with all these tentpoles, franchises, reboots and sequels, is there still room for movies in the movie business?

As we noticed in Oscar Season 2013, it is still the Old Abnormal for some: That is, movie stars like Ben Affleck and George Clooney, who made *Argo*—an original—and super-AAA directors like Steven Spielberg (with *Lincoln*) and Ang Lee (with *Life of Pi*) still get to make real movies, and thank heaven for it. Though the money is still tighter than before, the studios don't like to say no to these people. When they can't get them to make tentpoles, which they always try to get them to do—remember George Clooney in *Batman*? Or Ang Lee directing *The Hulk,* and of course Christopher Nolan's Batman trilogy—the studios will work with the stars' agendas and help finance their best projects.

After Kathryn Bigelow won the Oscar for *The Hurt Locker* (which made practically no money even after it won the Oscar), Sony financed her *Zero Dark Thirty,* and it is a commercial and critical success.

So James Cameron can make anything he wants; ditto Christopher Nolan and now Ben Affleck and George Clooney. The same is true of many others, whose mere participation in a movie makes it a marketable tentpole. Some studios will beg, borrow, or whittle down a budget to make these movies—and the audience is the better for it, so starved are they for fresh material. We need more movie stars who can produce and direct, and directors whose movies become Oscar-winning blockbusters. Can we live on this fancified diet alone? And will the trend thrive, or is it a temporary reaction to a starved domestic audience? And what of the rest of us, living off of Mt. Olympus?

This is one of the most significant differences between two eras—the Old Abnormal, roughly the 1980s through the early start of the decade, and the New Abnormal, from roughly 2008 on—though some forces began to congeal earlier. I have come to see these two eras as almost two different movie businesses. The differences are various, from what movies are produced to how we make them and for whom. The proliferation of giant franchises nearly year-round is both a sign of the end of the Old Abnormal and the imprimatur of the New Abnormal. The dearth of movies that used to fill the time between them is part of the collateral damage from the transition.

These huge tentpoles, $200-million-fueled missiles, are lined up on the studio distribution pads with their "must-have" famous names and launched like international thermonuclear devices toward foreign capitals where 3D is candy. International has come to be 70 percent of our total revenues in the New Abnormal. When I began in the Old Abnormal it was 20 percent.

The great great tentpole squall of May of 2011 was a dramatic—

if breathless for those of us with XX chromosomes—example of an in-between movie (one not designed for a summer release date) being tossed into a rough sea of big action movies: Judd Apatow's female comedy *Bridesmaids.* It was a movie with no stars to speak of, no preawareness, starring women, and likely to do bupkis abroad. What was the strategy? It was clearly counterprogramming for women. But was it an attempt to throw chick flicks overboard in the week of *Thor* to prove that women's movies couldn't swim with the sharks? It was the kind of summer that featured what I think of as "Man" movies—movies with titles that either contain the word "man" or at least feasibly could: *X-Men: First Class, Thor* and *Pirates of the Caribbean: On Stranger Tides;* all we were missing was Iron Man and Batman. How were four unknown (outside of television) women going to compete in this company?

This was the reality *Bridesmaids,* the unknown chick flick, faced on its May 13 release date. The weekend before, a sister romantic comedy, Kate Hudson's *Something Borrowed,* was flattened by the second week of Universal's *Fast Five,* the spectacularly successful action franchise about drag racers. It was still racking it up overseas and at home by spicing up its cast with the utterly brilliant addition of the popular action, and former wrestling, star Dwayne "The Rock" Johnson, and it showed no signs of slowing. *Thor,* opening directly against *Bridesmaids,* was expected to be a smash. It was tracking through the roof, as we say, expected to open at $60 million. Hiring "Shakespearean" Kenneth Branagh gave this Marvel silliness all the gravitas it needed to track well with what Hollywood marketing likes to call "older men": men over twenty-four. (Not just women get ageist angst around here.) It was going to bring in every male everywhere and their dates. By opening weekend, *Bridesmaids* was expected to open with $15 million at the box office at best.

If it performed as the tracking numbers suggested—between $15 million and $17 million—chicks were done for. Movies in the summer were expected to make $30 to $60 million on opening weekend to compete. *Bridesmaids,* made for a fraction of the cost of a normal summer movie, wouldn't have to reach this blockbuster bar. But it couldn't just fizzle out. How did this potential extinction come to pass? It's like we all went to sleep one day in Hollywood and woke up living in Tentpole City.

There is obviously more at stake here than bloody (well, not bloody, unfortunately for sales) chick flicks. The question really was, can the original movie with a good story get made for its own sake in today's Hollywood, as it could when I started? Could I get *The Fisher King* made with Terry Gilliam (the phenomenally talented and eccentric director of movies like *Brazil, Monty Python and the Holy Grail* and *12 Monkeys*) and the best script I ever had? (Ha! No way!)

When the late, great producer Laura Ziskin was asked by the *Hollywood Reporter* which of her great movies before *Spider-Man* she couldn't get made now—including the Kevin Costner political thriller *No Way Out* and Julia Roberts's seminal breakout hit, *Pretty Woman,* she answered, "None of them."

MOVIES THAT WOULD NEVER GET MADE IN THE NEW ABNORMAL
(EXCEPT AS TINY INDIES WE WILL CALL "TADPOLES")

Field of Dreams
Pitch: It's about a guy who builds a baseball field in Iowa to bring back his dead dad. *Pass.*

Forrest Gump
Pitch: A totally stupid, nice guy travels all over the world, selling shrimp and running into famous people as he looks for his screwed-up girlfriend—who is kinda over him, if she was ever into him. *Outta here.*

The Fisher King

Pitch: A homeless man finds redemption for a radio shock jock. *Can I get back to you on that? At Sundance?*

Driving Miss Daisy

Pitch: A happy and wise chauffeur in the South has an endearing relationship with his elderly charge. *Exactly how "elderly" are we talking?*

The Big Chill

Pitch: A reunion of sixties best friends celebrating their dead bestie. *So, wait, is it actually* set *in the sixties?*

The Graduate

Pitch: A returning college graduate has an affair with the wife of his father's law partner and runs away with her daughter. *Are you French?* Or, *Um, okay, we're not making Swedish movies here, unless they're by Stieg Larsson.*

Moonstruck

Pitch: An unlucky widow falls in love with her fiancé's brother. Romantic magic ensues. *You lost me at "widow" and nearly killed me at "romantic magic."*

I could go on, but it just gets increasingly obvious and depressing that the more we love the movie, the less likely it would get made now, at least in the studio system.

Everything was off-the-charts Abnormal, and we were still trying to play a game that wasn't playable anymore. It was a weird, changing, Darwinian time. Conditions were changing as fast as I could figure them out, and then would change again. Movies are now an endangered species in the very place that makes them. My son Oly, who now works as a literary manager at 3 Arts, echoed the sentiment: "Making a movie because it's good is so 2003, Mom." It struck me that *risk taking* itself was at stake. Hollywood, a town built by mavericks and rebels and mobsters, risk takers all, had now become utterly risk-averse. The very fact that a broad comedy like *Bridesmaids*—best friends coping with one's wedding, accompanied by actual pooping in a sink—had fallen into the category of risk taking was a sign of extreme distress.

This change in no way seemed temporary. It was strange and difficult in a systemic way that was killing producers and writers who weren't on the studios' new, hardwired agenda. When and how did this happen exactly?

We all knew that the studios had been pleading poverty for a while—since DVD sales had begun collapsing in the wake of the technological changes that brought piracy and Netflix et al. But who *really* believed their sob stories? They were *studios,* for crying out loud! If they were so poor, why were they making more wildly expensive movies and fewer of them? It seemed counterintuitive.

But there they were, right before us, the rules of a New Abnormal that could be easily discerned—a formula that every studio seemed to be following, and one which sometimes worked like gangbusters: The top seven movies in 2011 were all sequels (*Harry Potter and the Deathly Hallows 2, Transformers 3, Twilight Saga: Breaking Dawn 1, The Hangover 2, Pirates 4, Fast Five* and *Cars 2*). The model for all of this in the movies was *Star Wars,** from which George Lucas sprung six original movie blockbusters, including sequels, an origin story and sequels to the origin story. Comic-book writers had been doing this for years.

The studios took the formula and ran with it. They were shooting the moon, and often they hit the target. And when they hit, they

---

* *Star Wars: Episode IV—A New Hope* (1977), *Star Wars: Episode V—The Empire Strikes Back* (1980), *Star Wars: Episode VI—Return of the Jedi* (1983), *Star Wars: Episode I—The Phantom Menace* (1999), *Star Wars: Episode II—Attack of the Clones* (2002), *Star Wars: Episode III—Revenge of the Sith* (2005).

hit big. But how and when did they figure all this out? And what, exactly, *did* they figure out? There seemed to be three key components:

1. You must have heard of the Title before; it must have *preawareness.*
2. It must sell overseas.
3. It should generate a Franchise and/or Sequel (also a factor of 1 and 2).

What is the difference between a tentpole and a franchise? A franchise is the point of a tentpole: The first movie must make enough money to justify a sequel. If the sequel performs well enough, then you have another and another and *voilà*—you have a franchise. One wildly successful version is the aforementioned *Fast and the Furious,* which didn't have a famous title to begin with, but has no signs of reducing velocity after five installments. Another is *Pirates of the Caribbean*—based on a ride at Disneyland and Disneyworld—which is on its fifth iteration. *Transformers,* based on the alien car toys from Hasbro, has had three big hits at the bat and is still a player. *Harry Potter,* needless to say, had all the material for its sequels when Warner Bros. bought the property, and is, tragically for Warner Bros., now *finito.*

Back in the Old Abnormal, I used to make up movies with my favorite writers and pitch those ideas to the studios. If an idea was funny, fresh and could *potentially* attract talent (read: stars or A-list director) it could mean a sale. I used to be able to buy a book that had sold under a million copies and adapt it to sell to studios just because it had a great story. No more.

It was clear from talking to peers and executives that much, much more than the chick flick was on the ropes. Comedy was in trouble. It was dire for drama. But above all, it was the movie itself: the original one-off, nonsequel, nonremake, noncomic-book-franchise piece of business. That's what I have come to realize. This isn't about self-interest, my changing career, or what I can or can't get made anymore; this is about an industry that for more than half a century has been the caretaker of an indigenous art form possibly relinquishing responsibility for that art form altogether. Sure, it was always show *business,* never show *art.* But now it is *business* business. More and more, the Oscars are dominated by the independents. The studios seem to wake up once a year, don their finest and collectively remember what they are making isn't product or money, but film. Then they do a contrite walk of shame in the morning, and have amnesia by lunch. Movies are now an endangered species here.

The process by which this came to be is the knot that I will attempt to unravel in this book. This is a body-blow-by-body-blow account of what happened here during the past ten years that so fundamentally changed the movie business and where we are headed from here. People I started with in the business, classic producers and writers, look at me and then stare up into the sky. Why is it so different? Why has it become bone-crunchingly hard and so much less fun?

At least I can pin down one thing. It's one small step for womankind and the one-off nonsequel movie if *Bridesmaids* can open in this sea of testosterone and doubting Thomases. And I wasn't alone in my rooting.

Everyone in town reads the "tracking reports" like handicappers read the *Daily Racing Form,* but you should have seen the novice female screenwriters trying to figure out how to interpret the hieroglyphics two weeks before *Bridesmaids* opened. These daily and weekly reports are done by well-known outside market research firms as well as the marketing departments of the studios, and they are compared and averaged for outliers, similar to election polling. They measure "definite interest" in seeing a movie, "first choice" (i.e., "What do you want to see most this weekend?")

and "awareness" of the movie ("How many of you know it's out there?").

At first *Bridesmaids* tracked well. Then it seemed to "flatten," which means it didn't go up, even though they added TV spots. This stumped everyone. I checked in with my trusted source and colleague, Kevin Goetz, Hollywood's go-to market research guru in times of crisis.

Kevin Goetz is a marketing research legend, one of those guys many of us trust with interpreting the numbers and making the wise calls on inside-Hollywood baseball. He's been with most of the top market research companies, and I've had the pleasure of working with him on the research testing of almost all my movies. He is cherubic-looking, well liked and cutting-edge. You want him in the trenches when you need to figure out how to fix your picture or your marketing message, when your tracking—as with *Bridesmaids*—suddenly stalls out.

As I drove to work Thursday of opening week, I called Kevin: "So, Kev, how's *Bridesmaids* going to do this weekend?"

"Looks like it could be as low as fifteen. Could go high teens, if it picks up some big buzz from word of mouth. They came on strong but then they stalled, and nothing seems to be happening right now."

This is what all the prognosticators were saying.

"Nothing?" I asked, then added, "Call me if you see any buzz picking up as we get closer." God only knows what prevented me from bumping into the car in front of me. All the buzz was the same—and it wasn't good.

In Hollywood, "buzz" is a semitechnical term that means "everyone is talking about this." It can result from a multitude of things: word of mouth, great reviews, sudden media attention, a spike in tracking or an amazing television spot that clicks with the audience. There can also be bad buzz, but that's another thing: Everyone was saying that *John Carter*—the sci-fi fantasy flop—would be terrible months before anyone had seen a frame. *Gigli*—starring then couple Ben Affleck and Jennifer Lopez—provoked barely suppressed giggles around the globe even before it opened to no business whatsoever. That is bad buzz.

But good buzz is hard to predict and hard to generate, especially in a noisy summer market full of highly expensive advertising. Who knew what the buzz on *Bridesmaids* would be? It would have to be money to compete against the oncoming thunderous *Thor.*

My gal pals and I were placing wagers and consulting fortune-tellers and doing our own preawareness grassroots marketing. On the night the movie opened, I organized a small army with my dear girlfriend screenwriter Kiwi Smith (*Legally Blonde*). If I'm defined by *Hello, He Lied* because the title of my last book displays my cynicism, she's defined as "Kiwi Loves You" because her Twitter handle shows her refusal to see the dark side. We're a good team. Curly haired, slightly haywire, yet seductive to every gender, Kiwi is an ardent cheerleader for girl power.

Kiwi sent a rallying message to her entire email list that was so infectious, I sent it to my buddy Rebecca Traister at Salon.com, where it then did its social-networking proliferating thing. Kiwi was already a mentor and cottage industry to many young writers, and the thousands on her list reached out to their thousands to help us create a little femme-movie-ment. We convened a concerned (read "panicked") group of female writers, studio execs and actresses to meet first for dinner and drinks and then head to the ArcLight Hollywood theater on Sunset Boulevard, where we would meet with, we hoped, a larger group of female industry friends. Over dinner, texts were flying in from Kristen Wiig's manager that the matinees on the East Coast were "way overperforming expectations!" She knew that her client's life was about to change. At that point, Kristen was known nationally as part of the *Saturday Night Live* ensemble, but opening a movie would transform her career. Some of us veterans knew that overperforming matinees meant Friday night would be even better, Saturday more so. We started to throw back tequilas.

A gaggle of us, now tipsy, padded into the lobby, greeting flocks of other women and girls, until we found ourselves in a theater filled with—hallelujah, is this happening?!—"event-movie" electricity. Amid the raucous groups of girls (apparently we weren't the only ones who had this "get drunk with your GFs and go see *Bridesmaids*" idea) were an amazing number of guys—almost half the theater. In delighted shock, we smiled and waved to them. "We love you, *Bridesmaids* guys!"

By Monday morning (May 17, 2011) the number was $24.5 million, *$10* million more than was predicted. The fact that the numbers kept going up over the weekend meant that the word of mouth was great. Women had a hit. We claimed this as ours. We gave thanks that night that a genre had possibly survived.

This meant something big.

When an inexpensive ($32.5 million) original movie starring barely known women from television, whose stillborn death was predicted by all, survives and has legs in the hostile concrete jungle of noisy sequels and reboots, it is a cause célèbre. We felt this way about *The Help, The Town, The Fighter* and *Black Swan,* and about *Argo* and *The Silver Linings Playbook* this past year. We just want more original movies made because they are good. Because they are funny or smart and are being made by talented people. Where are they? Why are they so rare?

Why do movies like the first *Hangover* and *Bridesmaids* so surprise the studios? They are both classic high-concept ideas, which was the coin of the realm of the Old Abnormal. *The Hangover* is about four best friends at a bachelor party who get wasted and lost in Las Vegas and wake up in a hotel room with Mike Tyson's tiger and no groom. They have to find him and get him back in time for his wedding. It was something that would have sold in a comedy pitch by two writers in baseball caps. But now, in the New Abnormal, these movies that get made for under $40 million with no stars are the counterexamples, what the industry calls "lightning in a bottle." When they work, it seems like magic. But it's not magic. These writer-created original movies are simply funny. Finding them requires judgment, intensive script development, discerning writer and director choices and good casting—craft, in other words. Then unknown, the stars of *The Hangover* were paid under a million dollars for the first movie. Now each star can get a movie green-lit on his own and is getting $15 million for *The Hangover Part III*.

On the Monday morning after the astonishing first weekend of *Bridesmaids* (*Hangover*'s twin sister—four unknown women in a high-concept comedy), everybody was knocked on their collective asses, and as is common with paradigm shifts, many things happened.

The first thing that happened was that Kristen Wiig became a star.

Second, Melissa McCarthy, of CBS's *Mike and Molly,* who gave a breakout performance in the movie, became its second new star and is now toplining comedies.

Third, chick flicks were getting a second look all over town.

Fourth, 50,000 R-rated female buddy comedies showed up on managers' desks. However, it was a temporary reprieve. Much to our consternation, it did not presage a resurgence of chick flicks, romantic comedies, or even four-women buddy comedies. The success seemed to affect only the stars.

When an original comedy like *The Hangover,* a great idea with no preawareness and no huge stars, works so well—becoming a wildly successful sleeper hit that then spawns a sequel and perhaps a franchise—it could create a model that allows for other ideas like *Bridesmaids* to get made. And then movies like *Bridesmaids* allow for crazy, funny, broad movies to get a second look. I went to discuss this thought with pal Kevin Goetz, who had warned me of the industry's low expectations for the opening weekend of *Bridesmaids*.

We sat down to lunch at the South Beverly Grill, which has the best crab cakes in town. I wanted to razz him a little about *Bridesmaids,* but I also wanted the benefit of his insight. "Why do you think *Bridesmaids* overperformed? Don't you think it reflects a hunger for originals out there?"

"I think there was some late word of mouth on the picture that the tracking never picked up."

"But look, Kev," I shot back, "there were fifteen comments on the blogs this morning about sequel fatigue—these movies that are made for two hundred million dollars that are basically built for international. The movie stars won't be in them. They realize they're basically making product. Nobody comes to America to be a star in Russia and China. Who wants to be in that business? Penélope Cruz left Spain to be a star here, not in China. Eventually, these monstrosities of product will become burdensome for the actor to reboot, if not the studio. They will have to turn into *Law & Order:* a new cast each time, and a product where the title is bigger than the star."

Kevin smiled. "They don't need stars in Russia and China. They don't care about them."

I started to get it. So they can invent stars for tentpoles, pay them less up front and tie them in to infinite options for sequels, like with Chris Hemsworth in *Thor.* The franchise is the star and the movie already costs a fortune.

Kevin answered slyly, "I think both of us know that the reason to cast Chris Hemsworth as Thor originally had nothing to do with his numbers internationally."

And it was clear as a bell. "But now he has huge international numbers that allow him to make the other movies he wants."

Bingo.

This is what happens when the title is more important than the star, like with the James Bond franchise. And this is the reason for reboots: If they start over, they don't have to keep upping the salary of the lead.

Kevin said, "The studios are in the branded carnival business. Their job is to make amusement park rides."

"Really?" I asked. "We're in the amusement park business?"

He looked at me as if I were his very slow half sister visiting from Iowa. "Lynda. Never lose yourself. Don't forget this: We're in a business. If we can make six-hundred-forty-billion-dollar rides, why would we want to make two-hundred-forty-billion-dollar rides? It's a business. Widgets."

I have always known we were in a business, but making "widgets" had never occurred to me. I love movies, and a few $240 million rides had served me fairly well so far. The current contempt for that kind of profit struck me as deeply problematic.

This grand slam sensibility, along with the economic doom that caused it, has swiftly and fundamentally changed the culture we live in here in Tinseltown. I will show how in this section using *some* hyperbole, though not much.

CULTURE CHANGES OF THE NEW ABNORMAL

Casting in the Old Abnormal

Here's a bad version that gives a good idea of what changed.

In the Old Abnormal, you could have a really substantial casting fight:

GUY EXEC: I would never fuck her.
HIS BOSS: How old is she? A hundred?
CHICK PRODUCER: *(a laugh covering her alarm)* I think she's brilliant. But if you guys hate her . . .

FEMALE CASTING DIRECTOR: *(changing the subject)* What about Dude Z for the love interest? Marty just signed him for his next picture.

CHICK PRODUCER: He's hot!

GUY EXEC: He's so gay!

CASTING DIRECTOR: Do you mean literally?!

GUY EXEC: No, I just mean, like, he's so gay, like I would never see a movie he's in.

CASTING DIRECTOR: Let me send you some tape.

Casting in the New Abnormal

STUDIO HEAD: Who have you got for the guy?

DIRECTOR: I've been talking with Ray Liotta.

(Everyone stares at him as if he were from Mars.)

PRODUCER: He meant Robert Downey.

INTERNATIONAL MARKETING: He's worth thirty in Asia alone since *Iron Man*.

(Studio Head smiles, relieved. Emotionally joins the meeting.)

GUY EXEC: He's booked for two years. How's that possible?

STUDIO HEAD: We'll wait.

(Director sinks in his chair, emotionally departs meeting.)

INTERNATIONAL MARKETING: We break even before we open. Not counting Russia and China.

STUDIO HEAD: Who does? He's great in Europe and Japan too. Let's wait. We don't need the picture this year.

(Producer emotionally departs meeting.)

DOMESTIC MARKETING: Who's the girl? Hugh Jackman's daughter?

PRODUCER: *(to Studio Head)* You want cheap, or you want to spend money?

GUY EXEC: Why don't we get some Victoria's Secret model and save the money for the effects?

DOMESTIC MARKETING: Cameron Diaz or Emma Stone. I want some humor on the marquee.
PRODUCER: But it's a thriller.
DOMESTIC MARKETING: You make it, I'll tell you how to sell it.

As I've illustrated, there were urbane and constructive conversations (pardon my nostalgic interpretation) in the Old Abnormal, wherein everyone had a say and some sort of creativity was the order of the day. We all understood that these things were subjective, and we took chemistry and age into account, as you can see.

In the New Abnormal version, the age range between Emma Stone (*The Help* and *Superbad*) and Cameron Diaz (*Bad Teacher, There's Something About Mary*) is almost twenty years. Also note that there was no casting director in the room to point out that Cameron Diaz should play Hugh's wife, not his daughter. Domestic and international marketing make these key decisions much of the time, unless Steven Spielberg, David Fincher, or some other directing god is at the helm.

In the Old Abnormal there was always a ballsy, smart casting director in the room, originally from New York, with pictures and data on credits and ages. Usually a "she," she knew every New York actor, every director the actor in question had worked with and critical biographical gossip about the actor, not to mention a cheaper but great alternative for every part. At the studios now, her main function is simply to make the actors' deals after they have been chosen. (There are still some great casting directors working hard with the A-list directors right now, discovering actors and making subtle choices. Thank God.)

In the Old Abnormal, when we were casting pictures based on casting criteria, she was a key part of the discussion. At least for one moment during our profane conversations, "chops"—actual acting talent—came up. Chops conversations are the art of casting, involving the nuances of various specific performances.

With good studio heads, chops were always important. With good directors, even more so.

Example:

STUDIO HEAD: Does he have any chops?

CASTING DIRECTOR: I never thought so, but I saw his screen test for *Brokeback Mountain** and he blew my mind. He was all over that part. He was depressed. He was subtle. He was big where he needed to be.

EXEC: But he didn't get the part, did he? I found him wooden in *Toy Story*.

CASTING DIRECTOR: But he was playing a tin soldier. And it was animated.

PITCHES: A PRACTICE

Another Casualty of New Abnormal

Another casualty of the New Abnormal that forever changed the culture of Hollywood is the now-almost-extinct pitch meeting. Pitch meetings were the way we met and creatively played with one another; it was our commercial and social interaction—plus, there could be a prize at the end called a *sale*! With the studios' New Abnormal abstinence policies in regard to development spending and lack of interest in original ideas, this custom, which was a huge part of our work and social life, is now gone with the cold wind. The entire content of the workdays of execs, producers and writers has changed with it.

When there was extra money in the system, we all spent much

---

* Starring Heath Ledger and Jake Gyllenhaal; the story of a forbidden and secretive relationship between two cowboys over the years.

of our week collaborating on and then pitching new ideas for movies to the studios. Idea plus hot writer-producer equaled pitch equaled possible movie. But now, with their concentration on tentpoles for the international market, the studios know they are unlikely to find a "big title" in a pitch from a young writer with fresh ideas. Mattel and Marvel are better options.

In the Old Abnormal, studios vied for the hot new idea or writer they were hearing about from agents, and bidding wars sometimes broke out for them. (More gallows laughter.) Fifty percent of a producer's job and 75 percent of a writer's livelihood was a practice that subsided slightly and then finally stopped (with rare exceptions) in the aftermath of the 2008 writers' strike. But pitch meetings were once the superfood of the life of Hollywood. They made the town interactive, personal and social, and flushed ideas in and out of its system and into the market.

I met most of the writers I know through pitches. Most of my Los Angeles social life comes from the past twenty years of pitches and scripts (and sometimes even movies!). *Flashdance* started as a pitch, and Dawn Steel, who helped get that movie made at Paramount, became my best friend and ally, and eventually made me a producer. I pitched over half of my movies to studios first as ideas with writers, including *One Fine Day* and *The Siege*. I remember making up *One Fine Day:* I was raising my young son at the time and thinking, The only way I am ever going to meet a guy is if I literally run into him on a field trip. So I pitched the idea of a single mother on a difficult day at work who misses her child's field trip at the same time as a single dad does, and they chase the field trip around NYC together with their kids, falling in love—first to Michelle Pfeiffer, who became my partner, and then to Fox. We were all thrilled to cast George Clooney, who had to commute from the set of *ER*—which was only a problem the day he got a black eye at lunch playing basketball with the grips and I had to return him to L.A. with a shiner.

The Siege was based on a series of articles about the 1993 World Trade Center bombing in the *New York Times* by reporter Tim Weiner. I wondered what would happen to the civil rights of New Yorkers if a bigger threat stopped the city. I brought it to Ed Zwick, and we pitched it to Fox and Denzel Washington, as they had just made *Glory* together, for which Denzel had won his first Oscar. This is how we worked: Pitches were a vital life force of creativity that coursed through the bloodstream of the industry, pushing us to create new ideas with new minds. They stimulated the market, rendering the industry and each studio less of a bubble.

We got to know our generation and a younger generation. We got to know funny people and brilliant people. This was the fuel of development. A writer made a good living out of pitches that he sold that were never made. (But could have been, and might still be.) The studio now calls that fat. Writers called it a mortgage.

The absence of the pitch has radically changed the lives of all Hollywood execs, producers and writers. I imagine fewer dates, romances, marriages and partnerships, because that's how all of us met! (Of course, there was no Match.com, so you had to actually meet.) Everyone has fewer projects stewing, and there are precious few opportunities to make up new ideas and collaborate with your new or best friends.

To take you back to the Old Abnormal, or to rare moments within the New:

A pitch meeting consists of a team composed of a producer and a writer (or multiple writers) and another team of studio executives led by an alpha, in whose office it takes place. The producer-writer team practices for weeks before the event—a transactional-theater-meets-ritualized-mini-cocktail-party, sans alcohol. The drink is always bottled water, and the writers wear baseball caps, while the producer (unless part of a comedy writers' consortium) dresses up a bit more, in a nod of respect to the execs, and also to prove we can still afford couture.

The pitch has four stages:

THE PREP: The producer warms the room. There is much talk of family, dating, boyfriends, playoffs if the season justifies it, vacations and industry gossip (the harmless kind).

THE WIND-UP: The beginning of the segue into the idea. The wind-up is always led by the producer (or director if he or she is there) and prepares the execs for the tone of the pitch. It should contain a real or allegedly real event that is either autobiographical or ripped from the headlines that sets up the idea. Then the producer completes the brilliant segue, passing the baton to the writers.

THE CONCEPT: This is when the writers take over. They perform the theater bit of the pitch, which they've often memorized.

This is done in sketch format and is pretimed in rehearsal. The sometimes smiling, sometimes phlegmatic execs have short attention spans, and the moguls they in turn pitch to have even shorter ones.

THE WRAP-UP: This is the opportunity for the producer to lay out the way the movie fits into the marketplace, peppering it with examples of hot casting ideas and specific similar hits sampled for each studio. "It's *Tootsie*-meets–*Ocean's Eleven*!" Then you leave. Fast.

In the New Abnormal, whatever pitches are going in to the studios are accompanied by an array of materials: a reel of effects, a short film, a poster, a business prospective, or even a newly commissioned graphic novel. This is a virtual campaign the team must mount—out of pocket—to prove to the executive the commercial potential of the idea and its possible promotion strategies. Little is left to the imagination.

What the writer says is secondary to the campaign's ability to hook the execs with its potential big bull's-eye—its marketability. That is, if the team can get through the door in the first place.

Every so often in the New Abnormal, a studio decides they're open to a pitch. (In June of 2012, studios bought two, one in multiple bidding! A cause célèbre worth reporting.) In 2009, the studios were taken with Liam Neeson's *Taken*. ("They took his daughter. He has ninety-six hours to get her back.") It grossed $145 million domestically and $82 million internationally, and it cost $25 million to make. This looked like a "model," not a fluke. The studios put out the word that they were hungry for like-minded movies. It worked internationally, it worked domestically, it could be cloned, and Liam Neeson was cheap (then). The whole model could be done five hundred different ways and could be made for a reasonable price. After every conceivable family member was set up in an Insta-pitch ("They stole his mother. He has ninety-six hours to get her back." "They stole her husband," et al., ad infinitum). The first semi-iteration was released in 2011: *Abduction,* with Taylor Lautner (of *Twilight* fame, huge numbers internationally). It flopped, because it forgot to be about kidnapping his daughter or sister and was instead about something else too complicated to relay. While *Taken 2,* actually *with* Liam Neeson, was in production, it didn't deter three thousand producers and financiers from trying to clone it every other way imaginable. The sequel was finally released by Fox and producer Luc Besson, who assumes ownership of the movie four years after its original release in October 2012. The original *Taken* budget was $25 million, and Liam Neeson was paid $5 million to make the film—whereas *Taken 2* has an estimated budget of $80 million, and Neeson's fee is "not reported," which loosely translates to "so high the agent will not use it as a future 'quote'"—i.e., precedent—for other pictures: a considerable multiple of $5 million. On the weekend of October 7, 2012, *Taken 2* took in a huge $50 million domestic at the box office, the biggest weekend since *The Dark Knight Rises*. The former one-off thriller is certainly now a franchise for Fox, and every member of CIA agent Neeson's (Bryan Mills's) extended family will be kidnapped in *Taken 3, 4,* and *5.*

The New Abnormal, with its fewer movies and pitch meetings, its tiny expense accounts, and its centralized buying in the executive and marketing suites, has transformed the jobs of execs, agents and producers, as well as the whole process of how movies are bought and developed. All the lively interaction that went on between execs and producers to generate alliances and commerce, all the dinners and power lunches, went kapoof! Where are they? What happened? How did the rocking glamour capital of the world end up with execs acting like nerds from Silicon Valley? What transformed the lifestyles of the rich and famous, or almost rich and striving to be famous? Every portal became a wall. Business went indoors, and the thrill of meeting new people, forging new alliances and making up movies with new friends every month was gone.

A DAY IN THE LIFE OF THE NEW ABNORMAL: ONLINE

While pitches haven't been selling in the New Abnormal, a YouTube video by an unknown director can suddenly blow up on the marketplace, and there will be three studios bidding for it. (Without having yet met the director!) That would never have happened in the Old Abnormal, because there was no YouTube. Maybe execs are busy watching YouTube instead of hearing pitches. Our work is virtual.

Picture this:

The exec is in his office, surfing the net, between studio

meetings. He can get everything online, even "content," the New Abnormal word for material that eventuates on some device in the online universe. He gets his morning news on Deadline Hollywood, the compulsively read news blog that has replaced industry trades like *Variety* from the Old Abnormal. He checks into the Huffington Post for a sec. Then he goes to work, but not like we used to: He's still online. He gets director and writer ideas for his projects from freely shared online lists compiled by a multitude of execs, while we used to make them up from scratch. They get other vital data online, like whose recently turned-in Disney script "tanked," what director dropped out of what project, etc., via "tracking boards," also online. None of this used to exist, since we had no computers to speak of. (Okay, maybe we had computers, but they linked to nothing.) We created our own directors and writers lists from analog books, which led to mistakes like pitching my bosses several writers who turned out to be dead.

The exec checks into the tracking boards—email groups on Yahoo! or Google or on coveted private email lists—written by assistants, junior execs, agents and their assistants, all of whom are privy to way more chitchat than I am. The tracking boards are like an industry "cloud" brain. The exec goes on the boards for gossip: Who is getting fired? Promoted? What sold yesterday? We used to speak on the phone to hear this stuff. Then the exec goes to IMDb, the definitive Web site for credits, and he goes to Google or Wikipedia for any development content–type info he needs for a meeting. He is online so much, he emails much more than he calls. A call starts to feel like an intrusion.

With fewer pitches to hear, he or she has more time to do ever more work online. Research! Look for books! New Young Adult (YA) vampire series! This is a treasure trove of great ideas. YA is where the *Hunger Games* and *Twilight* series came from. Why talk to people when there are graphic novel sites?! Who needs pitches?

One exception to this new model is Comic-Con, when the town

empties for two days to promote its *-Man* movies and meet its fan-boys. Comic-Con has evolved from what was once a nerdy comic-book gathering to a huge, multimedia, star-laden promotional juggernaut for the fans, studios and gaming industry, where the next year's blockbusters are teased, promoted and fanned out to an ardent and important base of critical raving-mad word-of-mouth monsters who can make or break the industry's products. Everyone except me is in San Diego for two days.

And then there's the Soho House, a club perfectly located at Doheny and Sunset—which would be the center of town if there were one—where people show off their new clothes and prove they are still alive; but alas, to get in, you must be a member. Even at the Soho House, if guests are not (barely) eating or at the bar, they are on their computers or checking their iPhones.

While online, the exec can study multiplatform systems! And search for new chicks to cast on OkCupid or Match.com! Speaking of Match.com, so much of the business transpires over email, it's like dating, or what's left of it. You could stay in your bedroom in your sweats and go online and work—or pretend you're dating.

RARE MOMENTS WHERE OLD ABNORMAL AND NEW ABNORMAL MERGE

There are rare moments these days when things are suddenly the same as they used to be in the Old Abnormal. Of course, getting a green light is the same, as is the first day of production. But those are personal. There are times when we are all one dysfunctional family. Our traditional holiday, when we dress up like it's New Year's Eve and kiss each other on both cheeks and everyone comes out of the woodwork for good or for bad, is Awards Season. Then, for about a month's worth of parties, we see all our crazy uncles in the Academy whom we haven't seen since last year, or fired execs we forgot to call, or old frenemies, or the great face-lift a mogul's wife is displaying for the first time in public. These parties are supposed to gain our votes for the intended honoree by feeding us hors d'oeuvres as the nominees or intended nominees spread their fairy dust on us. This has been going on, with various Academy rule changes regarding who foots the bill, since . . . well, forever.

At these moments we can feel much of the distinction between the Old Abnormal and the New Abnormal twinkle away in the presence of the stars; our sense of community and our optimism are reborn with each new season. It is indeed our New Year. We make resolutions. We drink. We kiss people we don't like; we decide we like them after all. We make lunch dates.

"FRIENDING" IN THE NEW ABNORMAL

Over the last six months, my girlfriend Meredith (a talent agent at ICM, a blazing redhead with a toddler) and I have been trying to meet for lunch. So far, our efforts have been fruitless. Our assistants have exchanged 145 calls and 63 emails. Last week, we were on for 3 p.m., but I had to push to 4:30. She canceled. She rescheduled today. And I canceled: network notes call. This is the new relationship. The path to hell, my mother used to say, is paved with good intentions. Meredith and I are the New Abnormal. Is this why making movies isn't as much fun anymore? I can't even figure out how to have lunch with a girlfriend whom I actually want to see.

With so many people out of the office these days, timing is an increasingly difficult factor. I can't tell if people are sick, having manicures, working out of Starbucks, watching their kids at soccer games, hiding in home offices or just so rich they are on satellite on a boat somewhere, but I have never seen more people out of the office. This is because lunches are no longer necessary. They have become a vestigial courtesy. The young and networking, many of whom are off expense accounts, will work key lunches in when necessary. But many lunch hours are now spent checking calls while having a yogurt with gummy bears at Pinkberry. I only meet with writers, financiers, directors, actors (and friends). And yet, I really want to see my pal and her baby for lunch.

Phone calls have been replaced by emails, conversation has been replaced by chitchat and getting to know someone has been replaced by checking out their clothes and shoes. What about work? When you used to submit a script, you'd receive a thoughtful response. There was a possibility of persuading the executive with your charm or your relationship or even your well-articulated argument about how you would address the notes given in the response. There was a process.

Today, with some significant exceptions, one only gets an email pass that says, "This doesn't fit into our slate," or, "We have no slot for this." Case closed. It is rarely worth fighting back. Besides, if the exec gave notes, he might get a rewrite, and then he'd have to read it again, and chances are good that his studio's mandate will have stayed the same.

Why cultivate a relationship if it doesn't amount to anything, if you can't persuade somebody? If being funny and charming makes no difference, you might as well just send emails. So there are strikingly fewer meetings and strikingly less charm.

I once said to my manager son that his clients were all incredibly good-looking. Oly said, "Mom, we don't have time for charm. You have to just make a great first impression. People would rather see attractive people."

Truthfully, I don't know whether he actually said that or I just accused him of it and he laughed. The fact is, first impressions are increasingly important when people stop taking the time to get to know people. We used to spend fifteen minutes in every pitch meeting talking about families, sports, music or politics over fancy water. People don't have time to do that anymore unless it works into the pitch. This is mostly in TV, where during pitch season there is no time for more than three minutes of fast and funny chitchat.

Finally, few execs have the power to say yes anymore. They only have the power to move a movie up the chain in tiny, tiny increments. What fun is it for the exec to have a long meeting, after which they have to say no—an outcome they knew before the meeting even started? Better to email.

In the Old Abnormal, when there were more slots to fight for with more money available, the exec could team up with you and really make a case for a borderline movie, a "maybe," a script that everyone loved but wasn't a bull's-eye. Now the producer with an original movie who is fighting for one of these rare studio "slots" has to package it with a star or a director and that person's manager (in exchange for a producer's credit) to get any traction at the studio. They better make sure the star or director has a track record of big international numbers. The best way may be to skip the studios altogether. Or go to your parents, or take a run on some credit cards.

How did this happen? How did it become easier for someone who knows no one to make a movie for $150,000 than for someone who knows everyone to make one for $20 million? Or for a guy who last made a movie for $100,000 to make his next movie a superhero tentpole for $100 million? Nothing makes any sense. Battleships are falling from Mars. Tentpoles are launching and falling. No one knows what to make. What went wrong?

HOLLYWOOD'S WANING CREATIVITY

Short of the Week.com

TOP 10 FILMS (U.S. GROSS)

1981	1991	2001	2011
RAIDERS OF THE LOST ARK	TERMINATOR 2	HARRY POTTER	HARRY POTTER 8
ON GOLDEN POND	ROBIN HOOD	LOTR: FELLOWSHIP OF...	TRANSFORMERS 3
SUPERMAN II	BEAUTY AND THE BEAST	SHREK	THE TWILIGHT SAGA 4
ARTHUR	THE SILENCE OF THE LAMBS	MONSTERS INC.	THE HANGOVER PART 2
STRIPES	CITY SLICKERS	RUSH HOUR 2	PIRATES OF CARIBBEAN 4
THE CANNONBALL RUN	HOOK	THE MUMMY RETURNS	FAST FIVE
CHARIOTS OF FIRE	THE ADDAMS FAMILY	PEARL HARBOR	CARS 2
FOR YOUR EYES ONLY	SLEEPING WITH THE ENEMY	OCEAN'S ELEVEN	THOR
THE FOUR SEASONS	FATHER OF THE BRIDE	JURASSIC PARK III	RISE PLANET OF THE APES
TIME BANDITS	THE NAKED GUN 2 1/2	PLANET OF THE APES	CAPTAIN AMERICA

ORIGINALS   ADAPTATIONS   **SEQUELS**   REMAKES

ORIGINAL FILMS IN 1981	ORIGINAL FILMS IN 2011
7	0

THE ONLY ORIGINAL STORY IN THE TOP 15 FILMS IN 2011

#14 BRIDESMAIDS

FRANCHISES FROM 2001 WE'RE STILL SUPPORTING IN 2011

2001	2011
#1 HARRY POTTER 1	➡ #1 HARRY POTTER 8
#10 PLANET OF THE APES	➡ #9 RISE OF THE PLANET OF THE APES
#14 THE FAST AND THE FURIOUS	➡ #6 FAST FIVE

Chart courtesy of Short of the Week.com.

SCENE TWO

THE GREAT CONTRACTION

I was driving west in a classically horrible L.A. morning commute on my way to Peter Chernin's new office in Santa Monica, thinking about our regular lunches back when he ran the studio and I worked as a producer there in the nineties. Peter, who is now building his own media empire at Fox and had been president of News Corp. for over a decade, was clearly the perfect person to ask what had turned the Old Abnormal into the New Abnormal. First of all, he was incredibly smart about the business. But more important, I now realized that during those lunches, he was the first to warn me that the proverbial "light ahead" was an oncoming train. It was way before things turned obviously grim. Since I was reliably churning out pictures then, I didn't take his gloomy talk about piracy seriously. I just went around saying, "The landlord has the blues," and blithely fell into the future.

Peter wasn't exactly having a hard time making the transition. Once he decided in 2009 to leave the number-two job overseeing the News Corp. media empire, he became the biggest producer at Fox (one of the biggest anywhere), with guaranteed pictures and huge potential profit participation. His first picture was the tent-pole smash *Rise of the Planet of the Apes,* and he already had three television shows on the air. More recently, he released the smash *Identity Thief,* with Melissa McCarthy and Jason Bateman.

The long drive got me thinking about the contrast between the struggling Old Abnormal producers (and writers) and the soaring New ones like Peter. It was discussed at a fancy-pants dinner party I went to a week before.

"They're completely broke," said a studio head, when asked by me (of course) about how different things were these days. He spoke about famous players who regularly came to him begging for favors—a picture, a handout, anything.

"Why?" his very East Coast guest asked incredulously.

I recalled his exact words as I sat in bumper-to-bumper traffic. "They have extremely high overheads," he said to his guest with me listening in. "They have multiple houses, wives, and families to support. They've made movies for years, they were on top of the world and had no reason to think it would end. And then suddenly it did. They've gone through whatever savings they had. They can't sell their real estate. Their overhead is as astronomical as their fees used to be. They've taken out loans, so they're highly leveraged. It's a tragedy."

His natty guest looked unsympathetic, so I tried to bridge the worlds between us. "Okay," I said, "the Sudan is a tragedy. This is just sad."

I understood that it was hard to sympathize with broke producers when so many families were being tossed onto their lawns by bailed-out banks that had bullied them into bullshit mortgages. Meanwhile, New Abnormal producers like Peter were thriving, easily finding supersized tentpoles with the "preawareness" that was so craved by the New Abnormal, like his hit film *Rise of the Planet of the Apes*.

That is because those films were so well suited to their sensibilities and ambitions. But Peter was more than just a successful model of a New Abnormal producer. He had green-lit the two biggest movies of all time when he was head of Fox during the Old Abnormal.

Peter had earned his top-down as well as bottom-up perspective on the business by working his way up through publishing, then TV, to eventually run both Fox Broadcasting Company and Twentieth Century Fox Film. He became Rupert Murdoch's number two, overseeing the whole Fox empire, and shareholders clamored for the board to name him Murdoch's successor. But this was a job designated by Murdoch to go to an actual heir,* so Peter left to become a producer. He knew the business, as Joni Mitchell's great old tune said it, "from both sides now." More important, he was gifted with a brain both creative and financial in equal measure.

Peter's offices are as close to the water as you can get without falling in. He came into the lobby to greet me, always personable, never grandiose, but still a bit larger than life. He is the humblest of moguls, but that doesn't mean he doesn't have a strong ego— just not a damaged one.

We sat in his Santa Monica office with huge plate-glass windows overlooking the Pacific, where he happily relayed that he rarely crossed the 405 East-West divide. When I asked for his help in getting to the bottom of all this, I was reminded of how tough-minded he is. Even though we are old friends (we went to high school together), he had no problem challenging my buried premises. Maybe they weren't very buried.

"So how did we get here," I asked, "where things are so different from when we started? What happened?"

I leaned back a little on Peter's comfortable couch, and he sat forward to say, "People will look back and say that probably, from a financial point of view, 1995 through 2005 was the golden age of this generation of the movie business. You had big growth internationally, and you had big growth with DVDs." He paused to allow a gallows laugh. "That golden age appears to be over."

It was good we both could keep our sense of humor, the only way to survive the industry's crazy carousel of wild ups and

---

* Though now, after the hacking scandal, we shall see.

low downs. And this very carousel and its need for constant—bordering on psychotic—optimism to keep your projects going made it hard for a person like me to find a steady perch from which to see what was really going on. Peter, however, had one.

He seemed to be saying that the DVD market was critical to the life and death of the Old Abnormal. I knew the DVD profits were key, but it seemed to me like a classic case of the tail wagging the dog. "Why did those little silver discs go to the heart of the business?" I asked. "There have to be other key revenue streams."

"Let me give you the simplest math," he replied. "The simple, simple, simple math."

Good, I thought. Because my friends and I are not so great at math. I can guesstimate the budget of a big movie to within a hundred thousand dollars by reading the script, but I can't add the columns therein.

"The movie business," Peter said, "the historical studio business, if you put all the studios together, runs at about a ten percent profit margin. For every billion dollars in revenue, they make a hundred million dollars in profits. That's the business, right?"

I nodded, the good student, excited that someone was finally going to explain this to me.

"The DVD business represented fifty percent of their profits," he went on. "Fifty percent. The decline of that business means their entire profit could come down between forty and fifty percent for new movies."

For those of you like me who are not good at math, let me make Peter's statement even simpler. If a studio's margin of profit was only 10 percent in the Old Abnormal, now with the collapsing DVD market that profit margin was hovering around 6 percent. The loss of profit on those little silver discs had nearly halved our profit margin.

This was, literally, a Great Contraction. Something drastic had happened to our industry, and this was it. Surely there were other factors: Young males were disappearing into video games; there were hundreds of home entertainment choices available for nesting families; the Net. But slicing a huge chunk of reliable profits right out of the bottom line forever?

This was mind-boggling to me, and I've been in the business for thirty years. Peter continued as I absorbed the depths and roots of what I was starting to think of as the Great Contraction. "Which means if nothing else changed, they would all be losing money. That's how serious the DVD downturn is. *At best,* it could cut their profit in half for new movies."

I'd never heard it put so starkly; I'd only seen the bloody results of the starkness. The epic Writers Guild strike of 1988 was about the writers trying to get a piece of home viewing profits. It shut down the town for eight months, and estimates of what it cost the Los Angeles economy run between $500 million and $1 billion. They held out as long as they could, until all parties had bled out as if they'd been struck by Ebola. And still the writers got no piece of those golden discs. Then the writers struck again in 2007–8 for a piece of the Internet frontier, and won not much more than they did after the last awful strike, and we all watched its terrible and unintended aftermath play out during the recession and in the subsequent suspension of writers' and producers' deals.

"I think the two driving forces [of what you're calling the Great Contraction] were the recession and the transition of the DVD market," Peter said. "The 2008 writers' strike added a little gasoline to the fire." Well, at least my writer friends would be relieved to know that Peter didn't think it was *totally* their fault, as some in town were fond of intimating.

He went on to say, "It was partially driven by the recession, but I think it was more driven by technology."

There it was. Technology had destroyed the DVD. When Peter referred to the "transition of the DVD market," and technology destroying the DVD, he was talking about the implications of the fact that our movies were now proliferating for free—not just on the streets of Beijing and Hong Kong and Rio. And even legitimate users, as Peter pointed out, who would never pirate, were going for $3 or $4 video-on-demand (VOD) rentals instead of $15 DVD purchases.

"When did the collapse begin?"

"The bad news started in 2008," he said. "Bad 2009. Bad 2010. Bad 2011."

It was as if he were scolding those years. They were bad, very bad. I wouldn't want to be those years.

"The international market will still grow," he said, "but the DVD sell-through business is not coming back again. Consumers will buy their movies on Netflix, iTunes, Amazon et al. before they will purchase a DVD." What had been our profit margin has gone the way of the old media.

It hit me like a rock in the face. The loss of DVDs for our business had created a desperate need for a new area of growth. This was why the international market has become so important a factor in creative decisions, like casting and what movies the studios make.

We sat in mournful silence for a second before I realized that Peter probably had to take a call from China and I should go home and take a Xanax.

But then Peter said the most amazing thing. A P&L, if you're not a numbers person, is a profit-and-loss statement. Studios create P&Ls in order to explain to their financial boards, banks and investors how they are going to recoup their costs when they green-light films. It estimates how much money key domestic and international markets are expected to gross based on how "elements" (i.e., stars, director, title) have performed in the past in those markets, country by country. It also estimates how they will perform in various ancillary markets like DVD, TV, pay cable, Internet, airplane devices, VOD, handheld devices, etc., again based on past performance. If it all adds up to the amount of the budget or more, Go!

These are the quantifiers that studios use to rationalize their decisions, to put them on solid-enough financial ground on which to base predictions to their corporate boards.

"So," Peter said as I was about to leave, "the most interesting thing is what a few studio heads said to me privately about two years ago." He stopped to smile. "None of them from Fox, of course."

"Of course," I said. I knew he was about to share something very inside with me.

"They said to me, 'We don't even know how to run a P&L right now.'" The look on his face expressed the sheer madness of that statement. "'We don't know what our P&L looks like because we don't know what the DVD number is!' The DVD number used to be half of the entire P&L!"

"What are the implications of that?"

He looked at me incredulously, as if to say, Haven't you run a studio? Then he said very emphatically, "The implications are— *you're seeing the implications*—the implications are, those studios are *frozen*. The big implication is that those studios are—not necessarily inappropriately—*terrified* to do *anything* because they don't know what the numbers look like."

Of course they are. They're frozen, so the gut is frozen, the heart is frozen, and even the bottom-line spreadsheet is frozen. It was like a cold shower in hard numbers. There was none of the extra cash that fueled competitive commerce, gut calls, or real movies, the extra spec script purchase, the pitch culture, the grease that fueled the Old Abnormal: the way things had always been done. We were running on empty, searching for sources of new revenue. The only reliable entry on the P&L was international. That's where the moolah was coming from, so that's what decisions would be based on.

The Great Contraction explains the birth of the New Abnormal, and so many of the cultural changes that came along with it. Technology changes culture. Think of the way the all-embracing texting culture of the Japanese teenager created the first-person text novel (*keitai shousetsu*). The anonymous romantic accounts of teens written by texters were sent chapter by chapter as apps were being designed in real time to meet the needs of the growing audience. That birthed a genre that spawned "real" books and movies. Our industry reformatted itself with an application called "new revenue streams." A crucial question of that app was "what stars play in foreign territories," and the answer was, "whoever had a big hit there before!" Casting was not the only thing that technology changed, nor was the (disappearing) pitch. The big change was what movies get made.

TENTPOLES AND TADPOLES

Producers with scripts that don't fit the studio model are constantly searching for the crevices where money still exists. This leads to lunches and dinners with dubious people and wild-goose chases. I have a producer friend who has met with so many investors, he has a T-shirt that reads THEY CAN'T ALL BE FAKES. There are increasing numbers of rich kids with checkbooks and Russians with pretty wives who want a small part in a movie in exchange for financing the picture. And there are parties who will provide small pieces of "equity"—i.e., $30,000 here, $100,000 there—that can be pieced together by enterprising independent producers. These producers are willing to do the hard work to puzzle these chunks of equity into some kind of budget.

I spoke recently to the most prolific of tadpole producers, Cassian Elwes. A transatlantic transplant and former William Morris agent, Cassian is a funny, nonstop-action kind of guy who had three movies shooting when I last had drinks with him—two of them in Louisiana, one with a $20 million budget and one with a $4 million budget. Because the big one (of course) needs more money, it flew him here coach, he told me, but the little one was flying him back First Class!

The big tadpole shooting in Louisiana, *The Butler,* starred Forest Whitaker and Oprah Winfrey, each making $65,000 dollars up front. It's a movie *Spider-Man* producer Laura Ziskin had tried and failed to make at Sony before she died following a long struggle with breast cancer. A true story about the White House butler who served under every president from Eisenhower to Obama, and what it felt like to live to see the first black president. After Laura's death, Lee Daniels (*Precious*), the film's director, enlisted Cassian to help get it made, and he became driven to complete her dream. He raised all the money, and shooting began in the summer of 2012, a year or so after she died. The other movie is a tenth of *The Butler*'s size. They were puzzled together in the same impossible way that he does so well. By now he has a track record of making money for his investors, so he has an iPhone contact list full of go-to rich kids in town and elsewhere.

"It's painful making these movies, because any way that you do it now, you know it's got to be multiple investors, with at least three people each putting in one million dollars; it's literally like herding cats trying to get them all to agree on everything. My life is like, 'Okay, he agreed to this, so you should agree to that.' And then that investor says, 'Well, I don't know.' And then the other investor says, 'Well, if he doesn't do it, I'm not going to do it anymore,' and finally I get them all on the phone and go, 'Shut the fuck up, it's a million dollars!'"

But with so few movies getting made, agents and actors are willing to sign on to a tadpole and get paid less money if the script is really good. This has led to an underground movie community of upstart producers who never had a chance of penetrating the

Oz-like doors of now-broke Hollywood anyway. But they are making more movies (without guaranteed distribution) than their more established peers. I met a fabulous girl this year named Tatiana Kelly, who offered me a picture to direct. She had made three movies this year—good little tadpoles—when I had made none. How was that possible? Her big tadpole, made for $6 million, was called *The Words* (which she did with Cassian and her partner Jim Young) and starred Bradley Cooper, Olivia Wilde, Zoe Saldana, Jeremy Irons and Dennis Quaid. It was about a blocked writer at the peak of his success who discovers the price of stealing another man's work, and opened at Sundance, where it was picked up by CBS Films and shown in two thousand theaters in 2012. This is the Cinderella model for microbudget producers.

It's all about microbudgets, movies being made for around $100,000. I told Tatiana that I wouldn't know how to make a movie for that price with a gun pointed at my head. But here, technology changed the business again.

The biggest new thing under the sun is High Definition (HD). For starters, HD digital shooting eliminates film and printing costs, which cuts the costs even before we move on to its substantial other savings.

Film itself is expensive. There is no film in the camera in digital shooting. Everything is recorded digitally and can be downloaded anywhere—on set, at the studio, at the editing suite or onto the director's home computer. This makes watching footage and cutting on the fly possible. Additionally, when you shoot in HD, all the costs of printing are eliminated, so the "P" part of "P and A" (Prints and Ads) costs disappears. Historically, every film print had to be copied and shipped to theaters individually. This is costly for a wide release of 100 to 2,500 prints per movie. Soon every movie theater will be fitted for digital, as almost all are now, and when the encoding issues that protect against piracy are solved, the movie will be delivered directly online to digital projectors all around the world. For now they are delivered on coded cassette—still cheaper than film prints. The "A" cost refers to all marketing costs. The reason these two categories are always wed is that together they constitute all the hard costs of a movie independent of production costs. To independent filmmakers, securing Print and Ad money via a distributor is the sine qua non of a movie released properly: No prints, no ads, no one will see it! In general, indies raise production financing first, and then secure distribution, if they hit the festival jackpot.

Also, in digital HD shooting, postproduction effects become a breeze. Want to change a color? Sunset looks dreary or was shot on a cloudy day? No problem. Find the problematic pixels inside the dreary frames and colorize them on the computer. Do you have a flying stunt? Do it with wires and erase the wires by finding the pixels with the wires and erasing them on the computer. This is wildly less expensive than doing the same stunt on film.

Futzing with something on a film print is very expensive and complicated, but digitally, it can be done by kids on iPhone apps all day long. It's a whole new scale of innovation for cutting down the costs and speeding up the time of production. That's not to say every filmmaker is embracing the technology. Some of the best loathe it and believe it does not replicate the texture or experience of film. George Lucas, however, believes that eventually it will be possible to duplicate the texture of film by a "film program" that manipulates the pixels to do so.

When you shoot in HD, you can cut on set, which some directors love and some hate. Needless to say, this cuts down editing time. Most television dramas shoot in HD now, as the schedules are so tight. With the onset of HD drastically reducing the costs of making independent movies, they can be made on a recently issued credit card, or long-saved Bar Mitzvah money, or by hustling friends or parents. This situation drastically diminishes the power of the "gatekeepers," creates enormous opportunities for new distributors and opens the door to young talent via YouTube and other Internet outlets. We await filmdom's Justin Bieber: Just as the savior of the music industry emerged from his home to the world via the Net overnight, our next Scorsese or Fincher is likely to be shooting something unimaginably cool on his or her family's video camera that will pop up on YouTube and be instantly discovered the same way. It is inevitable.

We now have thousands upon thousands of tiny movies made on microbudgets, financed with personal credit cards. They are all vying to enter film festivals, and the very best of them will end up competing with studio films at Oscar time. Newbie producers without credits or experience run around like chickens with their heads cut off, getting scripts written for free, tying tiny pieces of promised cash together, trying to keep it all stitched up. Then they go to the big agencies and cast available actors who get paid nothing up front. They take on established producers without trepidation because it doesn't take a village anymore, just a digital camera. The actors, who secure the financing for these microbudgets (through their international numbers, of course), want to make these movies because studios aren't making dramas anymore. Or, to the extent that dramas are being made, they are mostly thrillers.

But with new video and online distribution outlets becoming viable options at the festivals every year, it is less of a feast-or-famine life for the tadpoles. In 2012, a few significant tadpoles broke into theatrical release from VOD purchases at Sundance: *Beasts of the Southern Wild, Arbitrage,* and *Bachelorette*—and the first two even went on to Oscar consideration. So VOD deals aren't the total losers they used to be; they're possible new routes to stardom, or at least solvency. This is a growing miniverse.

Increasingly, it is turning into a business of tadpoles, minuscule versions of the dramas studios once made, versus giant-sized tentpoles, made for the world. Of course, for the guys and gals with tentpoles and franchises going, they can't get out of production! No matter what they have to do—child's birthday, step-up ceremony at school. But that's a good problem, as we say.

There are a few highly sought-after sources from which to pull financing for "one-offs" still out there for producers who want a budget larger than a teapot. A few established financiers are making movies via credit lines established through banks and selling them back to the studios before or after they are made. In bizarre ways (understood only by people with MBAs), the funds get replenished and the investors are repaid, despite the box office outcomes of the pictures. I found one such investor, MRC, during the Great Contraction, and made my first indie with my son; his writing client and best friend, Matthew Robinson; and Ricky Gervais: *The Invention of Lying*. It was a philosophical comedy, starring Ricky and Jennifer Garner, about a world where there is no such thing as lying until Ricky's character invents it with enormous consequences. The script was Oly's client's; I'd known him since they were at Sarah Lawrence together. I was happy to help them get it made, if I could. Matthew had written it for Ricky, and I was fortuitously on my way to London and got the script to him. He loved it. Then Ricky offered to codirect with Matthew, and we had a movie. Soon after, Oly suggested Louis C.K. as the second lead, and I said, "Who?"* (This is one reason it's good to breed early.)

In the picture business, these sometimes hard-earned, sometimes lucky, moments require alchemy, extreme perseverance and the perfect alignment of stars and timing.

Some good movie movies were getting made at studios too during the Great Contraction, despite the gloomy P&Ls, and in the face of the crumbling profit margins. Why? Certain individuals (movie stars, primarily) are sneaking them through, at a price,

---

* Three years before his FX comedy show, *Louie*—my only excuse.

with the right ingredients. But some studio heads are trying to gut them.

My dear friend Elizabeth Gabler, with whom I made *Hope Floats,* and the head of Fox 2000—which I call Little Fox—spent almost ten years trying to mount *Life of Pi.* By the time she had Ang Lee attached, it was the height of the Great Contraction. She had no stars, a movie about a magical tiger and the human spirit, a big budget with lots of special effects and the bigwigs were jumpy. It was expensive and complicated and she adored it. It has just passed the $500 million mark worldwide, the biggest movie in her thirteen successful years there, and won Ang Lee an Oscar. Stacey Snider, the CEO and cochairman of DreamWorks Studios, green-lit *The Help* with a first-time director—a movie all the prognosticators pooh-poohed because it was a period piece about our racial history and therefore doomed overseas. But it was among the top five most profitable movies of 2012.

In 2010, Amy Pascal of Sony Pictures broke all "inside Hollywood" rules and green-lit a dicey baseball movie, Brad Pitt's *Moneyball.* It was another international no-no, since baseball is known to not perform internationally. But first she oversaw a rewrite, cut the budget and changed directors, all the while keeping Brad Pitt and holding down costs. Stacey and Amy were not afraid of tough calls on these projects. By January 2012, *Moneyball* had grossed nearly $90 million domestic. The next year Amy green-lit Kathryn Bigelow's *Zero Dark Thirty,* even though her Oscar-winning *Hurt Locker* had made very little money. This is fearless thinking in the tundra of the Contraction.

Sometimes studios support artists—particularly directors—in patronage roles and put them under contract like in the old studio heyday. (Paramount has a deal like this with Martin Scorsese [*The Departed*], and Warner Bros. has a working partnership, if not a deal, with Christopher Nolan [*Batman, Inception*]). I like to think of these as their Medici moments, sustaining an artist at the prime of his or her career. The best studio heads came into this business because they love movies, and for most, this is their favorite part of the job. But they wouldn't do it if they didn't hope to ultimately make money out of the situation, so for the right price and for the right talent, they get behind a writer or a director. When these guys hit it out of the park, we all win. I am not remotely religious, but I do engage in a little praying or rain dancing for these movies when they're released, as we all need them to succeed. When one works, studio alliances are created, like the phenomenally lucrative one Fox has made with Jim Cameron (*Avatar, Titanic*). This is the bull's-eye of the business.

But getting to the bull's-eye takes massive *cojones,* plus something ineffable. Faith, of a sort. When Peter Chernin described green-lighting and then living through the production of what was then the most expensive and difficult movie of all time, *Titanic,* it was enough to give me the bends. I realized how hard these jobs are. Even during the Old Abnormal, when there was some money to throw around, a project like that put him under unrelenting pressure.

"I lived a life that was two parallel roles," Peter said. "One was the most satisfying creative experience I've ever had. It started the moment Jim Cameron sat on my couch and talked to me, showed me some pictures and discussed this notion of essentially doing *Romeo and Juliet* on a boat. It was just the two of us for maybe four and a half hours. He told me all kinds of arcane facts about the *Titanic.* If you were a woman in First Class, you had a ninety-nine percent chance of survival. If you were a man in steerage, you had a ten percent chance of survival. You had twice as good a chance of survival on one side of the boat as on the other because that first side did a much more efficient job of loading the lifeboats.

"On my own gut level," Peter continued, "the movie was fantastic. I remember saying to Jim that first afternoon, 'The great thing about this movie is we have absolutely no idea if it's going to work. But I guarantee you that it's not going to be a middle movie. Because every guy in the world is going to say, "Jim Cameron sinks the *Titanic*." And every woman is going to say, "*Romeo and Juliet* on a doomed ship, fantastic!" Or every woman is going to say, "Some James Cameron boat movie, forget it!" Every guy's going to say, "Some period love piece, forget it!" And we're not going to know until we make it! I love it! Let's go do it.'

"So we green-lit what I believe at that time was the most expensive movie ever made. Then script, great! Dailies, phenomenal! An hour of cut footage after a few months, phenomenal. Best preview I've ever been to.

"The parallel universe, however, was arguably the worst experience ever. The movie was green-lit at a hundred ten million dollars. It went a hundred fifteen million over budget. *Variety* used to write this piece called '*Titanic* Watch' two or three times a week."

"The press was very hostile," I agreed.

Peter nodded. "I was considered not only the stupidest person in Hollywood—I was considered the stupidest person in the *history* of Hollywood. It was very much parallel worlds, where publicly, everything about the economics of the movie couldn't have been worse, but everything we saw privately was wonderful!

"Then we did a little shoot up in the North Atlantic to get the stuff that bookends the movie. Three months before we started principal photography, I was told that *someone spiked the soup with LSD*. That's not a normal call to get as head of a studio."

"Seriously?" I asked. Oh, God, I thought, how horrible that must have been for everyone. I vaguely remembered news accounts of a bunch of cast and crew members being taken to the hospital with hallucinations.

"You go through the playbook, LSD in the soup of the crew isn't in there," Peter said, nodding his head.

"No, it certainly is not," I said. "I've never heard of that happening before or since."

"Everything that could go wrong went wrong, and yet I kept coming back to, *I love this movie.* That's the sense in which you believe your gut. It was a fantastic learning experience for me because first, it made me fearless, like, 'Bring it on. It can't get any worse than this.' And second, it made me say, 'I really believe in it, go for it!' It turned out that the reasons I believed in it were the reasons that the movie worked. I found it incredibly interesting, I found it deeply moving, I found it exciting."

The picture became the biggest-grossing film of all time. And why? Remember the key thing Peter said.

"The DVD business is not coming back again," he told me. "But the international market will still grow." And grow it has, becoming king of the box office, and its main determinant. The tipping point was *Titanic.* That boat not only historically crashed into icebergs, but it conquered new lands that had never seen a Hollywood movie before. And this changed everything.

HAVE YOUR POPCORN WITH SOME CHOPSTICKS

How the Rest of the World Came to Rule America's Movie Choices

WATCH A MARKET EMERGE BEFORE YOUR VERY EYES

Jim Gianopulos, now chairman and CEO of Fox Filmed Entertainment, opened the two biggest-grossing movies internationally in history, *Titanic* and *Avatar.* Referring to James Cameron, he says that's "just hanging with Jim." He is a modest, grounded, smiling, Buddha kind of man. He raised a daughter on his own, and when you're with him, you wish you were her. But don't mistake kindness for weakness with Jim: He is a brilliant strategist, and Fox's phenomenal success worldwide is no accident.

I had no idea that Jim had actually been part of what ultimately amounted to one of the biggest changes our industry had ever seen, if not the biggest. He watched a new market emerge before his eyes. It was of course due to *Titanic,* the game changer.

Jim was head of Fox's international division when I worked there over a decade before. We recently spent a long afternoon discussing how the international market has come to drive the movie business in the New Abnormal, a very different situation from what prevailed when he and I worked together, though Jim's position as head of the international division was clearly vital even back then. We talked about Fox's role in spotting and exploiting the international side of things early.

Star TV, the international satellite television network that Rupert Murdoch started, was like the media equivalent of Seward's Folly at the time. "What!? You're buying a what? And it's a satellite thing?" Jim laughed. "And of course it was an enormous, huge financial success, and it now covers most of the globe in scope. That's something that has been a mantra here for twenty-odd years."*

Jim's rise has been exciting to watch. He was first promoted to cochairman with Tom Rothman, Fox's longtime president under Peter Chernin, when Chernin became a producer. But when in September of 2012 it was announced that Rothman's contract was not being renewed, Fox made Gianopulos the sole chairman and CEO of the studio, overseeing production as well. It is a testament to his talent, his value to Fox and the primacy of the international audience that Jim got the whole enchilada.

I sat in Jim's now much bigger office and marveled about how things had changed so much since we had worked together in the Old Abnormal. Back then we never took international into the equation when we decided what we wanted to develop. I asked him about the growing influence of the international market on the selection of the movies we are making now.

"Those of us who have been in the business for a while see it as a fundamental fact. We [the United States] are five percent of the world market. Ninety-five percent of the ticket buyers are out there. It does not take a lot of math to tell you that's where the future and the opportunities are. More and more time and focus has been

---

* Star TV's British affiliate, BSkyB, is 39 percent owned by Fox, a constant source of frustration to Murdoch, who has been recently thwarted in his bid to take it over in its entirety by the tabloid hacking scandal that threatens both his media holdings in Britain and the status of his heir, James.

devoted to how we engage these people, how we make sure our product travels."

"You guys have had to change the least," I said.

"Part of it was my background. But most of it was the parent company. Rupert was always a global adventurer, you know."

We smiled.

Jim first introduced me to the concept of "the rest of the world" being part of the movie business by promising me he was going to sell my Sandra Bullock/Harry Connick, Jr., dramedy *Hope Floats* "door to door"—from territory to territory around the world—because he loved it so much, despite the "international" turnoff of Connick's cowboy hat in the poster. It was a rule of thumb that movies with what movie people call "dust"—i.e., westerns, or movies in the dusty hinterlands—never worked abroad. Why this is, we don't really know. In the old studio days we exported our classic westerns. But in the modern movie business, the mere presence of either "dust" or cowboy hats—or horses, for that matter—is thought to make a picture dead on arrival, even if it isn't a western. Our movie was a romantic comedy that took place in a small Texas town, in which Sandy's character returns home to her mom after being dumped on TV by her husband and is then pursued by Harry's character, who has always loved her. Small-town Texas with a cowboy hat on the poster looked dusty enough to be a bomb overseas.

But that was before Fox revamped the campaign and repositioned it for the global audience, sans dust. And against all predictions, the movie made some money abroad. Very few movies play well in Tokyo, Berlin and Denver, but not New York and San Francisco! Then and there, Jim became my international guru.

When I started making movies in the Old Abnormal, international counted for 20 percent of the business. By 2008, when I left Fox, it had come to count for 50 percent. In the New Abnormal, for reasons you will see shortly, it has evolved into an astonishing 70/30 ratio, soon to career to 80/20. The model has turned upside down. It was obvious I needed my guru to explain how this happened, and why so rapidly.

Jim Cameron had pushed the frontiers, and without knowing it helped create a vital emerging market, as Gianopulos related:

"I said to Cameron, 'Here are the cities where everybody wants you to appear on this publicity campaign . . . are you up for it? You know we have to go to fifteen countries. I will join you for some of them, but not all. You've got to do it.'

"'Okay,' he said to me. 'But do you make any money in Russia?'

"'No' I said. 'Why?' I mean, this was 1997.

"'Can we go anyway?'

"'Sure, I guess so. But are we going to do all the other cities on the tour?'"

Gianopulos had to have that commitment first. It was key to the success of the international release. Doing publicity only in Russia was the sound of one hand clapping.

"'Yeah, oh, yeah, no problem,' he promised me. 'But can we go to Russia?' Cameron kept asking.

"So, what could I say?" Gianopulos said to me with that you-can't-say-no-to-a-thousand-pound-gorilla-you-love look. "The real reason he wanted to go was because he is a man of his word, despite Cameron always going over budget . . ." We laughed in mutual admiration of Cameron's obsessiveness.

"He is a man of integrity, and a commitment is a commitment," Gianopulos continued. "Jim had become very friendly with the Russian sailors on the research vessel on which he went down to the *Titanic*. And when they completed their shoot, he told them, 'When this movie is finished, I'm going to bring it here and I'm going to show it to you.' Well, it turned out the guys weren't in Moscow, they were in Kaliningrad, and despite all the years that I knew international, I had no idea where the fuck that was. It turns out it's a little tiny port that gives Russia access to the Baltic Sea. I think it's actually part of Poland. And I was very worried. Because this is after weeks of having been tortured by Jim about the quality of the theaters, about the quality of the projections; every print had to be pristine, everything had to be impeccable, as he is. This is one of the things that make him such a great and devoted filmmaker. So when we decided to show it in Kaliningrad, I called the London office, which patched us in to Russia. I asked them, 'Is there a theater in this place?'"

Then Gianopulos continued this conversation first in a funny Russian accent, imitating the man who ran the theater in Kaliningrad, then switching to his own voice.

"'Yes, there's a theater, but it's kind of more like an auditorium.'

"'Okay, well, is it any good?'

"'Well, it's okay, but they are fixing it up.'

"'Great, great, what are they doing?'

"'They are painting the seats.'

"'Okay,'" Gianopulos said, thinking, This is bad. It's not going to work. "They were just these wooden, like, Soviet school auditorium seats, so of course we sent a crew in and they put in Dolby sound, and all of these technicians outfitted this auditorium and made it a gift to Kaliningrad.

"It was really pretty cool. And of course all of Kaliningrad came, and it was a very wonderful, warm moment to see people who had been living under Soviet oppression and denied access to so many films, now hearing it in Dolby.

"It was an incredible event—to see these sailors who understood their role in the process but also were just so amazed to see this fantastic presentation. And then we went to Moscow, because as long as we were there, what the hell? In Moscow at the time, there was only one state-of-the-art theater. It was built not because the market demanded it, but because Kodak wanted to build a flagship to enhance their brand and their status.

"So they built this beautiful state-of-the-art theater that was well ahead of the market and well ahead of the audience, and it became the place to go. In Moscow it was like the equivalent of going to the Metropolitan Opera. People would actually dress up, and it was a very sort of elegant place to go regardless of what movie was playing.

"From that point, because of *Titanic,* Russia has become one of the biggest markets in the world, and it took not even a decade—closer to five or six years—for the market to open up. It was one of those moments in time, because of glasnost and all the changes in the Soviet Union and all of the investment and capital that became available—it became, and still is, one of the most lucrative markets. *It went from nothing to one of the top five markets in five years.*"

As you can see from Jim's pivotal anecdote, these new markets were and still are being created in real time as their countries' economies go through epochal transitions. In these vast, formerly communist territories, theaters are opening where none were before, and yuan and rubles are being spent with abandon by former peasant kids wearing 3D glasses as our state-of-the-art special effects blow up creatures and cars in their happy faces.

This new reality was created by what the economists call "the emerging markets." My afternoon with Jim Gianopulos showed me how these new markets emerged so quickly, and the long-term impact that emergence was having on our bottom line. Jim began to explain:

"Here, people go to the movies roughly four to five times a year. In Europe, the average is about two times per year. In places like Japan, it's once a year. So you can imagine if you took the eighty to ninety million people of Japan and projected them to the level of U.S. moviegoing, you would have five times the market. That's what's happening in various parts of the world. That's what happened in Russia, that's what happened in India, that's what happened in China. All of this massive growth continues. What's really changed, particularly in the last decade, is that whether you call it globalization or the gradual interaction of cultures all over the world, markets have developed to the point that people are enjoying more frequent moviegoing in places where the infrastructure has been built and is being built. China used to be completely closed off. There was nothing. It grew 30 percent last year, and 400 percent over the past five years."

This is what our kings are doing tonight. Thinking chopsticks. And caviar.

Brad Grey, the chairman of Paramount, went to Moscow for the first Russian premiere of an American movie, *Transformers: Dark of the Moon,* the third and most successful in the action/sci-fi franchise. It is a complicated saga, which I struggled to understand, involving a JFK cover-up of a crash landing on the moon in '61, why we really went to the moon in '69, a plot to build a space bridge from Earth to the moon's dark side (finally destroyed by something called the Control Pillar) and robots called Decepticons planning to dominate Earth. Russians adored it to the tune of $45.1 million. In his speech there in 2011, Grey declared, "Ten years ago, Russia only had a few dozen screens. Now it is enjoying such enormous growth that we think it's fitting to have the opening of one of our biggest franchises here. Russia is just one of several new markets opening up that are driving most of the demand for our movies."

China is another. It is now the second-largest market in the world, and it is predicted to surpass the United States to be number one by the year 2020. It had 11,000 theaters in 2012, and is expected to have 16,000 by 2015. Take this number in. Most of these new theaters are 3D and IMAX theaters, built to play our blockbusters. This has both transformed and cemented trends in the movie business. But the important thing to note is that these emerging markets are now driving the profit engine of the industry where DVD revenue once did. So have your popcorn with some chopsticks, and let's figure out what we're likely to see—and not see.

SAD NEWS ABOUT COMEDY

Comedy is often said to be a dead dog abroad. It's basically not a funny situation. The easy reason for the conundrum is that emerging markets (let alone markets with their own comedy tastes—say, France) and Americans do not have the same sense of humor. Humor is local. People like their hilarious indigenous customs, built around their own private jokes. But I have a ridiculous and stubborn Pollyanna streak and am constantly butting my head against these kinds of obstacles, looking for counterexamples, ways around them, loopholes. And arguably, they've arrived.

The successive successes internationally in the past few years of *The Hangover* parts I and II ($190,161,409 and $327,000,000 respectively) and *Bridesmaids* ($119,276,798) have broadened the market for broad high-concept comedies, even those starring broads. It has recently become possible to travel a breakout domestic success if it's a high-concept comedy, so: (1) Easy to get the idea. (2) Not too heavy on the big words or walk-and-talks. (3) Big bawdy "set pieces," preferably with Mike Tyson and a tiger and/or pooping in a sink. Comedy that doesn't travel is, as Jim Gianopulos says, "based on wit." Or "verbal." *Nicht so gut* for clever so-called writers. Jim added, "Someone slipping on a banana peel is funny in every culture."

WHAT THE HELL ARE *YOU* LAUGHING ABOUT?

In America we laugh at movies based on our customs. They could be college movies, prom movies, high school ritual movies or family vacation movies. But national archetype jokes don't travel. When independent foreign sales agent Kathy Morgan of KMI tried to sell our huge domestic hit *The Wedding Crashers*— about two buddies who live off of the joy and food of strangers' weddings—to Japan, the Japanese buyers were incredulous. "Why crash wedding?!"

On the other hand, in India, weddings are big business, big culture, big events. *Wedding Crashers* is being remade in India, where the idea apparently *is* funny, because Indians are as obsessed with weddings as we are. Though the specifics of our wedding cultures and senses of humor are wildly different, our obsession with weddings is the same. It is enough to remake this in the vast Indian market somewhere, with its distinct sense of humor. There are pockets of similarities and differences to be exploited and avoided everywhere. For example: Sometimes a movie's sensibility doesn't travel twenty-one miles, as in this famous story I heard from Jim Gianopulos and Kathy Morgan and a few others.

"There was a movie in France a couple of years ago called *Welcome to the Sticks*. It was a fish-out-of-water story about a guy from Paris who goes to this city in the south of France where he doesn't understand the local accent. It was hilarious to the French. The movie did a hundred million dollars there!"

This is an impossibly high number in France—which obviously made everyone think it could travel. So they exported it. First stop: the UK.

Gianopulos said, "It made ten dollars in the UK, right across the Channel. There was nothing about it they could relate to."

WHAT DOESN'T TRAVEL

- Rule 1: Chemistry on paper does not equal chemistry on-screen.

  Angelina Jolie and Johnny Depp, two of the very biggest (if not *the* biggest) international stars, couldn't save *The Tourist,* because he looked like a girl and she looked like a boy, though on paper they looked *amazing* together. The much higher international box office numbers—$210 million, compared to

$64 million domestic—couldn't help the movie break even because it cost so much for its astronomical budget and advertising costs.

- Rule 2: Sports movies can't jump—even soccer movies.

People would rather go to a soccer game than see a movie about one, the better to drink and brawl and riot. Forget baseball, basketball and football; forget the whole thing. This is why it took even a star of the magnitude of Brad Pitt so long to get the movie *Moneyball* made. Well done, Sony, for not caring and making it anyway!

- Rule 3: Dramas that explore, glorify or otherwise delve into our national history bore everyone but us.

They like their local and national history, not union-organizing stories, Green Beret movies, America in Iraq, name-the-country-where-we-triumph-in-sports-or-war stories, or Lincoln stories (with or without a vampire).

- Rule 4: Minimal awareness is insufficient—for example, second-tier caped crusaders such as Green Lantern and Green Hornet. Maybe green things don't work.

Universal just canceled *Clue* (which my late, great partner Debra Hill already made once for Uni in the eighties; I was her exec—we flew to Parker Bros. in England to get the rights. Everything old is new again), as well as a number of other movies based on Hasbro games (for instance, *Magic: The Gathering*). *Ouija* went from a tentpole to a tadpole with a budget under $5 million, to be made by the producer of *Paranormal Activity,* the abnormally successful faux-found-footage horror series about a couple who move into a haunted house; the first in the *Paranormal* franchise was made in 2009 for $15 million and grossed $193 million worldwide. Likewise, movies based on video games have an iffy track record (just as video games based on movies often fail). The two businesses don't yet understand each other. One reason is that movie people don't give their game rights to the best game developers, but instead to in-house lackeys. Great game developers who try to work with the studios or savvy film-makers don't get access to the film process early enough to make the games cool. When it works well. But video games are not board games, which may be "Old Empire." Mere awareness may not be sufficient. Awareness means games like *Mortal Kombat, World of Warcraft, Tomb Raider,* etc. We all have to be completely internationally aware, like Jell-O or Kleenex, if Kleenex were a video game being played by thirteen- to seventeen-year-old fan boys all over the world.

- Rule 5: Mixed genres don't work. Maybe if you're too many things, you're nothing at all.
  Cowboys & Aliens. Abraham Lincoln: Vampire Hunter. Wash-up ideas that look good on paper, but ridiculous on-screen. All in all, after a rare bidding war for the latter property among studios, the "winner," Fox, ultimately eked out $101 million worldwide on the picture, with domestic earning less than the movie's $66 million production budget.

- Rule 6: No cowboys, no hats, no horses, no cattle, and no dust are allowed. With aliens or without.

- New Rule: Apparently the above works with Tarantino only, or there's a new black/cowboy genre. Guessing Tarantino.

BROADS ABROAD

With Sandra Bullock, we're in very good shape. Meryl Streep, *mon Dieu, mais oui*. Jennifer Lawrence, due to the magic combo of franchise (*The Hunger Games*) and Oscar. Angelina is huge. She has big international gazoogies. And the more she sticks her right leg out at the Oscars, the bigger they get. They love our movie stars; they've always loved our movie stars, from the silent movies to Marilyn Monroe. Big stars = big bucks. They are a beat behind (one of my international sales-agent pals told me, "We love the stars of the immediate past!"), so the hot young things that the domestic audience loves won't sell. This makes casting hard, as Sandy and Meryl can make only so many movies, and Julia and Angelina have a lot of babies.

It should be pointed out that one of Sandy's points of adoration abroad, besides constantly batting her hits out of the ballpark, is that she is fluent in German, does an occasional ad campaign in Germany and does all of her press junkets in perfect German. Her numbers there are astronomical. (Her mom was a German opera singer and spoke German in the house.) So too with Jodie Foster, whose numbers are great internationally, along with her acting choices, which favor action. She is fluent in French, does an occasional advertising campaign in France, does her junkets in witty, jaunty French and lives in Paris part-time. Penélope Cruz and Javier Bardem both score high numbers in Spain. Milla Jovovich, not surprisingly, is big in Russia. A little cosmopolitanism goes a long way these days.

Our romantic comedies have often performed well in Europe, particularly in Germany, and also, interestingly, in Japan, despite the studios' lack of interest in the international market when making them. Gianopulos would say that the successes in this genre are typically star-dependent, and on average this seems true—thus Sandy Bullock's huge numbers abroad. The success of our syndicated television shows in France, Germany, England, Scandinavia, Australia and elsewhere has made our customs and stars familiar to many territories, and therefore our mating rituals are somewhat adorable. But there is doing well ($110 to $120 million) and there is doing great ($600 million to $1 billion), and the billion-dollar payday the studios are looking for doesn't reside in success in "Old Europe," as the studios say with almost equal disdain as Donald Rumsfeld did. The business there is too small to impress them.

More ominously, Sanford Panitch, of Fox's new international production division Fox International Productions (FIP), tells me that indigenous romantic comedies are the new rage; they are now being made based on local romantic customs in local languages with local talent for a lesser price. They no longer need our rom-coms for style, trends, etc.—movies have been replaced by the Net as cultural carrier pigeon. Without our biggest brand-name stars, our movies will be dinosaurs, replaced by local ones. This makes sense. As Gianopulos says, you can make a $5 to $10 million romantic comedy in any country in the world, in the local idiom, with local stars. But because of our technical prowess and the enormous costs involved, you can only make *Avatar, Transformers, Inception* and *The Dark Knight* in America.

YOUR MOVIES? WE CAN MAKE THEM!
WITH YOU!

We are great imperialists. We are also the best distributors. So call us the running dog of imperialist distributors.

Movies are a vital, critical and growing U.S. export. But increasingly, most countries want a larger share of their own movies to be released locally. Many countries, such as India (which has the most successful indigenous movie industry in the world), Australia, England, Japan, Korea, France, Hong Kong, Mexico, Russia and Spain, have bustling and historic film communities that severely limit imports. One idea to remedy this loss of income is to participate in local production in some way. What way? Finance and distribute! Each studio has distribution offices in each territory for its own releases, and some of these headquarters are becoming financing sources for local production and/or offering new opportunities for wide-ranging international distribution for local products. Capitalism at work!

Fox is enjoying fast success in indigenous production with its new Fox International Productions (FIP) banner under Sanford Panitch, which as of the date of writing has made more than $300 million in local-language box office. They are not remaking Fox properties.

One of their most recent hits is *My Name is Khan,* about an Indian man with a unique point of view and his great but ultimately ill-fated love for a single mother, which became one of the biggest-ever Bollywood films outside of India. According to Gianopulos, who along with Panitch gave birth to the division, during one weekend in February 2012 Fox International Productions had the biggest movie in China, the most populous country in the world, and the biggest movie in India, the second most populous country in the world. Now Panitch and FIP have planned, made and cofinanced European, Indian, Chinese, Japanese, Indonesian and Korean indigenous productions all around the world. What does he offer that they don't have? Global reach.

Panitch explained why it worked. "What you'd normally hear is, 'We don't need you, we have our own stories, we have money, we can get our films distributed, we've managed to do fine without you.' Bollywood is a perfect example of that. They don't need anybody. So why do we need you? The only reason we do need you is to get us into the United States and beyond our borders. Well, the answer is usually no, because your movies don't usually go from India to China. *My Name is Khan* is a love story about an Indian man with a tragicomic way of looking at the world who moves to San Francisco and meets a vivacious single mother. It played around the world. We proved it can work. We provide that."

They also had an executive with a producerlike mentality who thought up the division and let him run with it. He had a philosophy that worked.

"Let's study the market, just like you would as a producer," Panitch explained. He had grown out of the Fox culture before he ran minimajor New Regency Enterprises at Fox. I had known him for years, before he ran the world, when we worked together in the Old Abnormal when he was just starting. He was recommended to me by my great friend Dawn Steel.

Even back then he was the world's greatest information gatherer; he was the first person I know who kept compulsive files on a computer. It was in the eighties, and I had no idea what he was doing. And now, in a world where information is king, he reigns. "Other companies have tried and failed," he said as we chatted about the quick success of his division.

I noted that Disney tried, with *High School Musical;* it worked everywhere else in the world, so they made a Chinese version. But it only did $110,000 at the box office. "Why?" I asked him.

"You could say it's a strangely imperialistic point of view. Exactly the opposite of what we are trying to do. We are trying to figure out what would work in China; for example, what's the best-selling novel there?"

More and more, U.S. film companies are becoming global financiers and distributors, with coproduction and tax rebate deals (which incentivize local production through tax credits) commingling our limited cash resources and creating genuinely international product. We have built theaters to play our movies and the movies we finance with local filmmakers. If there is product, we should distribute it. Fox has long been doing this in Germany and Russia. Now it is doing it almost everywhere.

I cannot understate the advantage that Fox had with an infrastructure already in place with pay TV (cable and satellite) all over the world. They had offices with well-connected locals all over

Asia, the Middle East, China and Latin America who could hit the ground running and knew who was who in the local movie community. This is invaluable, as connections are vital in any business, especially a preciously gate-guarded one like the movie business.

Panitch told me one of the things he had learned in Bollywood. When we were developing movies together, one of the organizing principles of development was tamping down wild tone changes. In Bollywood they *require* wild tone changes: In their crime and action movies, they want dancing and singing, and in their romances they want action, guns and death!

I was agog. And then I remembered how I adored *Slumdog Millionaire*—Danny Boyle's Oscar-winning movie about a Mumbai teen who grew up in the slums and becomes the winner of *Who Wants to Be a Millionaire*—and its torture-romance-dancing hybrid, and I suddenly knew just what he meant. (*SM,* by the way, performed less well in India than anywhere else, but they realized their movies could win Oscars!) It's all getting to *know* you, and Panitch is FIP's master of the local meet and greet, globalize and monetize.

If there is an indigenous market to support, we will help finance it, then distribute the product and make money out of it. If there is money out there in a global movie industry, the studios need it. Dwindling cash means that any income is crucial.

WHAT WORKS BETTER THERE THAN HERE?

3D: The Great Conundrum

At first 3D was thought to be the savior of the business, the technological breakthrough that would compensate for the DVD disaster. But it was overused, slapped on pictures that weren't shot in 3D. Some insiders were investors, which complicated matters so much that at one point a famous mogul-investor suggested to Paramount and Scorsese that they release *The Departed* in 3D.

It was such the rage that every movie that was being made in the wake of *Avatar* and *Alice in Wonderland,* the medium's first two blockbusters, was going to be in 3D. But the onslaught of lousy conversions gave the process a black eye and exhausted the sophisticated young audience in the United States, and many very young kids in the domestic family audience rejected it as well.

But in emerging markets, 3D is another story. In China and Russia, they *Just Can't Get Enough.* The studios soon faced a puzzle in the wildly divergent appetites for 3D domestically and internationally. In the United States the appetite is diminishing from oversaturation; in the critical international audience, it is crack. Now it is necessary to make two versions of films, both 3D *and* 2D, so the 3D doesn't keep the U.S. audience away.

Then, in February 2012, something huge happened. The future president of China, Xi Jinping, ended his first trip to America in Los Angeles with a meeting with Vice President Biden and the MPAA'a chief lobbyist, former senator Chris Dodd. It's not where you start a trip, it's where you end a trip that counts; it's like *The Last Dance.* The fact that the meeting included Biden and was Xi's last stop indicated the importance of our industry's trade for both China and the United States. The subjects were our movie quota for Hollywood releases in China—twenty-one per year—and the revenue ceiling for American movies, now 13 to 17 percent. In a groundbreaking deal, which was not all of what everyone wanted but a great start, Xi raised the profit ceiling to 25 percent and added fourteen more American movies to the quota over the next five years. There is one restriction: Each has to be 3D or IMAX. "I think, overall, people feel like it's important to get movement here and then go back to the drawing board and push for more openers," said Dodd.

The fact that nothing but 3D and IMAX is allowed into China

will critically affect what we as an industry will produce as China pushes itself to become the number-one movie market in the world over the next five years. They want fantasy and action, and they will get fantasy and action. Line up those tentpoles and fire.

ALL ROADS LEAD TO CHINA

With its 1.5 billion newly minted capitalists, China is the dream girl of every dashing entrepreneur's business plan. But it has had no more ardent suitor than the entertainment business. Rupert Murdoch was an early trailblazer in the march on China, investing heavily in a satellite system, but left without the partnership he was aching for. Many less formidable suitors followed, to be greeted by opaque rules and customs and many layers of bureaucracy to penetrate.

My image is Hollywood as the Road Runner, bashing his head on the Great Wall until he could finally leap over to see who or what would greet him. Then he'd get the slow kind of runaround. And we courted China, even as it continued to be our most virulent pirate of DVDs. But gigantic progress has been made, especially in 2011 (though not so much on the piracy front). Even with the old quotas and caps on revenues in place, China's box office profits surged 64 percent to $1.5 billion in 2011, and are projected to be $5 billion in the next five years. You can see what all the road running has been about.

DEALZ, DEALZ, DEALZ

Last year some major American companies made early coproduction deals with Chinese entrepreneurs as partners, and that made big headlines in the industry trades. Things are moving so fast that this year Chinese moguls have come a-courting to us and look like our new white knights. China's Dalian Wanda Group bought AMC Entertainment in a deal that is worth $2.6 billion, so they are now American distributors. There is a new deal and a new partnership announced monthly. So vast is this new market that everyone wants a piece of this trade deal. It will be the focus of a large part of the studios' efforts.

A Chinese media mogul named Bruno Wu, educated in America and married to a gorgeous media star in her own right known as "the Chinese Oprah," is bringing $800 million of financing money to the United States to buy companies, finance filmmakers and get into the content business for both the United States and China. He made a play to buy Summit Entertainment (*Twilight* franchise), at the time the only studio on the block, but Summit chose instead to merge with the more familiar Lionsgate Studios, like itself a minimajor (as we call studios without lots). Wu is advised by the Creative Artists Agency (CAA; one of Hollywood's top movie agencies) at their Beijing headquarters, and is said to be looking at many different avenues into the U.S. market. Until I read the announcement, I didn't even know that CAA *had* a Chinese headquarters. Things are getting seriously global around here.

Among the big production companies that got into the China game last year was Legendary Pictures. Its CEO, Thomas Tull, has invested in the *Dark Knight* franchise, *Inception,* and the *Hangover* movies, so we expect his decision-making to be refined, despite the first choice for his venture, an epic about the building of the Great Wall. I take this as a getting-to-know-you kind of gesture. It will be directed by Ed Zwick, but is currently on hold. I don't know how these historical-epic coproductions go, but I have my doubts.

Ryan Kavanaugh of Relativity Media has a penchant for trouble (two alleged DUIs and many angry ex-financiers), which was extended to China early in his first coproduction there, *21 & Over.*

Their central location turned out to be in a verboten city, Linyi, where famous human rights defender Chen Guangcheng, a blind self-taught lawyer, had been detained since 2005. Worse, unbeknown to Relativity, they had become partners with the local party secretary who was responsible for his repression. Human rights activists went ballistic, and Relativity came under fire in the press— just what Kavanaugh didn't need. When you're working with the government, and by extension the party, you don't always know with whom you are dancing.

These clashes and confusions happen because the cultures couldn't be more dissimilar. The only similarities are capitalism and our mutual love for dumplings, and the Chinese seem to be better capitalists than we are. They are great at picking our products as they choose, like from a dim sum menu, while keeping two-thirds of the profits. Those capitalists in China who want to get their money out and who now have the new coproduction deals have to depend on Hong Kong's transparent financial market to get paid.

In the meantime, they are reaping all the benefits of the infrastructure and technology we offer them and using them to distribute their own created content as well as limited international fare.

It is critical that we remember that they are fundamentally self-interested (who isn't?), no matter how much money we may reap from their new cinemas—a lesson Warner Bros. and Sony learned in 2012. Both studios were shocked when China scheduled *The Amazing Spider-Man* and *The Dark Knight Rises* on the exact same weekend. This would have slashed the performance of each U.S. movie to the benefit of a homegrown Chinese contender. Dismayed, Warners refused the date, and at this writing, their international blockbuster, one of the biggest of the year, has not yet been given a mutually agreeable opening weekend in China. Tricky partners.

It was announced soon after this debacle that *Iron Man 3* would be a Chinese-American coproduction, and many a wise man was seen stroking his beard, thinking, Ah, this is the way to escape the summer blackout! But no sooner was it announced than the partnership was thrown into doubt, with the arcane rules of what qualifies as a "Chinese-American coproduction" being brought into question. That is, can those rules be reconfigured to apply to a Paramount tentpole?

IMAX made a deep commitment to China, building theaters, buying real estate, and making a partnership with China's largest movie chain, Wanda. All this was on the basis of the phenomenal success of *Avatar*. Richard Gelfond, IMAX's CEO, tripled the number of IMAX theaters he was building, even before he had any idea that a new deal would lift the quota. But he hedged his gigantic bet just a little and is working, like Fox International Productions, with local filmmakers. The first IMAX film not shot in English, *Aftershock,* made $100 million in China, half of what *Avatar* did, which is pretty remarkable for the first Chinese IMAX movie. Two more Chinese-produced IMAX films have been shot and are to be released. The first is *The Founding of a Party* (about guess what?), and the second, *Flying Tigers,* is about how the United States and China kicked Japanese butt in the 1930s and '40s. Gelfond seems to have a very good thing going in China, and this newly cut deal justifies his prescience.

Now they have the theaters we built together. They need our content (until they don't, a moment they are hastening as fast as they can). We need their screens and audience. We will lobby to raise the quota and the revenue cap even higher than in the recently cut deal. We will trade with the Middle Kingdom. There is no choice. They are our biggest partner in the New Abnormal.

FICKLE FRIENDS

In midsummer 2012, right in the middle of our vital tentpole season and in the wake of our groundbreaking deal with the soon-to-be president of China, Xi Jinping, there was a bad bump on Alliance Avenue. Some studios would call it a crisis if they were among those whose blockbusters were forced to be released on the same weekend, like Warner's *The Dark Knight Rises* and Sony's *The Amazing Spider-Man*. The studios brayed and cajoled and begged and fought for one to get a September release, to no avail. Instead of relief, American studios were greeted in June with strict enforcement of a new blackout policy for American films, whereby no U.S. movies could be released over the critical summer months. Therefore, the two valuable franchises were forced to go head to head on the same weekend, hurting both, though likely Spidey more. This was of course intentional, designed to discourage U.S. film viewership and encourage attendance at Chinese-made films.

Around this time a member of the powerful state-run China Film Group was quoted in the *People's Daily* newspaper saying: "We [SARFT]"* are "making a series of transitional protection measures, which we hope can provide for the development and growth of Chinese films by supporting their roots, and increasing their ability to defend themselves against imported films." He went on to say that he "hoped that one day Chinese audiences would tire of American robots and superheroes."

What's going on? A studio head told me that China, unlike other countries, doesn't have the patience to grow its local film community in the way so many other countries have as its movie appetite grows. "It is clear that the indigenous market always climbs to the top of the local box office after a growth period,"

---

* State Administration of Radio, Film and Television.

he told me. "But it takes time, subsidies and development. China doesn't want to wait that long."

Apparently it doesn't have to. It's all happening faster than a speeding bullet, maybe faster than the government can control. Shocking even itself, China had its first self-created blockbuster, which surpassed *Titanic* in the Chinese box office in 2013, grossing 1 billion yuan. And it was a *comedy,* kind of a Chinese *Hangover,* made for the equivalent of $1.6 million, called *Lost in Thailand,* about a bumpkin pancake maker and his travails on a trip in Thailand. The people loved that it was free of religion and politics, and that it was funny. It opened in a slot cleared of American competition (*Skyfall* and *The Hobbit* had been pushed) but still very much not how the Chinese Film board planned it. It was an indie—not a state-made film—a tadpole! No 3D!

A forward-looking new Sino-American model emerged recently with the film *Looper,* a futuristic sci-fi actioner made as a Chinese-American coproduction of Sony/TriStar/Endgame and China's DMG Entertainment. This movie was *not* a victim of the summer blackout; it opened simultaneously in China and the United States. This is certainly the way the Chinese would like to play the Hollywood derby: not with our imports, but by reaping the greater percentages of our coproductions until they can take over the means of production themselves.

There is another, deeper factor: If you read the news out of China, it is clear that the country is experiencing a serious economic slowdown, and seeing 68 percent of its box office gross eaten by American product may not be popular in the politburo or in the streets. The summer blackout reduced that number to 60 percent, a step in the right direction. Sanford Panitch told me that it is always wise to think of China as a huge corporation looking for market share, not as a country. Additionally, it is undergoing a political transition that entails some instability: Our deal partner, Xi Jinping, went missing in the summer before his ascension. He may have been practicing his acceptance speech, he may have had a heart attack, or could merely be suffering a bad back, as was rumored in the press. He is now the president. Hooray for Hollywood. But what we know about our partners is that we know nothing. There are those movie people who understand the Chinese better than others and take Sinosensibilities and sensitivities into account. They read the political winds carefully and give back as well as take out profits. These long-term players will reap more long-term profits out of their deals. Fox, of course, with its savvy indigenous production wing, is initiating a huge coproduction deal and will be able to release its Chinese-made films even during blackout periods, as *Looper* was. DreamWorks Animation and IMAX are also listening more and complaining less. As Jim Gianopulos, whose studio has been working with them the longest, told me, they are fickle friends.

SO, COMRADE, WHAT WILL WE SEE?

I am glad that I have found Legendary to be my comrade. We sincerely value this partnership and believe that this collaboration will not only produce countless fantastic films for our global audience, but simultaneously will allow the world to see China from a whole new perspective.

—Thomas Tull's partner in their *Variety* announcement.

All these coproductions are subject to strict government regulations. They must be shot in China, and more significantly, they must pass the government censors. This will be no small feat, apparently. People who've seen *Snow Flower and the Secret Fan* (an English-language film) tell me that foot binding never occurred in provincial China in the nineteenth century, as depicted in Wendi

Deng and her partner's coproduction of the classic novel. Or so say the Chinese censors. They didn't like the dirty laundry hanging in Shanghai in 2006's *Mission: Impossible III* either, so it was cut. They are even tough on their favorite kind of tentpole. The Chinese are tough on laundry!

Recently, while on the jury of a film festival in Beijing, director Jean-Jacques Annaud apologized to the Chinese government for his insensitivities toward Chinese culture in his film *Seven Years in Tibet*—about the Dalai Lama during the time of China's takeover of Tibet—in order to shoot his next film there; the *Los Angeles Times* reported that in *2012,* a disaster movie about an attack on the White House, dialogue was inserted for the Chinese version that extolled Chinese scientists as visionaries. It also reported that gratuitous compliments about the Chinese people or government are being inserted into scripts to please financial partners. Pretty soon, with Russia and China as our primary trade partners, we will have no bad guys in our action movies. Only North Koreans.

What coproduction will also deeply affect are the types of movies we're less likely to see from the studios, as Chinese box office dominance expands: Dramas. Period pieces. Romances. Anything remotely political. Comedies. All of our financially advantageous (especially to the Chinese) coproductions require extensive rewrites and polishes to please the delicate sensitivities of the Chinese partners. Even the science-fiction hit *Looper* had to be moved from France to China, sixty years in the future, when it will be the greatest superpower in the world! *There's* a subtle change. Not.

The impact of this new deal obviously cements the studios' reliance on special-effect-driven tentpoles. Without the new exports, the Chinese market was already moving from number five to number one. They want fantasy, and only we can make giant, spectacular fantasy. It is the thing technology has left us with which to refill our empty coffers. The biggest movie in history led the way.

Think of what *Avatar* provided the world. The $2 billion dollar fantasy was the ultimate ride; it was the thrill of seeing a perfectly used technology that was invented, literally, for one movie. It was something that could be done only in America at that point, by only one filmmaker. The creation of that technology converged perfectly with the outfitting of IMAX and 3D conversions in all the emerging markets. Suddenly, teens, kids and families from Indonesia to Peoria, from Kaliningrad to Beijing, from Kyoto to Brooklyn, were all hooked up to the rest of the village. It made everyone feel like they were in tune with everyone else at the cutting edge of technology. You had to see it, and you had the technology to know that, and we had the outreach to tell you that—wherever you were under the Earth's moon.

As for ideas—the government of China doesn't want the West intermediating ideas. The Web is hard enough for them to control, and now they have their own indie filmmakers. Their audience doesn't want subtitles, or our interpretation of Tiananmen Square. This is not our job.

How do we keep making movies for them and yet also keep making movies for us? With this potential industry-saving mandate, can we still make something other than tentpoles and sequels? Is the business systemically addicted? Are we addicted? What about those of us who aren't?

THE ORIGIN OF SEQUELITIS

Is It a Disease Without a Cure?

The *Ice Age* Paradox: *Diminishing Appetite for Sequels Here Is in Direct Proportion to the Increasing Appetite for Them Abroad.*

Here we get to the crux of the matter, where marketing meets international, where our taste diverges from "theirs." This is where the number crunching tells you what the studios are going to make, what they are going to continue to make (apart from their Oscar bait), why they've made what they've made, and why there is rarely something you want to see at the mall this weekend but everywhere else they're flocking to theaters in huge numbers. This is where the rubber meets the road to China. The question I am asked most frequently is, why do the studios keep making sequels? Here we go:

Jim Gianopulos slaps what I can only describe as a profoundly depressing chart in front of me. It is the grosses for *Ice Age,* domestic and international. It is clear they exhilarate him, as well they should.

"So here you go, look at *Ice Age,*" he says cheerfully.

A quick scan reveals bad news, if your angle is to reduce the number of unnecessary sequels from the movie diet. "This is fascinating," I say, scanning the numbers for confirmation of the end of the movie world as we knew it.

Jim reviews the numbers: "The first *Ice Age* does $175 million domestically, $206 million internationally. The second one does $192 million domestically, $456 million internationally. The third one does $200 million domestically and $700 million internationally."*

"That's crazy! That's crazy!"

He tries to talk. "Yeah. And what that shows you is—"

"You're going to make *Ice Age*s forever is what it shows you."

"That's for sure," Jim agrees. "But it also shows you the potential of the international market, when you have something that appeals broadly across many audience sectors. Something that is pure entertainment and enjoyment, that has the warmth and emotion that appeals to families, that has the wit and fun that appeals even to teens."

---

* The fourth one opened at $46 million domestic, with a global total of $385 million as of July 16, 2012.

It is about now that I want to stick my finger down my throat. But then Jim gets serious.

"But more than *anything,* when someone sees a poster, when someone sees an ad and it says *Ice Age* and he sees those characters, they know instantly what it is."

There it is. Preawareness. The enemy of originality.

"The problem is, even if international is now two-thirds of the box office, getting close to seventy percent—the population that we talked about is five percent to ninety-five percent—you can't spend twenty times the marketing internationally that you spend domestically. It's just too outrageously expensive. So when you look by any measure—by total rating points (this is how we measure TV buys), by the amount of the overall spend, by *anything*—you can't spend the same to get any particular person per capita abroad to be aware of your movie, to involve them in your movie and to get them to come to your movie as you would per capita in the United States. But when you have a sequel to a film that's recognizable, that they know, that they've enjoyed in the past, that's when you really tap into the potential. That's when the population potential and the audience potential really kicks in."

"Disease" is a term for any condition that impairs the normal functioning of an organism or a body.

So, ladies and gentlemen, I give you sequilitis. We are infected, and the infection seems to be killing some and making others very healthy. And wealthy. It will be with us forever. The question is, can the original movie survive despite it?

CREATING PREAWARENESS

DANCING WITH THE MARKETING STARS

Creative filmmakers and producers—those who care about original movies—are increasingly dependent on marketing wizards for the survival of movies not based on previously existing material. These films without "preawareness" are the endangered species of the movie business. Christopher Nolan's *Inception,* released by Warner Bros., based on an original script by Nolan, is one such film that many in the industry doubted would open at the time, as it had no famous title or comic-book hero to hang its hat on. But it opened like gangbusters due to a brilliant marketing campaign. This is why people like Warner Bros. president of worldwide marketing Sue Kroll are the new Hollywood stars.

Sue is a complex presence, full of mixed metaphors. She looks like a cameo in a locket but acts like a turbocharged Ferrari. Her demeanor is conservative, but she makes up the hippest campaigns for teen boys. "RELEASE THE KRAKEN!!!" read the ad line for the 2010 hit *Clash of the Titans* that was so widely and loudly repeated by young boys from coast to coast when the movie was released that it became an international meme. Sue made it up. She is equally intuitive and intellectual.

I saw her for the first time in September 2009, dancing out of an elevator at the Four Seasons Hotel during the Toronto Film

Festival with Matt Damon and her trusty ally and second-in-command, Blair Rich, in tow. I'd been dying to meet her. This is the famous Sue? I thought. It turns out Sue is more likely to be poring over research than boogalooing down hotel corridors; I'd just found her at a very uncharacteristic moment. They must have dared her to do it. Wouldn't you, if Matt asked you to?

At the top of the Warner Bros. decision-making team, she had been an inside star for fifteen years. She worked her way up through international marketing, creating Warner's worldwide *Harry Potter* campaigns, among others. Warner Bros. was not doing well with its U.S. releases in the mid-2000s (though its international marketing was thriving), and chairman Jeff Robinov got the idea to bring Sue back home from London to L.A. to run the whole shebang. It was a bold move, since the customary thing to do when marketing is in trouble is to play musical chairs and entice someone from another studio. Warner Bros. has been among the top in market share ever since. So I had my eye on Sue even before I was lucky enough to work with her.

Sue and her Warner Bros. team were opening Matt Damon's *The Informant* at the Toronto Film Festival, as well as the Ricky Gervais/Jen Garner movie, *The Invention of Lying,* that I was producing with my son, Oly. The two movies were sharing a press junket Sue was running, wherein the world's entertainment press gathered to watch our movies to review them and write features. Sue's team would try to affect the coverage by feting, wining and dining, and gifting reporters with their paltry movie swag and holding a press conference for each. The game played at press junkets is for the entertainment press to lap up all the perks, free meals and snippets of "intimate" milliseconds with the stars that they possibly can, while remaining as snarky and independent as possible and still manage to be invited back next year. These days there's a lot of satellite TV, and less mano a mano than before. And the swag is pretty much movie merchandising—a key chain, a board game, printed bath towels, all movie-theme dependent. The New Abnormal has taken the swagger out of swag, and the press is pretty much left with buffets and promotional tchotchkes.

Both *The Informant* and *The Invention of Lying* were destined to be "art" movies for Sue's studio. By this I mean the box office estimate was under $50 million domestic, no matter what happened. (That would have been a bonanza for *Lying*.) But from the look-to-conquer in Sue's eyes, you would have thought we were all Batmen. Well, she did have Matt. And that's pretty hot.

Sue spearheads each of Warner Bros. Pictures' campaigns personally, working closely with President Jeff Robinov and his production team in every aspect of a movie's release. Robinov, who started as an agent, has a keen eye for picking pictures. Making sure they get seen is Sue's department.

Marketing is the one hard cost in moviemaking now; the studios cannot change how much a television ad, a billboard, etc., costs. If the studio is smart and tough, they can lower a movie's budget and rein in production costs with a responsible filmmaker. But getting the word out—through all the noise of the other movies getting their word out—costs a fortune. Free advertising and publicity have become crucial. Getting the stars—if there are any—to do their bit on TV is a job in itself. But if the reliance on titles of famous books and fairy tales, superheroes, games et al. ad nauseam comes from their preexistence in the culture, then marketing creatives working on original properties must compensate for their product's lack of awareness with a campaign that captures the public's imagination.

Robinov also brought Sue Kroll onto his green-light team, making her a part of their early decision-making about what to produce. When the head of production and the head of marketing are on the green-light committee together, as is the case at Warner Bros. and now other studios too, there is more communication throughout the process. The whole team knows what it is selling from the moment it buys the script or idea and starts developing it. No marketing team can successfully open every movie, and Warner Bros. has had its failures: It couldn't get an audience to go to female-fantasy-actioner *Sucker Punch,* or get sufficient numbers to launch *Green Lantern* into franchise territory, despite Herculean efforts. But it has opened "original" movies—those without preawareness—as well as anyone ever has; for example, the Warner Bros. marketing team's phenomenally successful campaigns for *The Hangover* and *Inception.* By October 2011, *The Hangover I* and *II* had crossed the $1 billion mark, the highest-grossing live-action (nonanimated) comedy franchise in history.

In the hot fall of 2012, Warner Bros. also opened Ben Affleck's *Argo*—the weird, mostly true story of a covert mission to help six Americans flee Iran in 1979 by posing as a Canadian movie crew—at $19.5 million and helped boost it and Affleck into Oscar contenders. The original hit had passed the $100 million mark before the festivities had even begun, exciting writers and producers all around town. All they had to do was score Ben Affleck and they could make their favorite story!

Marketing is crucial to the life or death of a movie, and like advertising itself with its coveted Clios, it has evolved into an art form. *Making the audience think* they will like a movie is the job of the marketing department. If a campaign doesn't click, the movie dies a quick death. If the idea isn't a presold "title," its concept should be easy to explain on a "one-sheet" (a poster on buses, billboards and theaters). If it's not, it better have big stars' faces on posters to plaster all over the world. Now that marketing people are often in on development decisions, Monday-morning meetings when execs talk about the scripts that were submitted and read over the weekend could, in the worst case, go something like this:

PRESIDENT OF PRODUCTION: What script should we buy?
EXEC: I love this one! It's great!

PRES: What's it about?

EXEC: Blah blah blah. Blah.

MARKETING PRES: That was one blah too many. It won't fit on a one-sheet!

PRES: Pass.

If they don't know how to sell it, they won't make it.

SELLING *INCEPTION*

Inception is the perfect example of a movie whose concept won't fit on a one-sheet: A guy has a dream within a dream in which he's looking for his wife, who may or may not be trying to kill him as they are chased by a series of bad guys in a multilevel dreamscape . . . while he is trying to get back to his kids. *What???* A one-liner on a poster wasn't going to sell this movie. It was a classic marketer's nightmare.

So I visited one of my favorite pundits, Vinny Bruzzese, a marketing research expert then with the marketing firm OTX (now called Ipsos), one of the outside companies the studios use when they're out of ideas to discuss its prospects, for insight. Vinny, with his slicked-back black hair and Bronx accent, looks more OTB than OTX, and he was dubious, as he looked ahead to summer's prospects.

"Not big," he said. "Specialty movie . . . for cinephiles . . . too hard to explain . . . big cities . . . lucky to break $100 million . . . no *Dark Knight*."

It wasn't just Vinny who was thinking this way; that was the industry buzz before Sue Kroll and her team got ahold of the campaign. In the end, this one-off did $270 million domestically and $650 million worldwide once the campaign and the word of mouth on the film coalesced.

How did Warner Bros.'s marketing team take an unknown property like *Inception* and turn it into an unexpected blockbuster? They made it a must-see phenomenon. If you didn't have an opinion about *Inception* by Saturday, the day after it opened, you were simply uncool. As Oly put it, "I felt like they were saying, 'Trust me. You don't have to know what it's about. You just have to see it. Dreams. Christopher Nolan. GO.'"

So it was with the key demo (males ages twelve to twenty-four) all around the country. It was beyond water-cooler talk. It was the brunch topic in Chicago, the dinner party chatter in Austin and Denver. If you hadn't seen it by Sunday, you were in the theater Sunday night to be ready for work chat Monday. Industry analysts call this buzz, or "want to see." This buzz was created. How?

First, they turned Christopher Nolan into a star—not a movie star, but a cinema star. They built a mystique around him and then built a campaign from there. *He is one of a kind, a talent of a different caliber, pushing the boundaries of cinema. See the movie because of the director! He is the exciting element.*

No director besides Spielberg had successfully opened a movie based purely on reputation before. Spielberg's name has instant recognition and is for many around the world enough of a reason to see a movie. It is placed above the title like a star's name. In this case, the *Dark Knight* director wasn't coming at them with an obvious blockbuster, as he was with his *Dark Knight* franchise. He had a "drawer" script from ten years ago that clocked in at two and a half hours, a formidable running time, with an idea that wouldn't have fit on a poster designed by Christo and draped around the Golden Gate Bridge.

They concentrated on the director, the astonishing visuals and the originality of the movie. I asked Sue how they handled this marketing crisis over dinner one night at her regular Italian haunt in Los Feliz, a ten-minute drive from Warner Bros.

She explained, "Rather than attempting to answer all of the

questions within the context of our materials, we really encouraged a dialogue. We wanted audiences to struggle a little and invest in what the movie promised to deliver. If they had questions, that was a good thing. To us it meant that they were engaged and paying attention, and that ultimately drove our results. Our campaign was a slow build over a period of months. We had to create 'event status,' but that can't be done all at once when you have an original concept. By the time we got to release, it was an event, but it took careful planning to get there."

The campaign made these concise points:

1. This is an Event.
2. This Director (capital "D") who made *The Dark Knight* is the Real Thing.
3. It's about dreams.
4. This movie is cool.
5. Here's all the story you need.
6. It's action: mucho action.
7. Here's Leo.
8. He goes home.
9. The visuals are mind-blowing.
10. More action.
11. You have never seen anything like this.
12. It's romantic.

What makes a great creative marketing executive like Sue so good at her job is the same gift that a great creative production executive has: total absorption and the ability to discover something about each movie to fall in love with. But her gift is by no means reserved for highbrow material. She made hits out of *Clash of the Titans* and *The Hangover:* "Bachelor party buddies wake up hungover in a palatial hotel room with Mike Tyson's tiger but no groom!' Go."

• • •

Sony has its own marketing star in its chairman of worldwide marketing and distribution, Jeff Blake. The return of Julia Roberts was
a big deal for Sony. She worked and worked and helped open their
movie *Eat Pray Love*. But just as important was Blake's campaign.
It was beautiful, dreamy and everywhere. If you'd even remotely
heard of the book, you would have noticed the poster, the jew-
elry, the movie tie-in bookstore displays with Sony-merchandized
prayer beads. It was utterly female-friendly penetration. His
campaign for David Fincher's *The Social Network,* the story of the
founding of Facebook, was equally brilliant and helped the film to
open all around the world, like the global social phenomenon that
Facebook had by that point become.

Ten years ago we never knew the names of the heads of marketing; they were the guys in modest suits who came to previews.
Now they are the other rock stars, along with the studio heads. We
know they are vital participants in the studio process, and we hear
that they are called into meetings to decide on whether to green-
light a script! More important, if no one sees your movie, what's
the point of having made it? If that's the case, what's the difference
between a marketing head and a studio head? It doesn't matter, as
long as the marketing head believes in your movie. What does a
marketing head think about? How to read and reach the audience,
and, specifically, the segment of the audience that is going to like
your movie the most. This is a cultivated skill based on quadrant-
think. Everyone is part of this, like it or not.

QUADRANT-THINK

Quadrant-think is one of the main exercises that movie and marketing execs use to figure out whether they are going to make a
movie. Then they use it again to determine exactly how to sell the

movie by determining who would like it and who they should target. It's how they model whether a large enough base potentially exists to see the movie, or whether to cut their losses and unceremoniously dump it. (Release it in one theater in limited cities with no ads.)

It's HellOOO? Who's out there? Anyone? Are there enough of you who go to movies for us to make this thing? Or spend the ad money and release it?

Here's how it works: Think of the entire moviegoing public as a pie, divided into quarters. Each quarter of that pie is a different demographic flavor. The idea is to get as many quadrants of the pie into the theater as possible.

If there is not a significant portion of the pie or combination of pieces of pie that can be reliably targeted to show up, the movie will not happen. The more slices you can get, the more likely it is to get made. If the movie you want to make is specific enough, if it can target two quadrants to which it can easily be marketed, the marketers will know exactly how to reach those quadrants on TV and online. Then it might get made. It depends on which two. But at least you can make a good argument. Any kind of pie will do.

The upper female quadrant—shall we call it Apple Pie?—is composed of women over twenty-four, like me. We are the least frequently targeted quadrant because of our penchant for waiting until we have unloaded the dishwasher and done every other imaginable errand we have to do before we leave the house and go to the movies.

Vinny Bruzzese regularly tells me, "They rent," and he has the numbers to back his point.

We are only potent when combined with our sisters, nieces or daughters in the "lower" female quadrant, those under twenty-four: the Berry Pies. AppleBerries have made reliable hits over three decades. But forget making a movie for Apple Pies alone: They call those Lifetime TV movies.

The opposite of Apple Pie renters is the most coveted quadrant, the lower male—the Mud Pies, which encompasses boys ages twelve to twenty-four. They used to go to movies on Friday nights in droves. But they are going less often now, as they are buried in video games and the Net, gaming, searching, Facebooking, everything. The studios just can't give these boys up, kind of like your nutty girlfriend who won't stop stalking an old lover despite his obvious lack of interest. Every week there is an update about whether the boys' attention is finally back, and if not, what will draw them back.

When Mud Pies show up for a movie, they can make it a hit all by themselves, because they go en masse on the first weekend, when studios make the most money.* Moreover, the opening number instantly brands the movie as a hit or a flop. This is why they are still the key demographic. The upper male quad (over twenty-four)—let's call them Pecan Pies—loves political thrillers. They go to the movies more than my Apple quad, but rarely make a hit alone. When they combine with the lower male quadrant, you have a big hit. Pecan and Mud together make your Man movies, some of which cross over to lower female (Berry) as well, so they make date-night action movies (*Thor, Iron Man*).

When any two quadrants show up, like my favorite two, the upper and lower female, you have AppleBerry Pie, and it makes a solid domestic performer. We can make a hit without a slice of Pecan or Mud pie showing up, à la *The Proposal, Julie & Julia, The Devil Wears Prada, Something's Gotta Give, Legally Blonde, How to Lose a Guy in 10 Days, Hope Floats* or hundreds of others. If we show up in droves, you have *Twilight*.

With a film like *Bridesmaids,* or *The Devil Wears Prada,* or *Sleepless in Seattle,* where we drew in many Pecans who identified with Tom Hanks, you have a three-quadrant movie. If in

---

* The first weekend is the studios' most profitable because of the financial split with the theaters. From then on out, the exhibitors make more.

those cases we cross that movie over to a few of the lower (or upper) males by not making it absolutely toxic to men in casting, title or premise, we can make a big hit. Remember, these movies cost nothing. They require no expensive special effects, no huge action sequences. They are just casting with locations and sets. (And a *lot* of hair, makeup and wardrobe.) All of the aforementioned movies easily exceeded $100 million. Three-quad franchises based on best-selling intellectual properties, or IPs, such as *The Hunger Games* and *Twilight,* brought in some AppleBerry and Mud pies, but Berries came in droves. Berries pushed the first of each of these movies into franchise territory.

The Holy Grail of the business is the four-quadrant movie: *Avatar, Titanic, Toy Story.* These are movies that everyone wants to see. Family movies are often four-quadrant movies, such as *Shrek, The Lion King, Madagascar* (from DreamWorks Animation) and almost all of the Pixar movies. The Pixar formula, if it existed, would have already been copied, stolen or in some way breached. They make them up, they make them well and they never copy themselves. All are originals, and so far only two have gotten sequels—*Cars* and *Toy Story*—so Pixar doesn't seem reliant on the sequel model for success. Quite a formula. No formula. That's why they don't die anywhere. If you can hit all four quads, well, it's time to retire—but you can't because you have to make another movie *right away*. It's the start of a potential franchise! A four-quadrant movie is the point of the game. We call that a blockbuster.

GIVING TESTIMONY AT TEST SCREENINGS: CALL-AND-RESPONSE

We meet the quadrants—that is, the audience—and discover what they have to say about our baby at the first recruited test preview. The marketing department decides who will be recruited based on a conversation with the producer. "Who was the movie intended for? Berries? Muds? Pecans? Apples?"

Then they spread the word at the malls: what the movie is about, who is in it and what other movies it is like. Often they hire outside companies such as Kevin Goetz's Screen Engine or OTX to help bring in the audience and run the preview. Pretty much everything is at stake: the advertising budget, the release date, the entire destiny of the picture.

That's why I arrive at the theater looking like a deer caught in headlights for the first test preview of any movie, after driving during crushing rush-hour traffic for at least an hour and a half on the 101 freeway in the Valley. I then stare closely at the line waiting outside. I say to these people, but not out loud—at least, not very loud—*You are the most powerful people in my life. Please be kind. In fact, be wonderful.* Then I smile like an idiot at all of them. And somehow I believe this behavior will affect their test scores. Sometimes it works. Sometimes, oddly, it doesn't.

The test-preview process is the horrifying reality show we live through right after the first cut of the picture is delivered to the studio. So I've developed some superstitions. I always request Kevin Goetz to run the preview, to keep both the focus group and me focused. Everyone is there, including my director, whose feelings I am more worried about than my own. Also present are various divisions of the studio whose moods I have to discern. It's here that we find out if we are a hit or a flop and what we can do to make us closer to the former. This is a do-or-die process, as we find out through this thumbs-up or thumbs-down roller-coaster night whether we have a shot in the marketplace.

We arrive at the preview with the big marketing issues unresolved and on the line. But then something consequential happens: We begin our dialogue with the audience. Before this moment, the movie was all ours. We knew what worked, what we loved, what was funny, what was moving. Until this moment, we knew our movie. But once we share it with the audience and we feel them in the room, in our bones, our subjective experience becomes a joined experience. We see the picture with new eyes now, both ours and theirs. To me, more important than what we read later in the audience preview cards is what we feel in our gut, especially with a comedy, but also with a drama. Where were they laughing? Where were they bored, twitching, rustling in their seats? After this, we never see the movie in exactly the same way. The audience owns it with us. And this isn't all bad.

If we are sane, we realize that we've fallen in love with our movie during shooting. During the cutting process, some of our thousands of choices have become ingrained. We may have lost some objectivity. This is inevitable when the filmmakers are alone together in a small, dark room eight hours a day for eight weeks. This is our last chance to regain that objectivity, as well as an opportunity to go Zen and just listen.

This is a wise posture, because there is often a combination of ego and interpretive conflict about what the audience reactions on the cards say. At times, the written comments are so random they are uninterpretable. Conversely, a picture can get better, or at least improve its numbers, from very clear and consistent notes that the cards reveal. (This happens more often than not.) Sometimes the process devolves into an ideological battle about whether the audience, marketeers and studio suits should be factored into the filmmakers' decision-making process at all. But now that show business has become business business as the cost of movies and marketing has exploded, there is little if any patience for these debates; or, when they do happen, they take place among the filmmakers on the ride home, where we strategize as to what we are willing to do and where to hold the line.

Certain "arty" and "indie" movies get to avoid this fate altogether: Nonstudio movies can't afford this process, and even if they could, the point of independent production is to allow the filmmaker his final cut. That's what independent means. Even at the classics divisions inside the studio system, they will test for marketing purposes, and A-list filmmakers get their pick of which notes to listen to and which to ignore; that's the price of working with these kinds of directors. For example, Alexander Payne's *About Schmidt* did not test well at all. Movies like this cannot randomly recruit a target audience in malls, because that's not where educated grown-ups who love Payne's movies hang out on weekends. When filmmakers like Payne work inside the studio system, as with *The Descendants*—a delicious dramedy starring George Clooney about a dysfunctional family becoming functional—they make only the changes they approve. (It helps that *The Descendants* was released by Fox's Searchlight division, which specializes in smaller, specialty films.) This also happens if the movie tests over 90, which is terrific, believe me. The same goes for Darren Aronofsky, Paul Thomas Anderson, etc., when they are working outside of the studios. I highly doubt Anderson previewed *The Master*. But when Darren makes *Noah*—about the biblical flood—for Fox for over $100 million, he will be testing, because that is the fate of tentpoles.

Our call-and-response begins at this moment in back of the dark cinema as the first audience watches the picture. Testimony is given right after, in the recruited focus group, filmmakers and studio silent in their hidden seats, as the righteous speak of obvious mistakes, confusions, backstory problems, jokes that fell flat, continuity mistakes and problems or confusions with the ending. Hands are raised for numbers. Hearts sink or soar. You get an instant A or F (Cs are Fs, by the way). Our dialogue with America has begun.

This is not new. I found preview cards used by David O. Selznick, director of the 1939 movie *Gone with the Wind,* in the Fox vaults. These cards asked virtually the same questions we ask today. Based on some of my past focus groups, I imagined what Selznick might experience in the San Fernando Valley if *Gone with the Wind* were coming out now, and he had recruited the wrong audience—which happens all the time.

KEVIN: Hi, everyone. I'm Kevin! What's your name?

THE FOCUS GROUP: (*In sequence, raising their hands*) I'm Cindy! I'm James! I'm Donna! I'm Billy! I'm Andrea! I'm Diego! I'm Joe the Plumber!

(*Everyone laughs.*)

KEVIN: You can be honest with me. I had nothing to do with making this film. You won't hurt my feelings. It's only a print. It's not finished or color-corrected. They have lots of work yet to do. And much of the Civil War footage is still waiting for effects. So, what worked for you? What didn't work?

DONNA: (*Raises her hand*) Well, Scarlett is a total bitch. She tried to steal Melanie's boyfriend. And she was a terrible mother. I hated her.

(*David O. slouches in his chair.*)

KEVIN: Who agrees with Donna?

(*All the girls shoot up their hands in agreement.*)

KEVIN: (*Trying another tack*) Who was your favorite character?

DONNA: Ashley Wilkes. He was dreamy.

KEVIN: Okay, Donna. And Joe the Plumber—what did you think?

JOE THE PLUMBER: I thought he was a pussy.

DIEGO: Yeah, I liked Rhett. He was a gunrunner. Cool.

CINDY: Me too. I liked him. I was glad he turned that bitch out.

ANDREA: Rhett is way cooler than Ashley.

DONNA: No way. He's a drunk.

KEVIN: (*Sees this quickly devolving into a catfight*) Girls? What do you think the theme of the movie was?

ANDREA: If you string the guy along, you're gonna lose him.

JAMES: (*Derisively*) God. It's not a romantic comedy. It's a war movie.

KEVIN: Good. Guys? What do you think the theme was?

JOE THE PLUMBER: The South will rise again!

(The studio head can no longer see David O.)

KEVIN: How many of you would recommend this movie to your friends?

(Half the hands in the room go up.)

KEVIN: What would you change about the movie so that you would recommend it to your friends?

CINDY: I think Melanie should come back to life and get revenge.

(Girls agree, all cheer.)

(Filmmakers cringe in the back, looking at one another in dismay, and at Kevin hopelessly.)

KEVIN: What if I told you this was based on a famous book and we can't bring Melanie back to life?

(Girls are deflated.)

BILLY: I know that book! My mother loves it.

Sometimes you leave the focus group and want to shoot yourself or the person who recruited the focus group or the focus group itself, deploying a mental firing squad. Sometimes, a point Joe the Plumber makes is a point that the director made in an earlier debate. At that moment in the focus group, he glares at the studio exec in his seat. Or sometimes a point Donna makes is a note that the studio exec had been pushing, so he smiles at the director. But often so many points are made that it's a jumble, and everyone just rolls their eyes.

While all this drama and annihilation of our hard work is going on, a little man who sits pretty low down on the totem pole is standing in a hidden dark booth in the theater somewhere where no one can find him. He is frantically counting the critical numbers marked in the boxes on the preview cards that the recruited audience has just completed, trying to arrive at The Number.

THE NUMBER! THE TOP TWO BOXES!

When it's all over and the audience has written and spoken its critiques, the whole team meets in the same small, dark projection booth like a bunch of outlaws and grabs at the little man in possession of the papers with the numbers. Someone has calculated the bottom line. Nuances are for tomorrow. First, are we a hit? Are we a disaster? Do we have work to do? And will it be easy, or hard, painful lifting?

The "everything" number is decided by how the audience rates the movie on their preview cards. There are five options: "excellent," "very good," "good," "fair" and "poor." The Number is the percentage (out of the total number of cards) of viewers who check one of the top two boxes, rating it as either excellent or very good. Good doesn't count. Fair is bad. Poor is terrible.

The point of these tests is to find ways to push the "goods" into "very goods" by analyzing those "goods" and seeing what the issues are.

Another question asks whether you would recommend the movie to your friends. The top two boxes are "yes, definitely" and "yes, probably." Again, only these boxes count in gauging a Number, and again we try to push the "yes, probably"s to "yes, definitely"s. The lesser options are "might or might not recommend"; "no, probably not"; and "no, definitely not." Anything other than the top two translates to "I'll watch it on TV or when it comes out on Netflix, or forget about it altogether!"

Everyone prays that their number is over 80. Then they're safe. Most movies tend to test in the 60s. Average is low 70s. Mid-80s to 90 and up is a potential hit; 50s or worse, hide.

The data on the cards that we are interpreting in the dark booth are this: If you're not recommending the movie to your friends, why not? It is interpreted through questions like: If you could change one thing about the film, what would it be? What will *get* you to recommend this movie to your friends? (This question is asked in the focus group, often.) Who is this movie for? What was wrong or right about the ending of this movie? (Read: How much will reshoots cost us to fix it?) What characters did you dislike most? (Read: Off with their heads!) What did you not understand? (Read: Cuts? Or reshoots?)

Sherry Lansing was the best I've seen at leading these meetings. Calm and focused, never domineering or overriding anyone else, she could read and interpret the cards in four minutes flat, figure out how to fix existing scenes, what to reshoot and how to do it all for a price. And she knew how to make the filmmaker think it was his idea.

Years later, Sherry told me her secret: She actually had all her notes while she watched the movie and took little of the cards into account. She shared her notes privately with the filmmaker so he knew that she was saying what she really thought, not what the audience was saying. It worked, and quickly.

You can sometimes gain upward of ten points by fixing a bad ending, or clearing up confusions and muddles, with judicious editing. Sometimes a movie is just too long in places, and cuts and trims help. This is what we hope for.

Sometimes a reshoot is called for. This costs big money, but it's a drop in the bucket if it makes a movie work. Particularly a movie that cost a lot to begin with.

The Number is the bottom line, the whole point of the evening, what we leave with. If it's great, we have great spin, we soar. If it's terrible, if we have a flop, we keep quiet. If it's in the middle, we go to work and spin that it's great and inflate the number by ten points. It's kind of like someone's age or weight in an online dating profile: No one believes the Number.

Constant studio test screenings in the San Fernando Valley have turned locals into mini-Roger Eberts—they are by now expert critics, writing as though they had their own *Chicago*

Sun-Times column, TV show and blog, because every studio is testing their products in the same ten malls, and the same gene pool is
getting all the action. The call-and-response with the audience is
therefore a multilogue between these anointed geniuses (standing
in for America) and the filmmaking team of directors, producers,
marketing gurus and studio heads anxious for feedback. After
we get the Number, the purpose of the meeting in the dark is to
Figure Out What the Audience Is Saying and then to Figure Out
What to Do. It is a song we have all learned to sing, some of us better than others.

The audience's thoughts and confusions, and how the filmmakers, studio and marketing gurus interpret and debate those
thoughts, shape postproduction and the creative direction of the
rest of the movie. When David O. Selznick was doing this, the
directors left the picture when production ended, so the producer
was in total control, with no debates allowed. But now the interaction is mediated by a committee involving the studio chiefs along
with the producer and the director. It is a "process," as we say, often
with the audience in the lead.

By the way, if we producers don't like our score and want to
preview next time in Chicago or Dallas or Newark, where we used
to fly as a matter of course if we thought our movie would play better as "rural" or "urban," the marketing people will say no. They
will tell us definitively that Newark and Atlanta and Calabasas are
all the same place, and they can prove it with statistics. Therefore,
we are staying in the San Fernando Valley. There is no regional
America anymore, they say. And none of the studio people have
time to fly.

After we make agreed-upon changes, the new movie is tested
again and again (if it is not being dumped because it tested in the
40s) until the numbers are up as high as the studio's support (in
the form of reshoots and additional previews) will allow for. If a
studio gets a movie testing well, then later on it will spend, spend,

spend on advertising—which is why the process is so important to us producers and filmmakers. We try to be accommodating to the notes that make sense, because it is after these screenings that the studio sets the marketing budget. Carrot and stick are the tools that set the pace.

If the studio decides it supports the movie as a result of this process, it picks the release date (if it hasn't already) and commences the campaign. Where it places its ads—and even the message of the ads—has everything to do with what it learned in the tests. Hopefully, the campaign clicks and hits the target audience (quadrants!) right in its sweet spot. If not, this is what happens:

"They are down to a science in marketing, advertising and what we call 'materials,'" Vinny Bruzzese, who helps studios when their campaigns are in trouble, explained. "Once the movie enters the tracking, they measure the success of their marketing in a continuing call-and-response with the audience.

"First they test the movie's awareness vis-à-vis other movies coming out. If the audience is not sufficiently *aware* of the movie, they need to spend more on marketing. If there is not enough 'definite interest' in seeing the film, maybe the *content* of their material is off, and they need to rethink the advertising content quickly. If the first-choice number is low relative to the other movies opening that week—the most critical number for box office success—we research what it would take to make the movie the first choice, and we do it. If none of this works past the first weekend, the studios are stumped. They go to outside marketing companies or their marketing departments, and they punt. They change the materials or the one-sheet if it's early enough, redo the television spots, change the message."

This is what we were seeing during the *Bridesmaids* campaign when there was no movement in the lower and upper female quadrants, where the movie was aimed. But an early preview created word of mouth, and the spots playing during the NBA finals ultimately brought in guys (lower male quadrant) as was intended. *Bridesmaids* turned out to be an AppleBerry Mud Pie Super Smash.

Another fascinating thing that happened in the last minute before *Bridesmaids* opened involved a delicious concept that Vinny taught me: Definite Interest Intensity (DII). It's a way of determining how committed viewers are to seeing a movie, whether those who've expressed interest in the movie feel the pressing need to get up and go out to see it when it comes out (the point, in the end, of all these metrics). I love it, because I've won a few weekend shoot-outs with it—when my team started as underdogs and ended up opening as a convincing number one (*Sleepless in Seattle* and *How to Lose a Guy in 10 Days*). As soon as it was explained to me, it clicked. OTX came up with DII while defining a "constantly changing psychographic" to a studio executive who was stumped by "the audience's confounding craving for something different." Vinny explained DII to me one morning as we had coffee at a Silver Lake café.

"On a given weekend," he said, "two movies will come out, tracking at thirty percent. One will, out of the blue, outgross the other. One movie records a sudden uptick in intensity of interest through buzz, word of mouth, or hotness. This can grow, as with *Inception,* pop, as with *Bridesmaids* or emerge from a sneak, like with *How To Lose a Guy.* Suddenly, a movie reaches its target demo and it swells into a 'have to see' from a 'want to see.'"

Why?

"We came up with a measure to try to capture that," Vinnie explained. "DII is that measure."

Over the past years, DII has been shown to be extremely susceptible to increasingly clever viral campaigns drawn out for months online. *The Blair Witch Project,* a tiny 1999 indie, began to show the effectiveness of the Internet in building word of mouth when it pretended to be online found footage of a group of friends who disappeared in the woods while chasing a local legend. Even though the claim was bogus, the movie opened big through its virally created DII. As much as studios would like to create DII, it can't be engineered. It is something that catches on—a brilliant piece of marketing, a great viral campaign, a YouTube spot, good word of mouth—like with *The Hangover.* Everyone had to see that movie from the minute the trailer came out. With *Bridesmaids,* if you hadn't seen it on the first weekend, you were out of the loop. DII is hot stuff.

The breakout movie franchise *Twilight*—a romantic vampire love series mostly for teen girls—has phenomenal DII. Lionsgate marketing president Nancy Kirkpatrick, whom I knew when she ran publicity at Paramount, caught a jet stream of Definite Interest Intensity smack in the face before the first installment opened, and knew she had a big one: "This is really how it started—with something so silly and simple that it's kind of embarrassing. When we were developing the *Twilight* script—I think we had just green-lit it [it was released in 2008]—Stephenie Meyer, the author, was doing a signing in Pasadena, a book signing. So it's Saturday morning down at, you know, Vroman's Bookstore down in Pasadena. So I drive down there, at ten a.m. on a Saturday, and there were a thousand people standing in line. Now, this is a book that had sold about a million copies. It was a hit book, but it wasn't a *huge* hit book, you know? And I thought, Wow! Something's going on here. And I sat, after the signing, as Stephenie did a Q and A with the audience, and the people were obsessed: The detail they knew about this book and its characters! It was unlike anything I had ever seen before, other than, like, *Star Trek.*"

"So how does marketing harness that?" I asked.

"The way that I started thinking about it was, This is girl *Star Trek.* Treat them like a fan base. Feed them the information they want. And that's sort of how the idea of it began. And we just started fanning that flame; there were already fan sites, albeit small ones, up on the Web, and we invited those ladies to the set and started giving them not marketing materials, but information that they wanted as fans. And to this day, we speak to them like you would speak to a friend telling them about the movie. You know, 'I was on the set and this is what they did at dinner last night' is not giving the fan base marketing materials, because they know what that is. It's letting them feel like they're on the inside and you're sharing information with them as you would a friend."

Twilight opened at $69.6 million, stunning the industry but not its fans or Lionsgate or Nancy Kirkpatrick. They knew they had Definite Interest Intensity of a scale that would drown out other movies in the market that weekend (and many others to come). No one was talking about anything other than *Twilight,* even if he or she didn't know what it was.

It happened to me on a much smaller scale when guys were targeted to go see Owen Wilson and Jackie Chan in *Shanghai Knights,* a comedy action adventure with kung fu, which came on dead even with the tracking of *How to Lose a Guy* two weeks before it opened. It turned out that the guys didn't *have* to see their movie on the first weekend or the first night. But the AppleBerries and their dates to whom Paramount had targeted our movie had a growing *need* to see *How to Lose a Guy* because the buzz and word of mouth were starting to grow. (Believe me, it wasn't the reviews.) It was a great campaign, and Paramount, knowing how highly we'd tested (95), held a national sneak preview the week before it opened. That sneak carried us to number one, and the girls for that weekend beat the guys. By the way, when that happens, amnesia sweeps the studio nation three weeks later. Can they come up with something to measure that, the nonchanging studio psychographic? Okay, Lynda, enough.

You can lead a horse to water but you can't make him drink, as the cliché goes. Good marketing can lead all us equines to water. But if we don't like the movie, the velocity of opinion travels much faster than marketing's ability to paper it over. In the Old Abnormal, this wasn't true. The studios could get a full weekend in before the second-weekend drop from word of mouth kicked in.

Today, buzz is quantum. A thousand people will each tell a thousand people what they think of a movie opening in three thousand theaters simultaneously. They will BBM it, tweet it, Facebook it, and before you know it, it's around the world in sixty seconds. No matter how many TV spots feature the three good reviews, word of mouth from your six closest friends always wins. So the efficacy of marketing stops at midnight opening night.

This is what happened with the collapse of *Hulk*, directed by Ang Lee, in 2003. He had just directed the phenomenally innovative *Crouching Tiger, Hidden Dragon* and had directed the critically acclaimed *The Ice Storm* and *Sense and Sensibility* before that. So there was great excitement for a fresh take on this tragic tale of a geneticist who suffers an accident that turns him into a raging green monster whenever he gets angry. *Hulk* opened huge. Universal's marketing could not have done better.

Says Bruzzese, "Its DII was off the charts. It had the highest levels of 'first choice' ever. But most everyone who wanted to see the movie saw it between Wednesday and Friday of its first long weekend. On June twentieth, *Hulk* opened at $62.1 million! The idea of an arty director on a comic-book movie was initially attracting everyone—an exciting idea, not unlike putting Christopher Nolan on *Batman*."

But perhaps it was too arty. Word of mouth rapidly overpowered the drumbeat of marketing, and within milliseconds it seemed that everyone heard that the movie was slow.

Vinnie said, "It dropped an astonishing seventy-seven percent after its opening weekend, leaving the entire industry slack-jawed."

It turned out to be a four-quadrant movie for no one. The studios can aim for a huge bull's-eye on the target, and the marketing wizards can hit it perfectly. But what the exit polls will tell you as they continue testing on the first weekend is whether the audience will recommend it to their friends.

These exit polls indicate whether a movie will underperform, overperform or meet the standard model, just like in elections. Some movies are review-proof—the audience loves them even if the reviewers don't. But what the exit polls ultimately reveal, in the final call-and-response with the audience, is whether the movie has *playability:* whether the audience likes it and will recommend it to friends. Sometimes that's about whether the movie is "good"—but really it's about whether it's *embraced by the audience,* good or not. Good is subjective.

The thing about playability is this: No matter how churchy state has gotten, and how statey church has gotten, production makes the films, not marketing. Production picks the producers, the directors and the writers. Marketing can advise on what film to make, but not on how to make it. If the film doesn't *play,* is a stinker or the audience rejects it, marketing looks to production, though marketing historically pays with someone getting fired. That's because it's really hard to open a stinker when word of mouth is so far ahead of you that marketing cannot be effective. (Or, as in the case of *Hulk,* when it is no longer effective.)

Because production is more powerful, marketing often takes the rap for a flop, and that's how it goes. In rare circumstances, however, a great marketing whiz can open a lousy movie, and whoa, are these guys suddenly valuable!

Sony is thrilled with what Jeff Blake has been able to do with Adam Sandler's minor opuses like *Jack and Jill,* in which Sandler plays both his character and his character's incredibly annoying twin sister, Jill. It opened to $23 million in November 2011, despite nobody seeming to like it. (It scored a remarkable 3 on Rotten Tomatoes, an influential review blog, out of a possible 100.)

There aren't many people who can do this. He also opened *The Social Network* with a cutting-edge campaign with an ad line that was almost McLuhanesque in flavor: "We Are the Social Network." We were all part of the opening; it was an online, around-the-world Event. He took an original filmmaker-driven biopic (David Fincher and Aaron Sorkin) and turned it into an Academy-contending social-networking phenomenon unto itself.

Then there is Fox Searchlight, Fox's lean, small and very exciting classics division, run by Nancy Utley, who was first its marketing head and is now president of the whole thing. She made *Slumdog Millionaire* the belle of the Oscars in 2008, beating the bigger and better-financed Paramount entry, *The Curious Case of Benjamin Button,* a David Fincher–directed love story about a boy who ages backward. Searchlight is a perennial Oscar contender, as it proved again in 2011 with *The Descendants.* Two of the best studio marketeers I know are now working together at Fox: Tony Sella and Oren Aviv, formerly president of marketing, then production, at Disney. Aviv both conceived of Disney's hit *National Treasure* and devised its campaign, as well as running the early *Pirates of the Caribbean* campaigns. Aviv's successes earned him the more volatile job of president of production at Disney, where he ran into politics and then ended up back in marketing with Sella at Fox. Heads of marketing becoming heads of studios could become a trend, or the marketers are so powerful where they are, they will be encouraged to stay in their jobs and given more and more money, like free agents. With rare exceptions, these talents tend to stay where they are, under lock and key, with escalating salaries and ever bigger offices. They attract producers and directors, who, over time, come to recognize these new moguls as allies in the trenches and as one of the reasons to pick a studio. They would like their movies to be seen as well as made.

I went to see Vinny Bruzzese again. I wanted to know what to make of all the concentration on marketing. Was it a good thing or a bad thing?

He referred me back to the questions raised by philosopher Theodor Adorno. This was unexpected, but I always forget that Vinny is a lapsed academic. Fortunately, I remembered Adorno a bit from my undergraduate days: Frankfort School, 1930s, a critic of the culture industry.

"What *about* Adorno?" I asked.

"Does industry *gauge* what the consumer wants?" Vinny asked. "Or does the industry *tell* the consumer what it wants?"

"You tell me," I said. I figure he had insight from spending weekends on the phone with panicked or elated studio heads.

"I think the industry tells the audience what it wants," he said. "The good thing about market research is that it's an opportunity for the audience to tell the industry what it wants back."

"I love that," I said. "That is *audience* power."

He smiled and added, "And Adorno said there would be a breaking point of formulaic production."

"Have we reached that? Did Adorno predict sequel fatigue? Is that what you mean? Sequels tend to be very formulaic."

He nodded affirmatively and said, "Adorno also talked about commodity fetishism: being delighted with something because of how much it costs."

"Like a wildly expensive Kelly bag!" I said. "Women wait in lines to get them! Will people go see it just because it's so big? Like size determines value?"

Vinny was on a roll. "These products, Adorno said, these commodity fetishes, are characterized by standardization."

I remembered some Frankfort School too. "Commodity fetishes" are supposed to give us a good cry and let us feel restored, keeping us politically apathetic. Adorno, the neo-Marxist, was criticizing all entertainment as a distraction from the political— anything that gave us a good cry, such as a great movie like *Casablanca* or *Jules and Jim*. These movies could temporarily make us forget our oppression and lift us up. I want this, thank you. But these days, our entertainment diversions rarely even give us a good cry. They are momentary diversions, like the proverbial Chinese meal after which you are still hungry. You can't remember them by the time you get home.

The smartest studio people are beginning to recognize this sequel fatigue—this *"confounding craving for something different."* But in order to select "something different" and have the guts to make it in the Great Contraction, the studios need to have some confidence that this kind of movie will open. They need talented marketers to create campaigns as thrilling as the movies themselves "to make you think you want to see the movie before you know you do." The audience needs to want to see it enough to get out of their bedrooms, off the Net, off of Facebook, Words With Friends, fantasy baseball, four-player video games and off their butts and into the theater in droves with their besties. Otherwise, it's too scary to green-light it, and the industry will cater to the only reliable markets that they have in the wake of the collapse of the DVD market: the ones outside our borders. The international market craves our tentpoles and 3D and does not suffer any fatigue. They are eating up our product with "preawareness." The rest of the world likes things just the way they are.

This is why we depend on these new marketing stars who are the keys to breaking out movies that thrill with pure delight, not in how big they are, but in where they take us emotionally. Original movies are now an endangered species, under the marketing wizards' protection. If they make them, we must come.

Well before all of these critical trends became clear to me, I had the temerity to leave behind my comfortable home at Fox, where I had been for six years. Most of us who were lucky enough to be making movies inside the system thought that things were just abnormal in the way they had been forever in this land of outsized personalities and ambitions. I left Jim Gianopulos, my guru for international, and Fox's chairman Peter Chernin, the man I so admired and who at our semiregular lunches could break it all down for me, and set off for new horizons with a bigger deal at the studio around the corner from my house. I couldn't have guessed that the movie world—as well as the real world—was about to change drastically. Only a few bean counters could foretell a problem at that point. Another thing that I could never have anticipated was that my new studio, famous for its stable leadership, was about to undergo an eight-year upheaval that would make working there akin to working in a MASH unit. And those were the good years, when we knew who was who and what was what.

FROM PARAMOUNT TO PARANOIA

A Personal Odyssey Indeed

With any luck, this will be the only chapter in the book that will get personal, or mushy, like one of my romantic comedies that my son so avidly dislikes. This will be the only part that you will say is not really objective, or where you can hear the sound of axes grinding. But I choose to speak about my almost nine years at Paramount for a few reasons: It's where I first started to write this book, and it's where my journey went awry; in the protagonist's tale, Joseph Campbell and George Lucas tell us, the hero's journey is the story. It's also where I went to seek gold: Part of the lure of Paramount was that first-dollar gross points were offered me by its CEO, Sherry Lansing, for the first time in my career. It had been too long that I worked only for up-front fees and the sheer love of making movies and couldn't make real profits. Sherry's desire to see me finally get a bigger piece of the pie was very empowering. So I turned down other offers that look far better now. Hindsight is the most worthless of all varieties of vision.

During my almost nine-year tenure, I had eight bosses, saw almost all of them fired, suffered through most of their departures, got in the middle of some of their fights and cared for their junior execs as they wept on my couch (one of whom, now a senior exec, no longer returns my calls). Early in his reign, Brad Grey, the last of Paramount's series of chairmen, was under siege from a media and prosecutorial witch hunt. He disentangled himself, Houdini-like, from what looked like a serious mob scandal but morphed into eventual industry-wide amnesia, to the extent that there is now no sense that any scandal existed at all. Someone went to jail somewhere. Nowhere near Melrose Avenue, where Paramount houses its lot.

I pitched the same movies to all of my many bosses, made a flop with a hot director and a hit with a cold one and spent way too much time along the way smoking on Paramount's beautiful lawn with the execs, trading rumors about who was going to be fired. I lived through the writers' strike on its lot, waving to my friends on the other side of the picket line as I pretended to go to work.

I began at Paramount under the Jon Dolgen/Sherry Lansing/John Goldwyn regime in 1998. In its early days, this regime was the paradigm of the Old Abnormal at its best. Between Lansing/Jaffe and the producing team of Don Simpson and Jerry Bruckheimer, Paramount was the home of the Old Abnormal high-concept model. Simpson, who had risen through the ranks to become the head of production, was made a producer by the studio in the eighties to accommodate his, let's say, nontraditional lifestyle—he would arrive in the office when he woke up, which was often after lunch. He was brilliant at story and was considered by many to have given birth to the whole high-concept-movie idea (i.e., can you describe it in a "log line" no longer than a *TV Guide* description?). The studio packaged him with line producer Jerry Bruckheimer, and the dynamic duo—as they first called themselves—was born. Simpson and Bruckheimer made Eddie Murphy's breakout hit, *Beverly Hills Cop* (about guess what?), and two Tom Cruise hits, the naval pilot actioner *Top Gun* and the car racing hit *Days of Thunder;* the Michael Douglas bad-husband parable *Fatal Attraction;* and the "what would you do if someone offered you a million dollars to sleep with your wife?"–premised *Indecent Proposal.* All of these one-off producer-driven movies embodied Paramount and the Old Abnormal at their high-concept zenith. It was what they were good at and what they were known for.

Paramount's women-centered thrillers are still called "Sherry movies" in the industry, after those she made during her producing career—Jodie Foster's powerful rape-victim trial movie *The Accused, Fatal Attraction,* and *Indecent Proposal.* Those groundbreaking female "refrigerator movies"—movies you would still be debating when you got home and were reaching for leftovers in your refrigerator—were all about female social issues and empowerment, a hallmark of "Sherry movies." Often they were, or could be, *Newsweek* cover stories, as they raised issues of social debate. At the end of Lansing's reign, "Sherry movies" devolved to "women in jeopardy" thrillers like James Patterson's *Kiss the Girls,* in which pretty girls are kidnapped and forced to be subservient or be killed by a sadomasochistic psychopath. Thrillers like these, devoid of social issues, lost their "refrigerator" value.

Now, under Brad Grey, the eventual winner of the eight-year Paramount power derby, Paramount has emerged as the consummate New Abnormal studio, with the polar-opposite business strategy it had when I arrived. At the nadir of the Dolgen-Lansing regime, it was last in market share (the percentage of total box office vis-à-vis other studios), and striving for a high mark in profitability through its frugal—one could say risk-averse—business model. By 2001, seven years into his reign, it was number one in market share, with *Mission: Impossible* (started under Lansing and Goldwyn), *Star Trek, Transformers,* and *Iron Man* as its crown-jewel franchises, aimed directly at the emerging international markets (though it was the last studio to make franchises a part of its regular diet), a great triumph. But by 2012, Disney was number one in market share due to the phenomenal success of *The Avengers*—the number-three worldwide hit of all time—and Paramount had gone from number one to number seven, showing how volatile the market is. It also shows how hard it was to put a slate of tent-poles together for the summer of 2012: Two of its planned summer releases, *G.I. Joe: Retaliation* and *World War Z,* a zombie movie starring Brad Pitt, had to be delayed because they weren't ready on time. Missing the summer definitely makes a huge difference in your market share.

Despite the heaving and hyperventilating of a topsy-turvy box office race between studios every weekend, Grey's track record has been strong. His contract was extended to 2015, which will make it a ten-year run, only half of which comprised what the Hindu god Shiva would call "creative destruction."

When you think of how far Paramount has traveled, perhaps this saga is less a hero's journey than a close look at a studio under-going a gigantic transition, a turning of a battleship. Paramount is a studio with a complicated, brilliant octogenarian named Sumner Redstone holding tightly to its helm. Sumner still likes the ladies, and from what I've seen and read of his survival skills,* he may be immortal. (He says he is.) Always remember a lesson about Paramount I repeatedly observed: Whoever has Sumner has Para-mount. And Brad Grey, having achieved the prize of number-one market share, has Sumner.

Back in the Old Abnormal, the Sherry-Sumner relationship was a wholly personal thing. They were friends. They still are. But then again, the whole town has a personal relationship with Sherry, as do I.

Whenever we have lunch, I have to spend twenty minutes did-dling on my iPhone while every single person in the restaurant, male and female, young and ancient, comes to the table to greet

---

* Sumner M. Redstone, owner of the fifth-largest chain of movie theaters in the nation, says his greatest achievement was living through the Copley Plaza Hotel fire that burned 80 percent of his body. At age fifty-eight he was holding on to his third-floor windowsill, his right hand burn-ing in the flames, counting to ten, as he watched the single ladder rising toward him from a fire truck late on the night of March 29, 1979 (Robert Lenzer, "True Grit," *Boston Globe,* March 17, 1981).

Sherry as the most important person in his or her life. She holds court, like an eighteenth-century French regent (she is actually a twenty-first-century regent of the UC system), with every person in Beverly Hills. It's not noblesse oblige—she is too down-to-earth for that—but it is definitely regal, as she knows something about everyone's family. It thrills each of them.

She is the daughter of a Holocaust survivor, and it has deeply affected her character; she is utterly unostentatious and thrifty. She taught high school math and English right after college, before she began an acting career that she quickly quit because she decided she wasn't good enough. So she started reading scripts. I first met Sherry when I was an editor at the *New York Times,* doing an article on the new female executives in Hollywood. She was then VP at Fox and clearly the one to watch. A few years later, after a stint at MGM, Fox named her its first female head of production.

Not long after, she left Fox and partnered up with Stanley Jaffe. When Jaffe retired, Paramount recruited Sherry to be the first female studio head, to great hoopla and cover stories everywhere. She made fabulous copy, and was more than ready to do the job.

In 1987, my best friend, Dawn Steel, a charismatic, superalpha kind of female exec—hard-driving, instinctive, hilarious, controversial (she yelled)—was named head of Columbia, so then there were two. It was a heady, thrilling era for women.

I'd gotten close to Sherry when Dawn fell ill with brain cancer in 1996. Sherry is a person you want in your corner when you are sick. Her strength, courage and generosity are like those of no one else I've ever known. Though they had only recently become close, Sherry was immediately by Dawn's side. We took little weekend trips to Palm Springs and went out to dinner. When Dawn eventually died a grueling year and a half later, Sherry and I ended up as part of an all-female pallbearer group, further bonding us.

Ultimately, when I considered leaving Fox after six very productive years, having Sherry as a mentor/friend at Paramount was even more important than the great deal she was offering. Everyone needs a real friend at the top.

But the big pitch came when I dined with John Goldwyn, the president and head of production at Paramount, at Sherry's urging to both of us. His industry savvy, honed by his DNA (he was the grandson of Samuel Goldwyn, the "G" in MGM) and his gut instincts and learned experience, made him one of the keenest minds I'd met up with in Hollywood. At our first lunch, he taught me the Paramount philosophy as he had come to understand it. John believed deeply in what he was saying, and I sat there listening earnestly, as my life was about to undergo a sea change, and I am a land-loving kind of gal.

GOING UNDER

John Goldwyn:
President of Production 1991–97
President of Paramount Pictures 1997–2003
Vice Chairman of the Motion Picture Group 2002–3

My Paramount saga began at lunch with John Goldwyn the day *The Siege* opened, November 6, 1998. We were dining at a restaurant called Ca' Brea, a mid-level agent haunt with midlevel pasta. We sat there chatting away as Muslim antidiscrimination groups were boycotting my movie and demonstrating at the theaters where it was opening. As we lunched, Fox was surrounded by barricades because of a bomb threat, and the director, Ed Zwick, and I were being accused of a Zionist plot. John asked me what the movie was about.

He was handsome and lean and fiercely intelligent, and I use the word "fiercely" advisedly. His eyes engage and observe, strategize and charm, and it's always clear that at any second he can come in for the kill like a bird of prey.

I thought carefully about what to say to him, as things were kind of dicey at that moment. John later said he found me very cool and collected, rare the opening day of any $80 million movie, let alone such a controversial one. I was actually a nervous wreck.

Three years before 9/11, I was making one of the biggest movies I had ever made, with a budget of $70 million. We closed the Brooklyn Bridge and blew up a bus (which made my father incredibly happy—finally, some action in one of my movies!), but astonishingly we ended up with what you'd have to call a fatwah on both the director of the movie and me. *The Siege* starred Denzel Washington, Annette Bening and Bruce Willis, and was about a terrorist siege of New York City and the sweeping restrictions of civil rights it brought about. Suddenly, I found myself in production in New York under an alias. The only thing I liked about being undercover was my new name: Rebecca Austin. I liked it because it sounded so completely fake, like the pen name of a Silhouette novelist.

It was more the director, Ed Zwick, the protesters were targeting; they saw him as the boss and chief Zionist. For months we had been campaigning to win the cooperation of the American-Arab Anti-Discrimination Committee by hosting representatives at teas and halal meals in our trailer during production and sharing the script, trying to get all the cultural nuances of the Brooklyn Muslim community exactly right. My efforts were met with sneering contempt—"I won't eat this food; it's probably pork!"—but eventually there was some successful rapprochement, during which Ed and I happily made script changes. But we couldn't make the one they wanted most: to change the terrorist cell that bombed New York and held it hostage in the movie to domestic terrorists, à la the Oklahoma City bombing.

We explained that our script was based on a series of articles from the *New York Times* about the World Trade Center bombing in 1993, which was executed by members of cells in Brooklyn run by Sheik Rahman, who was now in a Brooklyn jail. Further research had been done about these still-existing cells by our screenwriter, Lawrence Wright. Our story began in Afghanistan, from our CIA blowback. So, you see, we said, we can change anything but that. We did point out that we had a sympathetic Arab-American Muslim FBI agent at the center of the drama, whose son was swept up in the overzealous profiling of Arabs that followed the crisis. It was a cautionary tale, we tried to explain; we wanted to prevent the loss of a minority's civil rights in the wake of a terrorist attack.

They stormed out of our final meeting. Toward the end of the shoot, hostile graffiti about the movie appeared in Brooklyn. After we finished principal photography, we had an ending problem to resolve and had to go back to New York for reshoots, at which time Ed and I began to get death threats in our email and at our offices. Everyone involved with the reshoots worked under an assumed name, and the name of the movie was changed on all location records.

The Anti-Discrimination League couldn't have been more off-base with their accusations of Zionist conspiracy. If we were Mossad, as they alleged, we were the dumbest Mossad agents who ever lived. We had shared the script and movie release dates with our enemy, and had first gone to writer Larry Wright because he was an Arabist who had lived and studied in Egypt. (He later wrote the Pulitzer Prize–winning book *The Looming Tower,* about Al Qaeda.) As for the chief Zionist conspirator, Ed hadn't ever even been to Israel, as far as I knew. At that point, I hadn't. Annette Bening, whom we had to fight the studio to hire over multiple bimbos, was extremely sympathetic to the Palestinian cause, and that affinity drew her to the character and the script in the first place. We explained over and over that the part played by Tony

Shalhoub—that of the Muslim FBI agent whose son is caught up in mass arrests and is defended by a civil-rights-championing Denzel Washington—was the whole point of the movie, but no matter how hard we jawboned, no understanding was created. We tried to create a conversation, but got a battle.

The press didn't help. They were wholeheartedly buying the then politically correct argument that we were "demonizing the Muslim/Arab community" with this movie. The sympathetic coverage was feeding the frenzy of the indignant antidiscrimination groups, even before anyone had seen the movie. By the time it opened, there was a bomb threat at Fox, our studio, which was under highest security. And worse, the theaters showing the movie were under bomb threats too. That can really inhibit business, and drastically did on opening weekend ($13.9 million), though the movie managed to rack up $116 million worldwide.*

I thought it was probably better not to mention to the then president of Paramount, John Goldwyn, that my studio was under a bomb threat. That might have made him a bit less eager to invite me over.

So I just smiled and said, "It's a cautionary tale about an imagined terrorist takedown of New York. Tell me about Paramount."

He started to explain why Paramount was a producer's studio. He quoted Stanley Jaffe, its influential ex-chairman. "Stanley had a philosophy," Goldwyn said. "He was looking for Paramount to be the place for people who are really good at what they do—directors, writers, producers—to feel supported, as long as they worked within the rules. They would be given the opportunity to pursue their vision, but that opportunity would be provided within a very specific set of financial boundaries. He was very clear about

---

* On September 12, 2001, it became the number-one DVD. My Orthodox rabbi friend woke me up on September 11, saying, "Turn on the TV, your movie is on."

that. And even if a picture didn't work, they shouldn't worry, because in a year or five, they would still be there."

It got me. Ultimately, it got both of us, in different ways.

I had been successful, prolific and happy at Fox (now known to me as "Paradise Lost") under the consistent leadership of Peter Chernin. Peter ran Fox in a way that made it possible for producers to figure out how and why their movie could get made. It was easy to determine how to get a green light based on Fox's business model because it was a vertically integrated studio, which means that Fox owned all the ancillaries: DVD domestic and international, foreign distribution and U.S. television via Fox and cable TV. It even owned Sky TV, an international station. Fox is a self-feeding content provider.

A studio is as rational as its business model plus its leadership. I later discovered that at Paramount, each picture was a brand-new business venture, a one-off that Sherry talked Jon Dolgen into green-lighting—hence the constant tension. But who knew? A lot of agents, that's who.

As I sat there with John Goldwyn at Ca' Brea, I thought, I can work with this guy. He was very intense, very sincere and very smart. And I could make a profit at Paramount. *If* I could make a movie.

Paramount gave me a wonderful little bungalow that used to be the security guard's station and that was also a piece of a stage, and I proceeded to transform it into a two-story fantasy office that felt like my house in Texas. Texas had always been my respite from work; I bought my limestone farmhouse in the hill country west of Austin with *Sleepless* money, and it's where I went to write and relax. I found New York to have the same dominance hierarchy as L.A., but Texas was a whole other country. And for some unfathomable reason, it was a country where this New York Jewish girl was 100 percent relaxed and at home. So, I thought, maybe if I brought some of those comfy vibes to my Paramount office, I could be relaxed there too. What could go wrong? Then, during my first week, I ran into a good friend on the lot whom I'd known for years, producer Sean Daniel, who'd made *The Mummy* and green-lit the classic *National Lampoon's Animal House* when he was head of production at Universal. "Welcome to Paramount!" he said to me heartily. We hugged.

"Do you like your new deal?" Sean asked. He had been on the lot for a while already. He was referring to my newly enhanced fee and first-dollar gross on the back end (as we say here).

"Yes!" I answered, beaming like a moron.

"Then kiss it good-bye!" he said, laughing a laugh I would come to hear often—the Paramount gallows laugh.

"But what do you mean?" I called after Sean.

"You'll never see it!" he called back.

Oh my God, I thought, my mind racing. They can reduce the budget by cutting the producer's fee right before they green-light the picture. I went ashen. Bingo. I'd heard about this at Paramount. They do this in the eleventh hour to bring the budget down. The producer never stops the movie after having worked so hard and long to get the thing going. With an entire crew hired and waiting, as well as actors getting measured for their costumes in the wardrobe department, we producers are much too responsible to everyone to stop the movie just to collect our full fee. Mainly we are way too excited to leave the studio and go to the set, where everyone we've hired is already waiting. So we say yes to our newly reduced fee and start picking a caterer.

THE FLOP

One of the most famous reasons a movie doesn't work is that it gets rushed into production before the script is ready. Usually this happens because a studio is trying to make a critical date, so they throw a series of writers at a tentpole and piece a script together like a patchwork quilt. When there are constant rewrites, actors get involved, the studio must approve the rewrites while you're shooting, the schedule must be rearranged to allow for the changes and often you must shut down. It's a mess.

This situation is to be avoided at all costs. The script should be locked so everyone knows what they are shooting each day. These days, the pace of normal (non-tentpole) development—such as it is—approaches glacial speeds, and every line and scene is investigated by unbusy execs like conspiracy theorists.

But back in the day, a hustling producer, a motivated exec and a hot element could push a small movie into existence—sometimes before it was ready. That's what I did in brewing my flop.

I made a crucial error on Sherry's watch. Early in my tenure at Paramount, I bought a book about a murder at Harvard called *Abandon*. I attached my *Siege* director, Ed Zwick, who'd gone to Harvard, and he attached *Traffic* writer Steve Gaghan, who had just been nominated for an Oscar. When the script came in, Ed wanted to make the film in Cambridge.

We scouted Cambridge and discovered it was too expensive to shoot there. The budget came to $60 million. The studio said $40 million. Impasse. So Ed passed the baton to Steve Gaghan to direct, even though Steve had never directed before, and Ed became a producer with me. We needed Gaghan to continue writing since he was hot as a firecracker after the Oscar nomination. First-time directors were difficult to get approved at Paramount, but the studio was willing to consider Gaghan, depending on how the script turned out.

Steve's script was full of delicious, smart dialogue. It was edgy, cool and mysterious. It was attracting actors and lots of buzz, all because of Gaghan's Oscar nomination for *Traffic*. The momentum was heating up the picture. I was stoked.

But the script had some key conceptual problems on which Sherry zeroed in, Sherry not being much affected by buzz:

Was it a teen *Fatal Attraction,* as she saw it? About a psychotic ghost ex-boyfriend? Or brilliant, overworked grinds gone awry?

The production exec on the movie—whom we will call the Hipster—was old friends with Steve (selling factor), so there wasn't much objectivity there. I had lost mine with overconfidence about past successes with writers turned first-time directors (Chris Columbus and Nora Ephron). I understood the plot issues Sherry pointed out, but was convinced that Steve could and would solve them during prep. Steve's considerable charm, intelligence, faux self-deprecating humor and indie credibility in an atmosphere starving for it made us all push harder without being sufficiently concerned about the questions being raised.

We all unconsciously borrowed the arrogance of the Harvard setting and decided we were an indie–art-movie–teen-horror flick—and that was so great! But none of us properly made a priority of fixing the glaring script issues. When we tried to resolve them and couldn't, we didn't stop everything else to resolve them. Instead, the exec and I pushed the movie into production, elbow to elbow, like offensive linemen protecting the quarterback—even though Sherry had well-founded fears about the movie and its must-see director. What was it about at its core? Was Gaghan ready to direct? I was recklessly insistent on both fronts.

I remember a dinner party I threw on the eve of the *Abandon* screen test, with all my best New York friends at this wonderful West Village Japanese restaurant called Omen where they serve tiny exotic tofu dishes for something like $36 each. When I got there and greeted my twenty or so guests, my cell phone rang. It was John Goldwyn telling me the movie was dead and the screen test must be canceled. I spent the next two hours on the phone, pacing outside the restaurant on Prince Street, until I could get the studio to provisionally reinstate the test, in lieu of my speaking to Sherry on her vacation in the morning. By the time I went back inside and returned to my table, the check had arrived, my guests were weary and ready to go home and they all thought I was cuckoo. In the morning I resumed pacing, but this time in my hotel room at the Mercer. I caught Sherry on a boat rounding some Caribbean island with her husband and the Dolgens.

"If you can't trust me to control the set of a twenty-two-million-dollar teen horror movie, what can I do?" I argued in order to allay her fears of a first-timer going out of control. Paramount was famous for not backing first-timers, and I was conscious of the responsibility in my hands. I feared that Sherry would rather choose a mediocre guy who knew where to put the camera and how to get through the day over an inspired artiste who couldn't tell a story or was completely disorganized. It was a preference she was often criticized for, and one that had become part of the conservative Paramount culture. My exec and I were proud to buck it, reckless though that may have been. Coming through for Sherry would depend on my developing trust with the newbie director. I knew how to do that, I assured myself. It was easy.

The studio wanted to shoot in Toronto. We wanted Montreal, the better to double for Cambridge and the Northeast, with its old-world charm. Plus the crews were artier. We got Montreal. Prep went well. Gaghan learned how to rehearse. He scouted. Any dicey signs were ignored.

On the first day of shooting I was having lunch in my trailer as usual, when the line producer, Dick Vane, walked in. Dick, an unflappable guy, is in charge of keeping to the budget and handling the day-to-day crises with crew and equipment. I'd never seen him stunned before, but he was that day. "He's still shooting," he said.

"But we called lunch," I said.

"He's doing shots that aren't on the call sheet." The call sheet is the list of shots that we have to complete for the day in order to make our schedule.

"Really?" I said. "What kind of shots?"

"Dutch shots."

"Dutch shots?" I asked incredulously.

"Yes, from the ceiling and corners of the ceiling. And the floor. All the actors and the crew are into meal penalty. And we're still trying to get the shots."

Meal penalties are what production pays the shooting crew and cast members for encroaching on their legal lunch hour. The rate varies from city to city, but to give you an idea, in L.A., the first meal penalty—for anything up to thirty minutes—is $7.50 per person, and it goes up from there. With a 250-person crew, that's a lot of Tootsie Rolls—or what we call "hot costs": unanticipated, unbudgeted costs.

"What happens when you ask him to finish the shots and then break for lunch?" I asked.

"Nothing."

We looked at each other for a second with growing comprehension.

Then Dick said, "It's going to cost us some nice coin on the first day, all these meal penalties." And we both knew that was the least of it. In all my years of producing, I'd never seen anyone shooting so far off the call sheet on the first day.

Buckle your seat belt, I thought. Sorry, Sherry. Bumpy ride time.

The murder at the center of the plot (the mechanics of which were unclear because the script was still being rewritten) took place in a dirty, dank tunnel beneath the city. We began to shoot on location in the underground tunnel system in Montreal. But when we found ourselves three days over schedule and nowhere near through the material we were supposed to have shot, I began to worry for the crew. We all knew there were unhealthy levels of asbestos in the tunnels, and the crew foreman—who is the head of the union on the set—looked grumpy.

I talked to the art director about re-creating a portion of the tunnels on the soundstage and finishing the scene at the end of the schedule, when we would know exactly what we were doing. I wanted the crew *above*ground. I was afraid we'd shoot down there indefinitely. We didn't yet have script pages for the climactic murders that also took place in the tunnels, so we couldn't prepare the crew or the actors. If we moved on to other material now, our writer-director would have time to figure out the murder and then explain it to the actors and prepare the crew.

There was some dissension about my decision. For some it was macho to just go for it, but it wasn't healthy or wise or economically feasible. I was the studio; they were the filmmakers. As late, great producer Laura Ziskin said, "The producer is the traffic cop between art and commerce." I had lost my badge on this shoot.

I had given special screenings of Bertolucci films during pre-production. I had catered them throughout with great food. I made sure everyone had wonderful places to live, held parties. But no family was born. The show was sliding into a cliché of us vs. them. From there, it could fall into a hole of incoherence. We all tried to help it pull together—every actor, the director, me, the cinematographer (the brilliant Matthew Libatique, nominated for an Oscar for *Black Swan*), the talented production designer Gideon Ponte, the exuberant and steady-handed line producer, the crew, the crew foreman, the sound guy; but with the director and the producer unable to fundamentally trust each other, there was only so much the picture could do to right itself.

It was my job to make the director trust me. He did not. That was the key task I'd had to accomplish, and I hadn't done it. We were oil and water. He did not feel that I was sufficiently on his side, a feeling that probably stemmed from my closeness with Sherry. But at this point I had to march onward and do what I felt was right for the production.

Having forced the argument, with the help of the crew, we moved the completion of the tunnel sequence to the end of the schedule, and the three gorgeous leads—Katie Holmes, Charlie Hunnam and Benjamin Bratt (recently broken up with Julia Roberts and gaming along like a pro)—all went mad, per the directions of the freshly rewritten pages. The cast and crew were by now exhausted, the actors and director feeling their way around the material, the stage, the characters. When we wrapped, I skipped the party for the first time in my career and left that night for New York City with a cute crew guy. It was movie number thirteen for me, and felt that way. Ultimately, it went a week over schedule and grossed $12 million worldwide, half of its production budget. As I tell myself at times like these, you learn as much from the flops as you do from the hits—sometimes more.

THE HIT

Sherry and John were great to me, each in their own way. Sherry wanted me to get rich and John wanted me to make pictures, and that is all you can ask from a studio head and her head of production. Both of them believed in me as a producer. I found out about *How to Lose a Guy in 10 Days* from mega-agency CAA because its client Gwyneth Paltrow had shown interest in a very early draft at Paramount. So I called Goldwyn about it.

John had Michael Hoffman in mind to direct it. Michael had been my director on *One Fine Day,* a movie I'd made at Fox with Michelle Pfeiffer and George Clooney about two single parents who meet and fall in love while traipsing around New York City with their children. So Goldwyn thought my developing the script with its current junior producer, Christine Peters—who had found the stick-figure book it was based on—was a great idea, and so we developed a draft, first with the brilliant Ellen Simon (Neil's daughter), then with Burr Steers (*Igby Goes Down*). The development process went smoothly all the way through, except for one thing: We couldn't find a guy.

Gwyneth dropped out during development, I forget why (I really do), and along the way Sherry and I fell in love with Kate Hudson, up and coming from her Golden Globe–nominated performance in Cameron Crowe's wonderful *Almost Famous*. We attached her to an intermediate draft, which wouldn't have happened at any other studio, as she hadn't yet been in a hit. Sherry had the freedom to pursue her gut casting instincts on a mid-range movie like this. We believed in Kate. But we still had no guy.

We tested and read a bunch of funny guys, some who are now stars, some not. But there was no chemistry. Kate liked Luke Wilson, but the studio was not so sure. When the script was finished, there was a showdown meeting with Kate and Sherry because Kate had not approved any of the guys we had tested. She was looking for a quality no one had shown in the tests. Sherry couldn't believe that she'd even given Kate a say in the process. Right before the meeting, I got on the phone and talked to all the agencies, trying to find a guy to lose. When I reached ICM, they threw out the name Matthew McConaughey.

I thought, Brilliant! Is he available? Why hasn't he come up before? Somewhere along the line, he may have been dismissed as not New York enough or too old for Kate. But Kate is much more sophisticated than her age would suggest, and it was a new name, a good name, and I went to the meeting with his name in my pocket. Kate was twenty minutes late, and her CAA agent was sweating, Goldwyn was fuming and I was trying to entertain Sherry. Kate flounced in wearing a fabulous new skirt, and Sherry put on one of her *very* rare stern looks. "Kate," she said, "if we can't agree on a costar, this movie is over."

Silence. Someone, I think it was me, quietly said, "What about Matthew McConaughey?"

Sherry said, "I love Matthew."

Kate said, "I love Matthew."

John Goldwyn breathed a deep sigh of relief, and said, "Is Matthew available? If he is, I love him too."

I said, "Yes," and everyone laughed. Then legendary ICM agent Ed Limato got us by the balls and squeezed to close the deal, as there was no movie without his client, a situation agents live for.

We hired Donald Petrie—who had helmed *Mystic Pizza,* Julia Roberts's breakout coming-of-age movie—to direct. Donald knows what is funny, though he hadn't made a hit in a while. But Sherry felt safe with him. At that point, that was enough for me. Once, during prep, my occasional partner, the equally fun, missing and mythic Robert Evans (*The Kid Stays in the Picture*), who'd made *The Godfather* and *Love Story,* called me with an emergency casting issue. I was in the middle of a script meeting but I picked up the phone right away.

"What's up, Bob?"

"No thin lips."

"Explain, Bob?" I asked. "I don't think I heard you."

"The actors, Lyn. No thin lips."

"I got it, Bob," I answered, and proceeded to cast Matthew and Kate with the lips they were born with. I saw Bob three more times during the making of the movie: on the first day of shooting, when he took pictures with the cast; on the last, when he again took pictures with the cast; and one fun time when he came to visit the set on Staten Island and regaled me in my trailer with wonderful tales that may or may not have been true about the making of *The*

Godfather. Who really cared? The stories were so delicious. *How to Lose* was always fun, and from the first dailies, we knew the chemistry between Kate and Matthew—thin lips or not—was crackling on set, on the monitor and in the rushes. The energy between them created heat, and that makes a hit. Sherry called. She was coming to visit, on day five, just for fun. This was good news. We all had the best time; production was easy-breezy, and so was postproduction. Sometimes, as my first book would say, you "ride the horse in the direction it's going." Sherry visited the first week, she declared the movie a hit and she was right. She had no notes at the preview. It scored a 95, and opened number one at $24.5 million. And kept playing. But Paramount had sold off all of their domestic and international rights in order to pay for the cost of production, only keeping the DVD rights. This was one of their few hits that year, and they had sold away most of their revenues. This was the Dolgen way.

In the weekly box office derby, Paramount pictures started to look like a series of flops, despite the fact that the studio had protected its losses by preselling rights. But Dolgen was oddly copacetic, even as forces stewed elsewhere against him.

Jon Dolgen, a Bob Dylan–loving lawyer who thrives on conflict, likes to play tough guy. He looks like a giant sloth with a full head of thick black hair. You could tell that he relished his scary image, which worked for him strategically, as did his famously dry sense of humor.

In 2000, right before my little hit went into production, Mel Karmazin, formerly of CBS Radio and Sumner's number two at the time, began squeezing Dolgen's resources (if that's what you want to call them) even tighter, perhaps to please the Viacom board, perhaps to throw off his competition for Sumner's admiration. Karmazin's move didn't unbalance Dolgen at all. Instead, Dolgen made tighter financial projections to the board, compressing the studio's budgets even further downward to impress the people upstairs.

Paramount was becoming an issue of contention in the boardrooms of Viacom. A fight was brewing for the number-two slot under Sumner at Viacom, and there were three hopefuls. Dolgen was one. His competition was with his immediate boss, Karmazin, who had no intention of going anywhere,* and CBS chief Les Moonves, with his great track record at the network—the perennial number one—who was also a rising corporate star. That placed Dolgen in a competitive mindset that locked him even more solidly into his penurious financial strategy.

The strategy the Dolgen-Lansing team pursued for Paramount had looked good for years: Protect your downside, minimize losses by selling off every ancillary market, maximize short-term profits—basically, profitize every picture as an independent business venture.

This strategy guaranteed that few pictures lost money in the green-light game that was the upshot of the intimate wrangling between Sherry and Dolgen. They were equals and partners. He believed in her gut to pick pictures; she knew he could squeeze every dime out of every territory and ancillary market to pay for each film. She would tell him what she wanted to make, he would give her an impossible budget number, she would cast the top players and pass on the impossible number (a bit lower now) to the production team. It was designed to work financially, but it didn't always benefit the picture creatively. But Sherry could often "save it in post." It was the most conservative model possible, and it successfully minimized losses.

As long as he could report profits to his board, Dolgen didn't care what the outside world thought. Critically, however, this conservative philosophy did not allow them to be competitive for the

---

* Though he later left for Sirius Radio in 2004.

best new material or remain in tune with the market as it began to drastically change.

Perhaps Dolgen could have competed in the studio box office derby and made it to the New Abnormal if he had been strong enough to buck financial pressures and make the bigger special-effects-driven movies that were coming into vogue. But he wasn't competing against the other studios. He was competing inside Viacom.

As Goldwyn and others saw it, Dolgen took pleasure in making his anemic financial projections work. He was brilliant at selling off rights, and had been doing it throughout his career. As a former business affairs executive, it was one of the things he knew how to do best. He was comfortable with the formula, and to be fair, it was still bringing in profits, if not market share; but the latter is what almost everyone considers to be the true measure of studio success.

THE BATTLESHIP IS MISSING THE DOCK

But if you remember, 2001 was the year of the first big new special-effects movies, those using next-generation CGI like *Harry Potter,* the first *Shrek* and the first *Fast and the Furious.* Moviegoers were falling in love with the amazing animation and special effects that the new technology was providing, and they wanted more. This was the moment when everything was coming up tentpole. The audience was saying yes, please, we want more and bigger. Paramount couldn't afford it, comprehend its importance or accommodate it.

The vaunted philosophy of fiscal restraint at Paramount was becoming obsolete. The one-off business struggle for each picture was keeping Paramount unable to compete with the rising costs of production, of actors and their entourages, of big special effects or of the blockbuster/sequel/marketing–driven sensibility that was now ruling Hollywood. The studio was unwilling or unable to play the game. It did not have the mindset, and Dolgen's eyes were elsewhere.

Goldwyn described the transition that took place when Paramount's old model ran up against the tidal wave of change:

"When Viacom bought the company in 1993, it was right before the period when there was a shift in what movies Hollywood was making. We went from pictures that were *crafted* to pictures that were marketing juggernauts. The craftsmanship of the pictures was secondary to the marketability of the *intellectual property,* the 'idea.' And that was not what Stanley Jaffe and the Paramount tradition dictated."

In using the word "crafted," Goldwyn is describing pictures that were made during the Old Abnormal, when Paramount and much of the rest of the industry made movies "because they were good" (not to say that Nolan's, Spielberg's and Cameron's movies aren't crafted, but plenty of tentpoles put craft after marketability). These movies were not made because they were based on a big intellectual property like *Harry Potter* or *The Hunger Games* or *Twilight* or a Marvel property—a big identifiable idea that could be promoted all around the world at once.

Sherry Lansing made movies she loved and believed in, and at the lowest possible cost. But no one who watched the transition to the New Abnormal at the time knew what on earth was going on. We only knew that technology now allowed for some very cool new effects that the audience wanted to see. The boundaries of what was technologically possible were expanding every day. And it was expensive.

Goldwyn said, "If Stanley Jaffe had stayed at the company, I'm sure there would have been a serious discussion about where this was going."

But there was not, apparently, any such conversation under Dolgen. Paramount couldn't compete in the marketplace for the hot scripts that utilized this new technology, for which all the other studios were clamoring. All this was garnering Paramount terrible press. They were under relentless pressure, from inside and out.

Goldwyn concluded, "I just think after a while the financial pressures became absolutely terrible. And the creative community at large was intensely aware of that. The big material started to go elsewhere."

Paramount was not keeping up with the Joneses. A change was gonna come, as the bluesman sings. And someone was going to pay the piper.

THE HIPSTER AND THE BLOCKER

Of course, there are many more people I had to work with other than Sherry and Goldwyn. There were the execs. At first for me, there were the Hipster and the Blocker. The Blocker didn't look like a blocker. She was always helping me, sending me writers lists to develop my new ideas, sharing her incredibly up-to-the-minute inside info with me, sending me anywhere I wanted to go to visit fancy writers. She was a seductress of development, with the coziest office full of candy and pillows.

I bought a book called *Can You Keep a Secret?* by Sophie Kinsella (*Confessions of a Shopaholic*), attached Kate Hudson and sent it to Nora Ephron. She loved it. I called the Blocker ecstatically, and she said something like, "I'm not sure we will hire Nora to write this." I almost fell off my chair. Then I started to boil. I began breathing exercises. "May I come over and discuss this with you in person?" I asked.

I had given this to Nora, the best writer I knew and also my dearest friend, and hadn't cleared it with the studio. I hadn't cleared it because never in a thousand years would it have occurred to me that the studio would be anything but overjoyed. The weirdness factor I'd been warned about at Paramount was rearing its head. I would go to John. I would go to Sherry. I would use up my discretionary fund to get Nora. I walked across the lot to hear what the Blocker had to say.

"Hi, Lyn. Don't be upset. You know we love you. Let's talk this out." I started laying out my argument, as though there were rational underpinnings for her decision. When I finished, she said, "Yes, you know we have great faith in you, and we love Nora, of course, but she just made *Lucky Numbers* for us, and it didn't work."

Lucky Numbers was a very uncharacteristic Nora movie based on an Adam Resnick script she loved about scamming the lottery, starring two of her favorite actors, John Travolta (from her hit *Michael*) and Lisa Kudrow, who she thought was (and in fact is) a genius.

"This has nothing whatsoever to do with *Lucky Numbers,*" I said. "This is a horse of a different color," or some such idiotic thing. I added, "I'm going to talk to Sherry."

Sherry *lived* not to get smoked out at times like this.

"If you like," the Blocker said in a cold voice.

I walked out of the office knowing that this was going to get complicated and I'd better call Nora ASAP. But if I wanted to fly to London, that would be no problem for the Blocker—just as long as I wasn't getting any work done. I called Nora and told her the story. She was furious with me, and rightly so. She withdrew.

What would have been a slam dunk at Fox was punched out of the basket by my own teammate at Paramount. And there was no referee to call goaltending.

•   •   •

The Hipster was another proposition altogether. We had the same taste. We had the same frustrations. We got along great, until we didn't, which was essentially a factor of the crazy politics of Paramount. Nothing was moving forward in the bad winds that were beginning to poison the studio, and one tough day I blamed the Hipster for my frustration. She responded by writing a scathing email about me to the big brass, which got her in trouble with the administration and got leaked to the trades and made us both look bad. Bryan Lourd—one of the controlling partners at CAA—got us to make up. Bryan is thought of by many as "the Lourd in town" because he represents so many of the biggest movie stars in Hollywood* that a good movie is hard to put together without him. Moreover, his personality is all Zen strategy and common sense. Fights are not Zen-like and follow no common sense, he made clear to both of us.

The tension was growing severe in the halls of the administration building; it was as though the pressure that Dolgen was feeling from New York were landing on Goldwyn, who was distributing it evenly among his execs, who were passing it down to their producers. Call it trickle-down hostility. All teamwork vanished. Craziness multiplied. Paranoia prevailed.

The execs were gathering in clusters outside the administration building, smoking and fuming. John was not getting along with his underlings. Something was brewing in his life and in the careers of his execs (as in, nobody knew who was going to get fired), and Sherry's reign was being questioned for the first time, as the numbers weren't good. She was eventually going to have to make a change. The flops of 2002 were numbing.

---

* George Clooney, Jennifer Connelly, Kelly Ripa, Mike Nichols, Scarlett Johansson, Todd Field, Tom Ford, Warren Beatty, Oliver Stone, Sean Penn, Robert Downey, Jr., Reese Witherspoon, etc.

FILM	BUDGET	BOX OFFICE (domestic)
The Core	$60 million	$31 million
Narc	$7.5 million	$10.5 million
Marci X	$2 million	$1.65 million
Dickie Roberts	$17 million	$22.7 million
Timeline	$80 million	$19 million
Paycheck	$60 million	$53.8 million

Source data from BoxOfficeMojo.com.

The above are the worst, admittedly, but there were few hits to offset them.

Goldwyn and Lansing were intertwined. Good cop, bad cop. He knew how she thought; she knew how he executed what she wanted done. He loved to say no; she hated it. It would be hard to sever them. But inevitably, after twelve years, Goldwyn's sometimes acrimonious though wildly successful run of protecting Sherry and bringing her "the fish on a platter from which to choose" (movies to make) was coming to an end.

The job of head of production, Goldwyn's position at the time, is to put potential pictures together for his boss by directing the development of the scripts the studio buys and shepherds through rewrites. He picks writers from the lists the execs assemble, approves the "take" the writer will attempt on the material, attaches (or tries to attach) "elements" along the way like directors or stars that make the script more of a movie. Then these "potential movies" become "fish on the platter" for his boss, the chairman, who greenlights the movies. Because half of the scripts will "tank" (come in under par), a third will fall apart as they try to become movies by losing their "elements" and the rest his boss will hate, he needs to assemble double the number of movies that the studio needs to release. That's a lotta sushi.

He does all that while the whole town is either at his feet or at his throat. There is no protection from a constant barrage of selling and yelling. It's a melee where deals, projects, and executives' mistakes are constantly blowing up in his face. If the slate of releases he puts together doesn't work, he goes down.

Goldwyn could be as charming as he chose to be, but he had a temper that occasionally flared. Once he stormed out of his office and drove due north for 350 miles without stopping or answering calls because someone on his staff had made him very angry.

The kitchen got very hot for Goldwyn as the town turned against Paramount and the pictures weren't working. The pressure got to him. This is how he related that moment to me a few years later:

"The culture I came into was very different than the culture that I left. It was not a fear-based culture at the beginning. It was 'this is what we stand for, this is what we are going to do, now let's make it work.' And then it became very much 'How the fuck do we do that? How the fuck did that happen? How can we not do this?'

"It went from being proactive and accountable to being at the expense of that accountability," John recalled. "As much as you want to be accountable, the last thing you want is to be accountable for decisions you feel unsure about. And that's what happened. That's when I knew I had to get out. I knew that I would die in that culture, I knew it, I knew it. I knew I was failing, I knew the pictures were failing and I knew that I did not have the stamina or emotional reserves to turn it around. I felt very guilty about the quality of the pictures. Maybe I was feeling a little too much personal responsibility for them. It was much more about the mindset of the place. Because when you are in that job and you're the head of production, you feel responsible for it. You can't help it. At some point, you're saying that it's your fault."

On top of it all, or underneath it all, Goldwyn was having a personal crisis that may have exacerbated the discord. You would have noticed early signs if you had looked closely. He was looking snappier. He had been married to the wildly popular hostess–actress/producer and town doyenne Colleen Camp for years. They had been a team, like one professional unit, throughout his corporate rise—but he took a lover. To complicate matters, his paramour was a man, and Colleen, in her shock and dismay, looked for solace in her friends. John knew he had to tell Sherry first, before she found out somewhere else. This terrified him, as the studio was teetering on the brink of radical instability. (The Goldwyns commenced a divorce amid swirling rumors and fought a grueling custody battle over a daughter they both adored. They are all now good friends, though there was great hysteria at the time.)

John, in something akin to panic, called Sherry to meet privately. Sherry remembers it with great compassion, as John was and is one of her best friends. She had no idea why he was in such a state when he came to see her.

"That's it?" she said, after he spoke.

"Yes," he said.

"You're gay?! This is what the problem is? You were being so dramatic, I thought you had embezzled!" She was incredulous. "We don't care."

John remembers the moment like it was yesterday. Sherry got up off of her seat and walked over to sit down next to him on the couch. She took his hands in hers. "I am so happy for you," she said, looking into his eyes. "Now you can have authentic relationships." He was moved and utterly relieved.

"But I also saw that he was distracted," Sherry said, as we sat in her elegant office at the Sherry Lansing Foundation on Century Park East. "He was going through an identity crisis and a painful divorce. I couldn't care less that he was gay," she added. "But there were problems. It was a seismic shift in John's identity and what he wanted to do with his life. He was going through this terrible time. I think his ability to concentrate on his work was compromised, as it would be with anybody. Whatever it was, it all was a perfect storm."

BAD 2003

I adored John Goldwyn. I remember the day he called me while I was having lunch with a "nonpro"* girlfriend (who was extremely annoyed by the interruption) at the Peninsula Hotel over Christmas and told me he was leaving. I knew at that moment that things would never, ever be the same at Paramount for me. Half my team was gone. The conversation, connected by his trusty assistant Eben Davidson (now a VP), who was rolling calls all day (phone calls are rolled, not placed, in Hollywood), however, was designed to assure me of the opposite. "I will be there for you and your movies," John said over the phone. "Sherry has no one in mind. This could even take 'til spring. I will be working with you. It will be a smooth transition, I promise; you will still have me."

But even as I was talking with John, agents were calling Sherry to discuss his imminent replacement. Would it be my good friend on the lot, producer and former Disney president Donald De Line? He was happy as a producer, and wasn't angling for the job. But Paramount megaproducer Scott Rudin† wanted him, and Sherry had made a recent hit with him and was interested. Jim Wiatt, longtime head of the ICM agency, was publicly throwing his hat in the ring. CAA, mostly via Bryan Lourd, was making a case

---

* Since the 1940s, the trades have referred to wives (or husbands) who don't work in the business as "nonpros" in wedding announcements, and the term has grown to apply to any situation.

† Now at Sony.

for newly minted Paramount producer Lorenzo di Bonaventura. Bryan—whom Sherry (and everyone) took very seriously—was a friend and ally of Lorenzo's, and had made his producer's deal at Paramount after his controversial departure from Warner Bros.

A year before, di Bonaventura, a charismatic mountain-climbing guys' guy, was the high-flying exec at Warner Bros. who'd brought in *The Matrix,* among other cutting-edge hits. Then it was widely reported that di Bonaventura had quietly jetted off to New York to make a play for his boss's job to the Time Warner corporate brass. He landed at Paramount as a producer.* CAA, understandably, saw him as a studio head.

This was all well and good, but who would I be for? I needed a horse in the race. I went home and cried. Then I called Sherry.

My horse would be my buddy, the charming, funny, popular and talented Donald De Line. I'd rooted for his underdog hit at Paramount, *The Italian Job*—a gold-heist movie remake starring Mark Wahlberg, Ed Norton, Charlize Theron and Mini Coopers—during that crazy summer of 2003 when all the big tentpoles (like Ang Lee's *Hulk*) collapsed and the one movie that had the legs and the least tracking (it *would* be Paramount, which wasn't making tentpoles) had cleaned up. I called it "My Big Fat Italian Job." Sherry was hoping to find someone who would eventually succeed her as cochairman with Rob Friedman, then president of marketing and distribution.†

Sherry loved Donald—hell, everyone loved him (except Brad Grey, as it later turned out)—but there was serious competition out there. Though CAA was lobbying for Lorenzo, they liked Donald too, as he also had a very commercial track record. I think in the

---

* He is now the immensely successful franchise producer of *Transformers* and *G.I. Joe.*

† Friedman went on to found Summit Entertainment, of the *Twilight* franchise, and is now cochairman of Lionsgate Studios.

end it was Sherry's "throw off her shoes" comfort with Donald that won him the job, after weeks of frenzied speculation, gossip and wrangling. After over a decade with John, that intimacy would be hard to replace, and I know she struggled with the decision. Goldwyn was in agony, but in the end, he is happy and more successful as a producer, as it suits his temperament and creativity.

CANDYLAND

The rainbow coalition of Sherry and Donald began in 2003. The producers were happy, the execs who had whined on my couch were happy; nobody would get fired, Donald's would be the era of kindness and all would be well on the lot again. Sherry could still reign over the happy Christmas party, and there would be less smoking and moaning on the quad. The Blocker was going to stay, Donald told me, but she was going to be a new, gentler, happier Blocker, reinvented in Donald's image. She had promised.

Really? I asked.

Really. Everyone on the lot was saying so. She'd gotten a promotion. It was like Candyland.

Then Donald hired a new senior exec, whom we'll call "Cookie." She was a tiny ball of fire who brought no small anxiety to the women of Candyland. Donald was crazy about her and thought her wildly commercial, though the stories that preceded her from her prior studio were just wild. Sherry didn't get that "throw off her shoes" feeling from her. The Blocker sensed the possibility of herself being blocked. I was open to Cookie, as she was even shorter than I am. Perhaps she would help me get *Can You Keep a Secret?* going. The option on the book was coming up.

Cookie cultivated long lines of people outside of her office. A meeting would go like this:

YOU: It's about a girl who's terrified of flying.

COOKIE: I'm terrified of flying!

YOU: So many people are! So she gets totally wasted, and sits next to this gorgeous guy on the plane . . .

COOKIE: Good.

YOU: And tells him everything about herself.

COOKIE: Can you get Hugh Grant?

YOU: I didn't tell you that the guy ends up being her boss!

COOKIE: If you get Hugh Grant, I can get it made.

You leave exhilarated. All you have to do is get Hugh Grant. Kate Hudson and Hugh Grant want to work together! Perfect! And then you realize you don't have a script. And you need Cookie to sign off on a writer. And there are thirty people waiting outside her door, and you can't get back in for two weeks. And of course you can't get Hugh Grant before the option runs out.

Sometime around mid-Candyland, Donald called to offer me a movie he wanted to make, with a director already lined up. He knew it wasn't perfect for me, he said, but it would round out his slate. Great, I said, what is it? I was jazzed.

It was called *Step-Dude*.

Okay, it didn't have a great name.

It was about a cougar who falls in love with a guy her son's age.

Okay, it had a dicey, creepy, uncomfortable premise.

But it was really funny.

Okay, funny enough. And I hadn't had a picture in a year now. Too much turmoil. The director was having a hard time getting a cast. Could I help?

My son, Oly, in his twenties at the time, was aghast when I told him the premise. But he played poker regularly with the director. So that was one thing. What thing? I don't know. I thought it would be fun to location scout New Orleans in a van, such was my frustration with my efforts to get *Can You Keep a Secret?* made. *Made?* Hell, even to hire a writer! Now Kate Hudson was pregnant! Nine more months.

So we went scouting for locations in New Orleans. While in the van, we heard that Owen Wilson—the director's best friend—had passed on the script. Then we heard that Seann William Scott—my friend—passed. Then my line producer quit for an Adam Shankman movie. Was this a present, or a trick? I spent months trying to put together a movie I didn't love. I stopped. This was not my job. Making movies I love is my job. Why wasn't it happening? In the meantime, I started to invent some more movies that Donald and I could both like and that I could get around the Blocker. But then, of course, someone got fired and there was a hot new boss, so I got a little distracted.

HIP "R" US

When I think back on the glory days of Tom Freston's reign—all eighteen months of it—it seemed then like he would be at Paramount forever. And why not? He was so cool! He founded MTV! He was a homegrown Viacom star! We were all proud and excited. He came in as the beloved son, waving the MTV banner high, this network he'd founded for proud papa Redstone. He led with his chin, superconfident and New Age, an entrepreneur who could run a conglomerate! Handsome and edgy, he dressed like a rock star and jetted around with Bono or Mick or whomever, wherever. Freston's loyal longtime staff at Viacom's starlet division, MTV, saw him as their Steve Jobs. Out with the stodgy old, in with the new, and he was the cutting-edge face of it. He had Sumner's personal mandate to recreate the brand, and he came in branding away, naming MTV and Nickelodeon the lead faces of the New, Cool Paramount. He seemed to have a bemused contempt for everything Old Paramount, both in style and substance. Apparently the old administration had treated the film division of MTV shabbily, and that would be rectified both by MTV's independence and the wholesale reinvention of the sensibility of the studio: Hip "R" Us. There were a lot of unhip holdovers around, and they were looking nervous.

DOLGEN GETS THE SQUEEZE PLAY

What happened to Dolgen is that he suddenly had no real job. One morning he woke up to find Viacom divided into two divisions. Tom Freston was running the movie division and Les Moonves was running the television and cable division, and it wasn't clear what was left for Dolgen to run. He resigned days later. Sherry was bereft.

It took Tom Freston a while to figure out what he wanted in a new team. In the meantime, he promoted Sherry into Dolgen's job. Suddenly she was going to Walmart to discuss DVDs, running P&Ls, basically doing the financials. She hated Dolgen's job, it was taking her away from the movies, taking her away from getting her hands inside the celluloid, the scripts, the packaging, fixing it in post—everything she loved and was good at. But she figured that she might be able to wait it out until Tom got to know the team she had put in place—Rob Friedman and Donald De Line—and appreciate them as she did. She hoped to convince Tom to promote them to her job. So she stayed in Dolgen's job for eight months, despite the fact she would have preferred to retire sooner, start her foundation and spend more time with her husband, director Billy Friedkin, where she could relax and throw off those wicked work shoes—and not read another financial projection for Paramount ever again. She wanted more than anything to leave gracefully. But as she dutifully performed what was expected of her, Tom Freston knew she was unhappy doing Dolgen's job, so he began scoping out his future options, as is the prerogative of any new CEO. Meanwhile, all of us producers on the lot experienced more debilitating confusion.

Freston reached out to some industry players to fill the top job, notably Stacey Snider, Steven Spielberg's partner at DreamWorks. Behind the scenes, however, it was a bit weird. In a very collegial way, Freston said to Sherry one day, "Let's start a new team. You and me. You fire everybody."

Sherry answered, "Why?"

Firing people is not Sherry's style.

She said to Freston: "But don't you understand? Next summer is going to be the biggest one in the history of our company. And that summer was created by Donald De Line and Sherry Lansing and Rob Friedman and everybody. What are you talking about?"

She was referring to 2005, the summer that was to see Paramount release *War of the Worlds,* which did $245 million worldwide. Sherry remembered what were to be her last days at Paramount. "And in fact, that was the single biggest summer we'd had in years. But he wanted to fire everybody. And I thought, Huh? I'll tell them I'm not going to renew and I'll stay until they find my replacement. If you remember, that's when I kept pushing for Donald and Robbie [Friedman] to be copresidents." While Freston was reaching out to big industry players like Stacey Snider, others lobbied for the job. "And then," Sherry added, "they ended up with Brad Grey."

Freston took everyone by surprise and chose mega–talent manager Brad Grey (notably Brad Pitt's manager and an exec producer on *The Sopranos*), whose name had never been in active contention. Grey managed many big clients and needed months to get out of his contract at his company, Brillstein-Grey Entertainment. During the long transition, from January through March, Donald and Sherry continued to try to put movies together, but none of them happened. She remembers it as a very nice time in which she was perfectly happy and felt no pressure. She and Freston "coexisted," she said. "You know—you decide! Tra-la tra-la! I was perfectly happy. And soon after, I left for a lot of reasons. You know: Been there, done that. Wanting a new life."

All I remember about Sherry leaving is two things:

1. She resigned. She didn't get fired. Period. End of sentence. End of thought.
2. Who didn't come to her good-bye party? I made a list. The place was packed. The gate guards cried. The people she honored every year at the Christmas party for forty years of service cried. Richard Fowkes, head of business affairs, who had been there for three decades, cried. The Blocker and I embraced and cried together.

To her credit, the Blocker was a fantastic person to have work *for* you; all of her bosses adored her and her up-to-the-second inside information that I too would often be privy to. In moments like these, we were on the same team—the sad team. Sherry's key players would be gone once Brad Grey came in and got to remaking things in his image.

The Old Abnormal was dead, along with its unforgettable queen and her unmatchable leadership skills. No one was ever fired right before Christmas vacation under her tenure, as Richard Fowkes was that year. But times were a-changing. And henceforth they would change very, very quickly.

HIP "R" US GOES TO SUNDANCE

The first picture chosen by Freston and his choice of studio head, Brad Grey, was *Hustle & Flow,* an urban picture they picked up for distribution at Sundance and embraced with a splashy "Here comes the All-New Coke" for the New Paramount branding debut. Starring Terrence Howard and directed by Craig Brewer, the movie was an elegy to a "dope" pimp. Though it had won Sundance, it was too cool for the rest of America. With the power of the MTV brand, a huge marketing campaign and a hit, Oscar-winning song, "It's Hard Out Here for a Pimp," the first test of the team's instincts brought in $23 million worldwide. They followed it up by hiring the very Irish Jim Sheridan to direct rapper 50 Cent's life story, *Get Rich or Die Tryin',* still pursuing the hip-hop music tie-in. With a $40 million budget, exclusive of prints and ads, the movie grossed $46 million worldwide.

Despite the fact that *War of the Worlds,* which Sherry and Donald put together, did as well at the box office that summer as she had predicted, soon after Brad Grey arrived, many of the people on Sherry's team were starting to pack. In July, Rob Friedman* was gone, and Rob Moore was running his marketing and distribution divisions as well as business affairs.

I was still not getting my movies made. I had a terrific, action-packed, true-life, high-seas adventure by a great screenwriter that everyone loved, but it had no traction; I had a drama with an Oscar-winning screenwriter about an intelligent-design case in Pennsylvania that was the equivalent of *Inherit the Wind;* I had a comedy with two hot writers, but nothing was going anywhere. Was it the internal drama here? Or the Blocker? I wasn't sure, but

---

* He went on to cochair Lionsgate, which produced *Twilight* and *The Hunger Games,* after it was bought by Summit.

I needed a do-over. I woke up in the middle of the night and decided to make a dinner date with Donald.

"Donald," I said over Dover sole at the restaurant Il Sole days later, "I love the Blocker. She's sent me on many great wild-goose chases to visit unavailable writers. She is adorable and hilarious. But she is killing me."

"Great!" said Donald, in his loving, enthusiastic, totally supportive way. "No more. We will take her off your account tomorrow."

That night I went to bed without tension for the first time in five years, as Donald jetted off to London to check on a picture, *Watchmen,* a movie being produced by veteran producer Larry Gordon and his partner, Lloyd, and directed by Paul Greengrass (*Green Zone, The Bourne Ultimatum, United 93*), based on the DC Comics limited series. Donald thought the script had gone awry.

And then I learned a fatal law of Paramount: *Never*, *ever* jet off to London when there are politics in the air. For it seems (to me) that as soon as someone upstairs gets the travel voucher, your hours are numbered. That was Donald's final flight for Paramount. As he flew east, his contract was terminated, his office was shut down and mind-blowingly serious hardball was being played. Who knew what when? I was so horrified by what was going on that I actually took notes, like a reporter at an assassination who can rely only on her training in an emergency.

Donald flew to London with Cookie, and they met with the director and the production team. It was a tough meeting. Basically, the studio didn't like the script Greengrass wanted to make, and they had to shut down the movie. When Donald returned to the lobby of his hotel, the Dorchester, he got a message from his office that Gregg Kilday of the *Hollywood Reporter* had called him six times. That is *never* good. He called the reporter back, and Kilday asked, "How do you feel about Gail Berman coming in to run movies?"

Donald said, "What are you talking about?"

"They've hired Gail Berman," said Kilday.

"No, Gail Berman is in television; you obviously have it wrong. This is why you're the *Hollywood Reporter* and not *Variety*. That she's possibly coming to run television sounds right."

Donald hung up the phone and called Nancy Kirkpatrick, then the head of Paramount publicity and a smart, plugged-in, fabulous woman who was a great pal of all of ours.[*]

"Nancy, why has this guy called me from the *Hollywood Reporter* with this story about Gail Berman?"

"I got the same call. I know nothing, and I'm not kidding."

Donald hung up the phone, and a minute later, the *Hollywood Reporter* was calling again. "I'm really sorry. This is all so weird that I'm telling you this, but I got it confirmed by Fox."

At that point I found out, because Donald called me from London. My heart was beating hard. I knew that my brother, Rick, knew Gail (they did *Malcolm in the Middle* together—he was packaging agent, she was head of Fox TV) and Peter Chernin well (Gail was then working for Chernin at Fox), and would know the skinny. I offered to call Rick; in a millisecond he confirmed it. Gail's deal to run motion pictures was done, closed. I was in shock. Rick told me not to worry. Worry? My heart was palpitating. It was way beyond worry. Execs were starting to pour into my office like it was a suicide prevention center. Candyland was over.

I called Donald. By then he'd already had it confirmed. He said to me, "Okay, Houston, we have a problem." He hung up the phone and called Brad's office.

"Brad's not here," he was told.

"Well, it's really important. I need to speak to him."

"He's at the dentist."

Phone calls were streaming into Donald's hotel room—press,

---

[*] She is now president of worldwide marketing at Lionsgate under Rob Friedman.

other studios, everybody. I was talking to him and his sister and the Blocker—who was hysterical—constantly. Donald's head was spinning. And why not? He'd been fired, without really having an opportunity to get to work with Brad and be rejected for a good, sound reason! They'd barely had any meetings at all. And he was told by the press, not by his company!

When Donald finally reached Brad hours later, Donald said, "I got this call from the *Hollywood Reporter* telling me you've hired Gail Berman."

"Yes, that's true," he said.

"Oh, okay. Well, so what does that mean for me?"

"Well, that's what we need to talk about."

"So you've fired me."

"No, no, no."

"But you gave her my job. If you gave her my job, then I'm fired."

"Well, we want you to be here. We want to talk about opportunities."

"Okay. None of this makes any sense to me, but I'm getting on the next plane out of London, which unfortunately is not till tomorrow morning. I will come off the plane and go straight to your office at Paramount."

I remember Donald telling me that Freston sat in the room with Brad the next morning, after a sleepless night—a terrible night—saying that he was a big fan. I was such a big fan of Freston's at the time that it meant a great deal to me, who knows why.

In the meeting, the team explained they had wanted to make Donald a producer, and he said, "Thank you, but no." He didn't want to stay at Paramount. It would be incredibly uncomfortable for him, as they can imagine. And that was that.

At dinner with Cookie that night, he got a call from *Watchmen* producer Larry Gordon. "Oh, kids! Welcome to Hollywood!"

Donald told him, "Yeah, well, we just shut your movie down. Go get your friend to fix it. Not my problem anymore."

Donald went on to become a very successful producer at Warner Bros., producing *Green Lantern,* Ridley Scott's *Body of Lies,* the bawdy *Observe and Report* and the buddy comedy *I Love You, Man.* So one studio's attitude at a given time doesn't necessarily affect your fortunes elsewhere. But these guys were in a hurry to create the new Paramount. One, two, three, no time for thee.

I asked Sherry about that moment. What struck her the most, she said, was how content she had been the very second before she heard. She had planned Chapter Three of her life so carefully, leaving her "people" in place, determining the nature of her philanthropy—everything perfectly laid out by careful design. But as my mother always said, the best-laid plans of mice, men and women went awry. This is how Sherry remembers hearing that Donald had gotten fired.

"I had been gone for three months, or something like that," she said. "I remember so clearly that I had gone to a meeting at the United Nations. I was so excited they were asking me to do something. My first meeting was with President Carter, whom I happen to love. We were talking about global-this and global-that and guinea worm, and I was so happy."

I could see that "guinea worm" delighted Sherry: The very thought of it being a parasite she could do something about and not a movie in crisis overjoyed her.

"I was in New York," Sherry continued. "Amy Pascal [cochair of Sony and one of Donald's best friends] called and said, 'How is it?' and I said, 'It's everything I thought it would be. I found salvation, you know. I just left the center; it's everything I wanted for the third chapter.' She was so happy for me. Then I said, 'What I really feel good about is that all of the people I love are fine.' You know, I thought they were. And then I went back to the hotel and there were seven messages from the trades—some from this person, some from that person—and then one from Donald, saying that they had fired him."

It still amazed her to think of.

At the time of Donald's firing, I was in my office, surrounded by my suffering executives. They could smoke in my bungalow, so it was a popular hangout. Plus, they knew they could get the dish from Donald's camp at my place. A big bear of an exec was actually crying—"Woe is me! What am I going to do?" Nobody knew what horrors would come next.

Cookie called me, sounding devastated. She asked how Donald was handling this.

"Bad," I said. "Not good; but okay," I added, carefully.

COLOR WAR

The guys upstairs would have to be smarter than Hip "R" Us and other assorted "MTV meets pimp" movies. They needed to insulate themselves from the front line of decision-making. That's where Gail Berman, the brilliant Fox programmer, came in. She was responsible for the long-running, critically acclaimed hit *Malcolm in the Middle,* about a gifted middle child; *House; 24; American Idol;* and the general rise of the Fox network. Her job there was to find America's taste, and she was Brad Grey's choice to replace Donald. I knew her a bit via my brother, Rick Rosen. They were great friends. I would live to see another pitch.

In the meantime, on a critical metalevel, the Freston-Grey-Moore team saw into the future. They determined that the Dolgen-Lansing regime was very domestically oriented, selling off their foreign rights to pay for making a picture. Remember, in the Old Abnormal, international only counted for 20 percent; their thinking hadn't really changed with the times, even though they held foreign rights on some of their early franchise efforts like the Tom Cruise vehicle *Mission: Impossible* and *Lara Croft: Tomb Raider,* based on the video game of the same name about a fearless, tomb-raiding archeologist, played in the film by Angelina Jolie, who, needless to say, is quite a babe.

The new team quickly decided to retain their foreign rights and set their sights on the international market. That was a key move in the turning of the battleship Paramount. They began to concentrate on their in-house franchises, generating another *Mission: Impossible* in 2006 and pushing the *Star Trek* franchise into gear, a task the old regime had struggled with. But there were many growing pains and strains to come before the turn was complete.

One day early in the Gail Berman regime, we were told that we would have all-new executives. I guess it was just too cozy the way it was. Gail got this idea that we should all break up into teams of new executives, and she would reassign our projects to these new teams. Each team would handle all our ongoing projects plus any new pitches or ideas. And each would have a color, like red, yellow, blue or green. Really! No more pitching to the executive who would most take to your idea, who loved comedy or drama or sports, as it was done at every other studio for the last *fifty years.*

We were all starting from scratch, repitching our one- to six-year-old projects, picking new writers, creating new treatments, leaving our allies—it was a total disaster. Cookie called to explain. "This is so great!" she said. "You will love your new exec! This is an exciting new direction."

I just couldn't believe I was pitching *Can You Keep a Secret?* all over again to the exec on the Yellow team, whom I'd never met. We rebelled and named ourselves the Khaki team. This was early in the soon-to-be-troubled relationship between Gail and Cookie. But that was in another country and alas, now they are friends, to screw up a great expression.

At one point, when we were working on the Khaki team, Cookie called me again with great news: She was bringing in her best friend in all the world to run the studio with her. (I had been thinking that Gail was running the studio.)

"Really?" I said. "Who?"

"Brad Weston," she said. "It's a secret. But you will love him. I've known him all my life."

I couldn't help but wonder whether this meant I would have to pitch *Can You Keep a Secret?* to yet another person that month. I was distraught, so I called my brilliant agent and key ally, Kevin Huvane, of CAA, who knows everything, always.

"Kev, who is Brad Weston? Is he coming here? Will I like him? And is he a good guy?"

"Yes, yes, yes. I will set up a meeting with you two. This is good. He's sane."

So there I was, a week later, in this incredibly calm Zen office, with a bald (the shaved-head variety), hot guy who ran ten miles every morning and claimed to love romantic comedies.

"So she meets this great-looking guy on a plane," I told him, "and because she has horrible plane anxiety, she gets totally wasted and ends up telling him every tiny secret about her life— completely embarrassing, gross things. In the morning she goes to work, and he's her boss." I'd never gotten so much of the story out before.

"What if she sleeps with him?" suggests Weston.

"Interesting," I say.

"Pick the writer you like, and I'll hire him."

I *was* going to like this guy!

Brad immediately commissioned a talented British writer, Ol Parker (later the writer of *The Best Exotic Marigold Hotel*), and we got to work meeting with book author Sophie Kinsella, which involved fun trips to London, where the *Shopaholic* writer, our new screenwriter/director and I had exciting story meetings, where we reinvented the script, and went on many fun shopping trips, where we undermined my bank account. Brad even inquired, without prompting, about long-languishing projects that I'd been working on in creative solitude. He was going to be the first creative ally I had here since Goldwyn had left. It was beginning to feel like Christmas.

I started a project on the Dover "Scopes"-type trial, in which intelligent design was put on trial in a Pennsylvania courtroom. Cookie said I could do it if I landed Oscar-winning writer Sir Ronald Harwood (*The Pianist, The Diving Bell and the Butterfly*), and much to her shock, he agreed. Then the three of us proceeded to have the most horrid pitch meeting in history, after which Sir Ronald determined he would never pitch at a studio again. I then hired Ron Nyswaner (*Philadelphia*) who wrote a terrific script, which I sent to Tom Hanks. But soon movies like this were not going to be made at Paramount anymore.

In the midst of this creative bliss, our option on *Can You Keep a Secret?* was quickly running out, so Oly was on a crazy deadline. Within two months, the script came in, and I loved it. I sent it to Weston. He said, "Get it to Kate ASAP, and we can figure out what to do about the option." So off it went. We made the option cutoff within days, and then . . . Kate was too busy to read it. I called. I emailed. She sent back love and smiley faces. But she was too busy to read. When she finally did, she passed, much to my shock. And after all that huffing and puffing, Kate said no, and the author didn't renew our option. Development hell—full of sound and fury, signifying nothing. But my little failure was nothing compared to the cataclysm about to occur at the very top of Paramount.

THE END OF THE SHORTEST MOMENTOUS ERA

Tom Freston's firing couldn't have been more unexpected.

This part we all heard: One bad weekend, Tom Cruise (who'd had a long-standing and *very* lucrative deal with Paramount, which included the *Mission: Impossible* franchise) jumped the shark on Oprah's couch, on national TV. This not only appalled the nation, it appalled the Redstones, and Sumner went public and fired Tom Cruise by press release. Firing a star asset by press release is something the chairman rarely does, particularly without consulting his top execs—in this case, Brad Grey and Tom Freston—who run the studio day to day and have movies with this star, and many more movies with his powerful agency, CAA.

Freston, thinking he was family, is said to have visited the Redstones over the weekend to protect his executives and object to his boss. According to insiders, whatever conversation followed this confrontation led to Freston's firing. Some say Redstone objected to being confronted on his actions, that he felt he was the boss and able to act unilaterally when he chose to, vis-à-vis his studio and its actors under contract. CAA was said to have been up in arms and screaming and yelling at Grey and Freston about the public firing. "Who cares about CAA?" was Redstone's position in this version of the story.

Freston tried to explain to his boss the importance of the *Mission* franchise and that he should work with his team. Redstone reportedly said that Cruise was "over," "that was that" and "the conversation is over." This conversation may not have happened; it is industry scuttlebutt. Redstone stated publicly that he fired Freston because he had not made a timely bid on MySpace, the non-Facebook social networking site that was up for grabs, but that Freston considered to be in precipitous decline and not worth Viacom buying. But no one believed that story, as Freston and

Sumner were too close to end their relationship over a deal. The Tom Cruise story is what we all heard, and it is thought by most to be true.

This could be another part of the story:

Sumner, it was said by many in his office, could often be heard shouting, "Where's Freston?" Freston, the former Afghani rug dealer who loved to jet around the world with rock stars, apparently, even as co-COO of Viacom Entertainment, didn't change his lifestyle all that much. Why did anyone think he would? That's what everyone loved about him. Tom Freston's work ethic was not Sumner Redstone's work ethic, which could kindly be described as 24/7; Freston's might be described as unconventional/out of the office/hard to reach in St. Barts with Mick.

Whenever someone gets fired, it's the culmination of a number of issues. In this case, it was likely Freston's lifestyle. The very thing that made Tom Freston so special and interesting and enabled him to found MTV—going to concerts all over the world, hanging out with creative types, brainstorming with rock stars— drove Sumner nuts because Freston wasn't a "sit in your office and do Dolgen-type financial projections" kind of guy.

But the heir apparent—the new surrogate son—Viacom CEO Philippe Dauman, was that kind of guy. In his most public discussion of Freston's firing, reported in the *New York Times,** Redstone said he fired Freston for Dauman. "It was a crying session for both of us when I said, 'Tom, look, you've been great, but the board and I have decided that Philippe is the best man to lead the company.'" And presto chango, the *Times* article went on to report, Freston's hemp chairs, dark blinds and Jamaican music were replaced with Dauman's spare office of taupe, white and heavy wood.

Underlining this thinking is something I once heard from an

---

* September 22, 2012.

assistant, the best of sources. Sumner called Sherry once, screaming about Freston, "Why the fuck didn't you tell me he's never around?"

She answered, "Why the fuck didn't *I* tell you? It's not my responsibility to tell you."

Freston had been offered the top job at Viacom in the past and had turned it down. His ambivalence had been good intuition. In any case, Freston was gone the Monday after the Tom Cruise weekend. All of MTV wept. Again, the town was stunned. Brad Grey and his new deputy, Rob Moore, went on. Rob Moore could eat a lot of real estate on Melrose. And there were rumors he wasn't happy with someone else.

MEETING WITH VAMPIRES

I was getting the feeling that Brad didn't like Gail so much anymore. First of all, it was the way they looked when they walked across the lot together: It wasn't just that she looked like Big Bird looming over his Ernie, but he looked trapped, like he was trying to escape. I heard from excellent sources that at some point early in Gail's tenure—maybe when she was forming her producers into color groups—Rob Moore, who had been crowned president of distribution, marketing, business affairs and home entertainment in 2006, had already essentially usurped her green-lighting position. In addition, the whole film industry was complaining about her phone list—as in, they weren't on it. She was dining with *television people*! If you could hear the utter disdain with which this was whispered, you would think she was meeting with vampires in the dark of night. I could imagine that Brad was hearing this and not liking the fact that Important Movie People were grumbling. This is somewhat ironic, particularly now, knowing that TV darling J. J. Abrams, of *Felicity, Alias, Lost* and *Fringe* fame, is now among the lot's biggest filmmaker attractions, and most of the movie people who were so disdainful then are now doing TV.* I assumed Gail's preeminence in TV was one of the reasons she was recruited.

My last encounter with Gail at Paramount took place at what turned out to be one of the more surreal meetings I had ever attended. It was supposed to be a green-light meeting on a movie that Gail had tried to give me, *Angus, Thongs and Perfect Snogging*. It was an adorable script by the gutsy and talented English writer-director Gurinder Chadha (*Bend It Like Beckham*), based on a well-known British young adult book called *Angus, Thongs and Full-Frontal Snogging*. I was thrilled to go to England to do it. (Read: I loved the script, and would have done anything to leave the lot.)

Gurinder wouldn't hire Emma Roberts to star, as Nickelodeon wanted (because she had a hit Nickelodeon series at the time), which probably cost us a U.S. release. I supported her decision in an effort to bond with her, which eventually failed. But Gurinder and I were getting along swimmingly at the time, and we were waiting for Gail and Cookie in the huge main conference room at the administration building. There had been financing problems we had overcome with the help of Paramount International, and we looked like we were there on budget with an all-English cast of unknowns, as Gurinder wanted due to the excellent numbers in the UK from her hit *Bend It Like Beckham*. We were waiting excitedly for the go-ahead.

Cookie arrived; the two execs from the Khaki team were there; but no Gail. A half hour passed; the assistant called and said it would be another few minutes. Forty-five minutes of gossip, small talk, chitchat about Gurinder's pregnancy and scheduling passed, but still no Gail. At the hour mark it became weird, and Cookie

---

* Abrams was recently hired by Disney to reboot *Star Wars*.

left the meeting, never to return. At an hour and a half, Cookie called me into her office. With a look I can only describe as abject horror mixed with manic delirium, she told me that Gail had been fired. I was in shock.

"Oh my God," I said. I loved Gail. I had helped heal her relationship with Cookie. I thought her instincts were really great, and growing by the hour. I couldn't handle this.

I went to Gail's office. I hugged and kissed her. She was upset but relieved; a pro. In shock, but not. But still we talked for a while and commiserated about Paramount. I returned to my meeting and said, "All bets are off for now. I will check in with everyone tomorrow." I went home, took a Xanax and watched three nights' worth of *48 Hours Mystery* (I hoard them for insomniac nights like these).

Within hours, the red-hot rumors were that Cookie and Brad would be copresidents. They were both to be promoted to Gail's job. The copresidency situation could be really bad or really good, but it certainly didn't feel stable. I was going to lie low until it all washed out.

Which was unbelievably fast, even for Paramount. You could say it happened at lightning speed. Within what seemed like minutes, Cookie too, despite her plans to run the studio with her best friend in the whole world, was gone. There was a sense that she and Gail were let go together, like a two-for-one sale, and this infuriated me.

From my vantage point, this was entirely sexist and unfair. Gail was apparently fired for political reasons not really of her own making. She had gotten tangled up in Cookie's complicated political imbroglio without her knowledge. Gail was terribly naïve, really. The fix was in for both of them, though neither of them knew it. A catfight could be blamed, but in fact they were both expendable to the powers that be. They were noisy, they were women, they were in somebody's way. So on the day of my strange *Angus*

Thongs meeting, January 10, 2001, both were summarily fired, in a cold un-Nike-like whoosh.

Brad Weston looked like a seasoned corporate survivor, hanging tough in the top spot. For a moment he became the sole president of production, and spent his time both infighting and literally fighting for the movie *The Fighter*—the Oscar-nominated story of fighter Micky Ward, starring Mark Wahlberg—like he was in one corner.* But who was in the other?

As I sort out the chronology in my mind, I realize I've left out a whole president who suddenly turned up. This *was* Paramount, after all. This seems negligent, I know, but there were so many. There were copresidents and presidents of divisions and presidents of MTV and a lovely senior vice president of Nickelodeon Movies. But this was a real president: John Lesher, whom I'd known earlier in his career as an Endeavor agent. Brad Grey had recruited Lesher in 2005 to run Paramount Vantage, its then to-be-reinvented (there's that word again!) classics division. Lesher had streaked out of the gate with his ex-clients' prepackaged pictures, and seemed for a time to have more movies in production than Paramount itself.† In one impressive year, he had two movies, the Coen brothers' *No Country for Old Men* and Paul Thomas Anderson's *There Will Be Blood,* competing against each other for the Best Picture Oscar. (*No Country* won.) When Lesher ran Vantage, he seemed, for good reason—from many on the studio lot's point of view—to be Grey's and Freston's favorite acolyte.

Apparently, Freston's demise spelled the eventual demise of Vantage, his baby. And "suddenly" (like everything at Paramount in those days), Lesher was a president of big Paramount too, and my new friend, Brad Weston, who liked romantic comedies and let

---

* Eventually his administration would lose the movie; he was forced to abandon it in what we call "turnaround." But Paramount later picked it up for distribution after Relativity Media financed it.

† In the same year Vantage also released *Year of the Dog, Black Snake Moan, A Mighty Heart, Into the Wild* and *Margot at the Wedding.*

me play alone on my passion project, was suddenly in danger. Grey had given Lesher the top job at Paramount, now that Vantage was effectively closing, perhaps as a kind of trade-off for his tenure at Vantage. Would he know how to make regular movies? And would Weston work as a subpresident under Lesher?

But even bigger things were brewing. As the Moore-Grey team refined its formula (Super-Moore was now vice chairman), the huge deal it had made with Spielberg's DreamWorks in 2006 fell apart after only two years. It had been acrimonious almost from the start. It didn't take long for Spielberg and Grey to get into battles over autonomy, and DreamWorks left bitterly in 2008. Paramount took custody of many scripts and a shared hit in its divorce from DreamWorks, *Transformers.* Each studio got custody of forty of their shared scripts, with the right to cofinance. Eventually, parts of this divorce settlement, including a new head of production who moved from DreamWorks to Paramount to oversee their shared inventory, would complete Paramount's transformation into the New Abnormal paradigm.

Adam Goodman, the former president of DreamWorks, became president of production after Lesher was fired, and remains there to this day. Brad Weston, at lunch with me recently, credited Goodman with finding a new kind of inexpensive franchise for Paramount, *Paranormal Activity,* which, he pointed out, brings the sensibility of reality TV to movies. A handheld horror franchise on its fourth incarnation (at the time of writing), its "you are there as this is really happening to real people" conceit is as cheap to make as it is scary and fresh. (Or was.) Goodman was a nice good-bye present from the departing DreamWorks.

But an intervention was about to take place on a scale much grander than anything we moaned and groaned about when we smoked and gossiped on the quad. It would ultimately entail sweeping cuts to the studio's overheads and practices that the most ambitious deficit-hawk type would never have dreamed of suggesting. None of it was really planned. None of us saw it coming. When we heard the foreboding sound of tom-toms in the air, we never suspected that would be the onset of an ill-timed war that would interrupt and then change business as usual forever.

THE CATASTROPHE

The Writers' Strike of 2007–8

I recall Halloween 2007 very clearly. My lunch date had to cancel because he had to evacuate his parents from their burning gated community in San Diego. The crazy Santa Ana winds were kicking carbon dust into my face from the thirteen fires that were raging out of control up and down the coast, and that's not counting the one that was about to consume the entire town: the writers' strike.

The 1988 strike was Vesuvian, lasting six months and costing the industry half a billion dollars. It is remembered as "the Bloodbath." The financial consequences had been so dire that neither side had fought again until now. But the sides were redrawn as a new revenue frontier was opening up—the virtual one—and if the past was prelude to the future, the future was grim. The trace memory of that strike had the town shivering in the ninety-eight-degree heat nineteen years later. Both camps were entrenched as the Writers Guild of America (WGA) contract was expiring that night.

The ghetto was hyperventilating. In Hollywood at times of industry-wide stress, everyone is a ghetto Jew. The tens of thousands of Irish, blacks and WASPs were all running around like the pogrom was coming down from the hills into the hood. The prospect of future work ceasing if the writers went out on strike was terrifying.

For weeks before the strike deadline, the two sides had barely spoken, each viewing the other as something akin to aliens. The writers were still reeling from the battle of 1988, when they fought mightily for a fraction of DVD profits and lost. The writers still wanted a piece of that pie, but it was gone, baby, gone. At least the writers wanted some payback for the slice of DVD revenue they missed in '88 by taking an aggressive posture toward "new media"—i.e., the Internet, in the form of online streaming. In truth, the value of the revenue stream had not been definitively evaluated by either TV or films at that point. There were guesses, estimates, based on models pulled out of models. It was 2008, and deals of consequence are just now, in 2012, being made—and they are still not predictable enough to be projected onto any profit-and-loss statement. But who believed this then? Not the writers.

The AMPTP, or Alliance of Motion Picture and Television Producers—by which we mean the studios' and networks' negotiating body, also known as the Moguls—was hostile to these fundamental incursions into barely existing profit streams. They saw one on the way out—DVDs—and one just barely on the way in—the Internet. So they began the negotiations with "rollbacks," a common and (in my humble opinion) repugnant management negotiating strategy. To me, Malcolm in the Middle, it seemed like a gigantic pissing contest: Whose industry phallus, if you will, was bigger—the Moguls' or the Writers'? This may sound like a Polish joke, but this is the only season when the Writers, usually at the bottom of the industry totem pole, can take on the Moguls and slap them silly. Potential work stoppages are deadly.

The $64,000 (not modified for inflation) question was, were the Writers willing to go out for months on end, losing millions for many, for what might turn out to be a few dollars per year? Or was there really a pot of gold at the end of the Internet rainbow worth holding out for, as they suspected?

For days on end leading up to the strike, the Moguls stone-walled. Some decried it as a tactic—perhaps they were waiting for the DGA (Directors Guild of America) contract to expire in June. The DGA was always considered a more "mature" (i.e., less hotheaded) negotiating partner by the Moguls, which, needless to say, infuriated the Writers. When the two sides did communicate via the media or other intermediaries, their numbers were so far apart on the so-called new media that they hardly seemed to be in the same industry. The Moguls were dying to talk to someone they thought understood what they were saying (like directors). The Writers wanted a piece of this gigantic frontier.

The Moguls said, "What frontier?"

The Writers snorted, "We *know* you are making forty billion dollars now! Give us a piece!"

The Moguls sneered, "These numbers are from where?! Who *are* you people?"

They were talking moon rocks and refrigerators. Everyone was going batty.

This is how crazy it was.

OCTOBER 2007

Right before the strike deadline, when movie people were dashing to finish scripts and turn them in to the studios (thousands of hastily completed scripts dated October 31 were simultaneously submitted to the Writers Guild and the studios' production and legal/labor departments), I was standing in the parking lot at Disney after a development meeting with a Barbie of a writer, discussing the issues of the potential strike. Suddenly I found myself practically shouting, "It's really true! They have no money! Their DVD library is gone! They are living from movie to movie!"

She shouted back, "They have zillions of dollars! They make all these blockbusters! Don't you read what they tell Wall Street?"

"What are they going to tell Wall Street when they need financiers? That they're broke and have no future?"

She yelled, "The Internet is the future!"

I yelled back: "There are no Internet profits yet! Everything is downloaded for free! Because of piracy we are all going to go broke! There will be no more movies!"

And then we burst out laughing, realizing that neither of us had any idea whatsoever what we were talking about, that we were both simulacra of our side's positions, repeating unadulterated propaganda.

We all turned in our scripts as commanded by the studios, just ahead of the strike deadline. There we were, writers, producers and agents, all complicit with the Moguls' intention to stockpile material to get through the strike. But we all had to try to survive and get our movies made, right? The actors' and directors' contracts didn't expire until June, and the plan was that everything that made it into inventory could shoot up until that final date. The networks claimed they could live without the crucial showrunners through reality programming, "unscripted television" that was cheap to produce. Showrunners, the writer-producers of television, guarantee the scripts will be ready on time and that the show will be delivered in time to air. As television goes, they are invaluable. Reality TV wasn't taken seriously at the time, and the creative community pooh-poohed the networks' strategy.

The night before the deadline, after stonewalling the Writers Guild until the final moment, the Moguls met the Writers' leadership to make their so-called generous offer. They took the "rollbacks" off the table. This is the way Moguls negotiate: They start from less than zero, so that getting to zero is a triumph. This is business as usual for Moguls in Hollywood. The Writers could have their residual payments back—the checks they receive for the reairing of their shows. But they could not have what they wanted in DVD and Internet profits. The Moguls thought they were being beneficent. This was a concession of sorts: The residual issue is fundamental to writers; it had been brutally fought for in the two longest strikes in movie industry history, in 1960 and again in 1988. Eliminating residuals had been called a nonstarter by the guild. Now the nonstarter had been removed, so maybe negotiations could start. For a day, everyone in the ghetto was saying there wouldn't be a strike.

Luckily for me, I have a brother, Rick, on the inside, and as the head of television at the huge agency WME,* he repped many of the showrunners at the crux of this strike. They would likely be the first to see some Internet ad revenue if they won concessions, as their shows were already replaying on the Net. So they keenly watched the new media issues.

During this critical juncture, Rick and I sat on his Bel Air porch. It was a gorgeous day; the wind was kicking up, and I commented on the lovely, bonfirelike smell permeating the air. It reminded me of Texas in the fall. Little did we know that it was the odor of people's kitchens on fire.

After some beating around the bush, I asked the big Q. "Will there be a strike?"

"They [the Writers] have to give something up," Rick said. "The producers did"—referring to the Moguls—"and now they have to. That's how negotiations work." So much for inside information.

The WGA had thus far dismissed the Moguls' offer. The ghetto was now holding its collective breath. Some were choking on ashes

---

* William Morris Endeavor.

(the fancy Westsiders, who live west of La Cienega), and the rest of us were just choking.

The Writers met the next day, November 1, and took a vote to authorize a strike should negotiations come to an impasse. The Writers Guild had elected a militant leadership headed by Patric Verrone, an animation writer who had been on the WGA board. But everyone believed (hoped?) there would still be serious negotiating to avoid a work stoppage and picket lines at all the networks and studios. Was this still possible?

The Moguls thought the WGA negotiators were provincial and naïve, and the WGA negotiators saw the Moguls as immoral liars, much like progressives view the Tea Party and vice versa. These views of one another solidified early. Verrone was elected to avenge the losses of 1988. The Moguls' rollback of residuals inflamed an already incendiary situation. The Moguls felt that the expectations of the Writers were numerically way out of line and emotionally biased. The Writers had been lied to in the past about DVD revenues and believed that they were being lied to again.

The stage was set for . . . well, let's say, *not* a party. The Moguls waited for a counteroffer. And waited.

Days later, everything changed. For a year, everyone had been planning production schedules around a "worst-case scenario": a June walkout of all the unions (WGA, DGA or, more likely, the Screen Actors Guild (SAG), who, according to the Moguls, were the Taliban of the unions). If they could keep talking through June, the network showrunners—even if they couldn't write— could keep up their producing duties, and the studios could shoot the scripts they had stockpiled. The Moguls were confident they could eventually reach an agreement with the DGA, which would "grandfather" everyone else into the best deal they could get. The DGA had the best relationship with the Moguls, and there was a history of pleasant negotiations between the two. This gave the

DGA confidence that they could get the WGA and SAG the best terms, and perhaps avert a walkout altogether.

But the Writers were not so sure they were going to go along with the strategy. There were suspicious mutterings questioning whether the more powerful (in film) Directors had the Writers' interests at heart. (Do they on set?) Then suddenly, on November 4, the Writers exploded a nuclear device. They walked out.

I tried to figure out how this happened. After reading his book about the future of screenwriting, *What Happens Next,* I sought out Marc Norman, a WGA negotiating committee member. The reflective Papa Bear–like Norman, who cowrote the Oscar-winning film *Shakespeare in Love,* sat with me in my office for hours discussing union strategy.

"We didn't really anticipate or plan it," said Marc. "We saw no reason to wait for the—let's call them unpredictable actors."

I asked him if he thought the directors were too cozy with the Moguls. He smiled. "The timing wasn't premeditated. It wasn't highly debated. We thought, Why are we waiting for them? Why don't we go on strike?"

This totally unexpected move left the network heads exposed without a new season, or sufficient episodes for the fall's upcoming shows. It was the middle of pilot-writing season, and scripts could not be rushed. Big hit shows went unresolved. As for the studios, any unfinished and unsubmitted scripts had no chance of getting made that year. This placed the Writers in a better negotiating position than ever before. No leisurely wait until June. No orchestrated nice-nice negotiation.

Suddenly, I absorbed a new fact: The Writers had, for a moment, stumped the Moguls. I sat in my office and reevaluated everything. *This was good!* I was on the side of—*work!* Maybe the Writers playing hardball would make the Moguls cave!

Sure.

The Writers thought the studios would run out of material

for their summer and winter blockbusters, and they were counting on the failure of reality TV to fill the audience's appetite for
good television. In fact, on November 7, two days after the Writers
hit the picket line, the town's ace reporter and soon-to-become-
much-more-than-that, Nikki Finke, warned otherwise. She had it
from good sources that the TV brass was happy to trash the entire
2008–9 season, which was already looking like a stinker. Was that
posturing or truth? We were falling down a rabbit hole and giving
birth to an Alice.

THE MAKING OF A NARRATOR

One of the most fascinating things that happened during the
strike was that it grew its own narrator, and then its own Norma
Rae. Nikki Finke was already something of a phenomenon: the
town's top columnist, breaking news reporter and *terrorista* if
you got on her wrong side. Her Web site, then self-owned and
called DeadlineHollywoodDaily.com (now deadline.com), was a
must-read well before the strike, but it became much, much more
during the strike (and even more afterward; its popularity forced
the perennial trade journal *Variety* onto the block by 2012 and
into a weekly by 2013). It became the town square, our industry
bulletin board, our way of communicating, slugging it out. It has
remained so ever since. But it was a remarkable social and political phenomenon during the strike. At its peak in January and
February, there were 90–105 comments per update, and often
10–20 updates per day on every side. Everyone was leaking there.
The longer the strike went on, the more vital (and ultimately
valuable) Nikki's Web site became.

In the tradition of the great Hollywood reporters from Hedda
Hopper to Walter Winchell, Nikki inspired fear, respect and devo-
tion among her sources and readers. Some sample entries:

Comments

You are the bomb, Nikki. Hope you're feeling better—glad you're back . . .

Rock on, Nikki.

I know this is so last week, but I have to say it anyway: You go Girl!

Do they give Pulitzers for online writing? You rock!

Nikki's news was inside and up-to-the-minute. She had the detailed reports from every secret or public meeting and official or off-the-record negotiation. And she had a point of view. Nikki's readers tagged the *Los Angeles Times* and *Variety* as shills for the Moguls, while Nikki was their fearless, populist leader. When she got sick, people were virtually apoplectic over the absence of information.

The most riveting aspect of the Web site were the comments. The town fought it out on the comment board: exhorting fellow strikers, criticizing each other for not picketing enough hours, calling out names of potential scabs, accusing posters of being Mogul imposters who undermined the will of the masses by slipping in antiunion economic information about new media. Ultimately, an ugly class war broke out between the trade unions and some overly frenzied Writers about what a union was and the value of each other's work, though some less drenched in ideology chimed in on the crew's behalf.

The politics got baffling. It was much like the Stalinist-vs.-Trotskyite years, as my grandfather explained them to me: the narcissism of small differences. Years later it makes for an astonishing social history, and Nikki Finke's Web site and her fans will guide us through the wild Mr. Toad–like roller-coaster ride Hollywood took for a while, crash-landing only in time for the Oscars.

THE FOUR SEASONS OF THE STRIKE:
THE ARDENT FALL

The Writers walked out onto the picket lines that formed in front and in back of all the studios and networks on November 5, 2007. They were having the most wonderful time on the line (as opposed to online). They were having romances. Bromances. They were making alliances, forming writing partnerships and spawning webisodes and fresh concepts for movies and series by the thousands. One girlfriend, a talented screenwriter, was having the best social life of her career. Imagine a bunch of isolated people who usually stay home all day long staring at their computers suddenly coming together at the studio with scores of cute, like-minded people and being fed pizzas by their agents, all with a single purpose: Defeating the Man! They had a cause! And they were getting fed for free and they had to be there and they couldn't write. Nobody could make them write. And there's nothing a writer loves more than being forced *not* to write.

I remember driving past Kiwi Smith (you remember Kiwi from the *Bridesmaids* premiere) and Marc Klein (*Serendipity, Mirror Mirror*) in the line in front of Paramount, two great friends and collaborators, as they yelled, "Lynnie! Lynnie! Wave and honk!" As the granddaughter of a beloved labor-organizer, crossing my first picket line was pure agony. I had to honk and wave to Marc and Kiwi and all my friends, and then I'd drive through their line to my office. I thought the world was coming to an end.

But for WGA leaders Patric Verrone and David Young, who had been elected on a "get ready for a strike" platform, the world was an opening oyster. They had an enthusiastic, untapped labor force in a new generation that had never picketed before, and the public was on their side. Verrone was in full command of morale all the way through the rank and file.

"It's like we were catching a tailwind from Enron," Marc

Norman, of the WGA strike leadership committee, told me. "One of the things that was interesting about this strike—and I mentioned it in a piece I wrote at the time—was that for the first time, we had a sense that the public was kind of on our side. If there was any public interest at all in the Writers Guild—which there never is—it was on our side. We were the beneficiaries of luck. There was an antiestablishment, anticorporate mood in the country. And we could portray ourselves as Clifford Odets's peace workers going against the owners."

They had all the people power.

Celebrities were joining the Writers on the picket line, creating juicy, national publicity, public relations you can't buy and general whoop-de-doo, while the Moguls hired PR agencies to help them build a counteroffensive and put out viral videos, all to no avail. They accused the union of using scare tactics, and then leaked to the newspapers terrifying things about what the strike would do to the economy. The more they tried to look like the good guys, the more they looked like the bad guys.

Deadline Comments Board

I'll explain . . . It's the AMPTP accusing us of using tactics that they themselves have employed.

The AMPTP is refusing to negotiate.

The AMPTP leaks rumors of a nine-month strike to local news outlets, who then report the rumors as news, so as to create financial fear among writers and all the other unions as well . . .

Comment by Writer who earned 60K in '07—Tuesday, November 13, 2007, 3:00 p.m. PST

Soccer moms drove by the studios after picking up their kids to honk and wave at the Writers, and the Moguls were the butt of jokes on late-night comedy shows. If you liked artists, you were for the WGA. Hillary and Barack both supported the Writers. The Writers' agencies sent Krispy Kreme doughnuts to the picket line even as their expense accounts were canceled and their bottom lines began to cave. This didn't stop the anger directed at agents as a group from being vehemently expressed on the comment board as if they were the source of the Writers' anguish. Those striking Writers who didn't have agents took the opportunity to hate agents even more. It was a pointless diversion of fury that nevertheless flourished on the board for days.

In the midst of it, in the absence of any negotiations whatsoever in November, people searched for a hero, a glamorous Superman.

Deadline Comments Board

Where's Hollywood's favorite son? No, not Tom Hanks—the Governator! He's the only one with the clout, the pro-business and pro-talent reputation, and the power to solve this.

His office said today they don't want to get involved. Tell him to get off his butt and back to Hollywood so all his old friends can get back to work.

Comment by Mr. Wants a Good Deal—Wednesday, November 7, 2007, 4:32 p.m. PST

The Governator, Arnold Schwarzenegger, still thought of as the Terminator in his former (and now current) Hollywood home, stayed far away, apparently too busy for a legacy. In the Old Abnormal, this impasse would never have happened. As in Washington, where, prior to the congressional debt-ceiling debate of 2011, the process had been pro forma for years, labor relations here had been pro forma for years, and everyone knew how to get along. This degree of labor strife is a semirecent phenomenon. For decades, labor negotiations were handled by the guy at the top and his Fixer. They had "everyone's" interests at heart—that is, making movies. There was a Big Man (in the African sense) who ruled the town, Lew Wasserman; he founded MCA and eventually merged it with Universal. He had a Fixer named Sidney Korshak, who was a labor lawyer (and much, much more) with ties to the teamsters. Korshak had even represented Jimmy Hoffa.

According to former Paramount head Bob Evans in his book *The Kid Stays in the Picture,* "A nod from Korshak and the Teamsters change management. A nod from Korshak and Vegas shuts down. A nod from Korshak and the Dodgers can suddenly play night baseball." For the purpose of labor relations in Hollywood, he was a strike fixer. Between Wasserman and Korshak, they kept the negotiations on track for decades. They set the parameters for the studios' and the union's expectations, and things went swimmingly for a long time.

Pre-Wasserman, the glory of the WGA, founded by pioneering screenwriter Frances Marion, was earned repeatedly, notably in the famously arduous 1959–60 six-month strike, when writers first won residuals and a basic health and pension plan. Then, through the relatively harmonious seventies when Wasserman and Korshak ruled, they added significantly and rather painlessly to those gains. Until, that is, the Bloodbath of '88, when the Fixer and the Big Man were no longer in power and the Writers' DVD demands struck at the bone marrow of the studios' profit margin.

There was no fixer like Sidney Korshak for this strike. Early on, Jeffrey Katzenberg tried and failed, and no one else arrived thereafter. That is, until Nikki exhorted the agents to come to the rescue.

Nikki realized that agents were professional mediators, and in the absence of Superman, we needed the top-seed agents to step in. They were obviously already talking among themselves, as they had everything at stake. Someone needed to rise up and fill the vacuum.

Deadline Comments Board

Excellent idea, Nikki. I was having this exact same conversation today on the picket line. The only problem is . . . it makes way too much sense. They'll never go for it.

    Comment by A-Dub—Wednesday, November 7, 2007, 4:45 p.m. PST

I am a TV agent. I would be happy to work on this. If empowered, I am sure a deal could be made. Remember, artists pay agents 10% to provide a buffer between talent and studios . . . now we see why that's important.

    Comment by tvagent72—Wednesday, November 7, 2007, 4:49 p.m. PST

Although I agree that the Moguls hate agents more than they do the talent, the suggestion has a lot of merit simply because it would show the extent of the economic disaster that this strike is about to inflict, if it hasn't already . . . Agents and the agencies are a very large part of this economy. Theirs is as vested an interest in resolving this fight as any of ours. They are part of the economy.

    Comment by JimBo—Wednesday, November 7, 2007, 5:16 p.m. PST

The agents' businesses were in jeopardy, and they decided they had to give it a try. They selected CAA's smooth Bryan Lourd to step into the fray, and on November 21 he began weeklong round-the-clock secret negotiations at his beautiful home in Benedict Canyon. They couldn't have been in better hands. The Bayou-born Lourd is as cool under pressure as anyone in any town. I have never seen him lose his temper or his resolve, and I've known him for almost three decades. He gets along equally well with lords and cooks and is strategic, tactical and relaxed. His house has so much room—it hosts the best Oscar party every year—there is space to cool off and to conspire. Nikki quoted an insider on how he was playing it, mid-talks: "He keeps asking what everybody needs. This is what Lew Wasserman used to do during these things. Wasserman would say, 'I want to know what you each need. I don't want to know what you want. Tell me what you need.' There's no arbitrary end to this. Everyone only leaves if Bryan gives up and goes home."

I can assume nothing about Bryan going home (since that's where he already was), but his private discussions coincided with the resumption of formal negotiations on November 26. To the great relief of the entire ghetto, the two sides met almost every day up to December 8, during which the town read Deadline Hollywood as though it were the Talmud. In the morning, we davened (prayed like the Orthodox, rocking back and forth) to the column (even if we had no idea what that meant). All day long we compulsively checked in, and in the evening we searched for meaning in the crumbs of information Nikki gleaned from the gods.

The talks went on for days and days. We didn't know if the strike was ending or continuing. At first it seemed like nothing was happening. On Day One, the Moguls resubmitted their original proposal regarding online streaming (Internet downloads), which they felt had been "misunderstood." The Writers felt deeply insulted by this. Misunderstood? Did the Moguls think they were dumb blondes? Stalemate occurred. Then there was an exciting moment when we all held our collective breath as the Moguls promised an offer would be forthcoming by the end of the day. The Writers' reps waited until sundown; no new offer came, and they watched the last of the Moguls' cars slip out for Chanukah. After seven days of nothing happening, the talks broke down amid great acrimony on both sides. Winter was coming, and the sky wasn't the only thing getting darker.

FLASHBACK

I'm no biblical scholar by any stretch of the imagination; I know a lot more about science than I do about religion. But I think I can date the beginning of the movie business apocalypse to when people started speaking in tongues. People who'd known each other forever suddenly stopped making sense to each other; their sentences were long-winded, illogical and determinate. They whispered in restaurants and seethed at one another. Lawyers and agents lied to clients about what they really thought, so inebriated with ideology were the clients, and so fearful was everyone. Producers sat behind the closed gates of empty lots—many for the last time—speaking against their self-interest, just like the honking teamsters who wouldn't know a residual payment if it smashed them in the windshield. But they honked highway solidarity as they watched the last of the L.A. productions shut down and their jobs disappear.

It was the Tower of Babel. No one knew what everyone else really meant, only that "the bosses" (in the thirties sense) were greedy and must have a lot of money, because after all, they were studio heads. What were they doing inside those rooms upstairs while we were down here fretting?

We weren't allowed to meet with Writers, or even really socialize with them. I snuck a dinner with two girlfriend-Writers in Silver Lake and spent all evening being shamed by them. Some Writers left town completely. One great Writer went to Fiji to avoid dealing with it. But Writers who didn't support the strike weren't allowed to say it. Producers either. There was a sense of political correctness that was unlike anything I've ever experienced. You *had* to toe the line. You *had* to honk your horn. You *had* to turn in your fellow Writers if you knew anybody who was writing. But nobody was writing. No one was even making sense.

Deadline Comments Board

Fuck the Moguls. For some reason, they have decided to destroy their businesses. It's time for their shareholders to revolt. And just like the defiance against the Edison Trust 100 years ago, this business will change because the filmmakers, not the big corporations, decide to change it.

Comment by ReelBusy—Monday, December 24, 2007, 11:36 a.m. PST

FORCE TRÈS MAJEURE

Starting in late November and continuing through Christmas into mid-January, the studios and the networks started canceling Writers' deals. This was legal under a clause called "force majeure," which means having been struck an unexpected blow from above that disenables us to perform our fiduciary duties. In production, we often use this clause on insurance claims—like when the wardrobe trailer burns down while we're shooting, or when our major star gets kicked in the head by a horse and can't shoot for a week because she has a hole in her face, or when an earthquake or hurricane or lightning has struck down or blown away our set. In this case, force majeure was not a bolt of lightning from above, but from below: the Writers' strike. On January 12, the date on most contracts, they would legally be able to cancel even more deals than those they canceled in late November.

Deadline Comments Board

Force majeure. They're just stalling till they can clean house.

Comment by Unemployed—Wednesday, November 28, 2007, 8:02 a.m. PST

LOL!! I called this two weeks ago!! I said they are going to work the force majeure but they have to make it appear as if they are trying to negotiate in order for that to stick in the face of lawsuits from writers. This was all VERY obvious to everyone but the naive writers, who seem to think we're living in a fairy-tale land where corporations give a damn about you and your feelings ("it's all about respect and fairness—bwaaaah!" LOL). Your strategies suck. The fact that WGA leadership is scratching their heads in this negotiation, trying to figure out what's going on, is proof of that.

Comment by ChuckT—Wednesday, November 28, 2007, 8:13 a.m. PST

MERRY CHRISTMAS, HOLLYWOOD!

Let's Not Talk!

Not making an offer at Christmas during a recession was a low, ugly, smart blow, bent on dividing the unions, sowing dissension and undermining the WGA's PR with the town. The Moguls may have been bad at PR for a time, but they keenly understood their leverage. It worked. They scared the bejeezus out of everyone during the holidays. All of Los Angeles could see that there would be no work gearing up after Christmas or in the near future. The Writers felt duped, as they were hoping to negotiate and instead were forced to wait through meaningless talks and watch their own leaders get blamed for their collapse.

While the Moguls handed out their lumps of coal, they began to suspend Writers' deals, and any other deals they could legally suspend under the force majeure clause. The suspension of deals was saving them money and leading them toward a new business plan, one that jibed with the future and the recession and their loss of DVD revenue. Quietly, they opened talks with the DGA, and many flew off for holiday.

FADING FEBRUARY

After Uncle Scrooge sent all the workers home hungry at Christmas, the IATSE (International Alliance of Theatrical Stage Employees—i.e., crew!) got really angry. Restaurants were empty. There were stories in the *Los Angeles Times* on the local economy starting to tank, and working Writers were getting *utzy*. Some were feeling guilty, some just liked to work and for some, the arguments just weren't working anymore.

The party was fading in some quarters, going strong in others. It wasn't as much fun on the picket line. It was getting older and colder, and nothing was happening. Most of all, the very powerful faction of showrunners, the writer-producers who run series on television, wanted to go back to work. They had the most at stake. If their shows went off the air for too long, they could easily be forgotten and end up canceled, especially the new shows.

On Nikki's board, an ugly below-the-line/above-the-line war broke out between members of IATSE and of WGA about what a union was, and it was pretty demoralizing.

The working stiffs commented like this:

Deadline Comments Board

The WGA screwed up royally. All of the crew on my show supported the writers, and all of the Teamsters were going to walk. When we all arrived to work at 6:30 in the morning on day one of the strike, which was a Monday, there was no picket line to cross. The writers didn't start picketing until 9 or 10, and that was a big slap in the face for all of us . . . Instead of crossing a picket line, I felt like I witnessed a monthlong celebrity pizza party. For instance, one day a young woman in yoga pants and a red top was passing out popsicles to teamsters and btl [below the line] workers as they crossed the picket line . . . This strike is supposed to be supporting the "middle class" writers, but is destroying the middle class of this industry. I don't understand. Jon Stewart is scabbing, Leno and Conan as well. I don't understand how this can happen, and it just shows that it's every man for themselves . . .

Sincerely, Camera Assistant who has lost $20,000 in wages and over 500 hours that go into my pension and healthcare.

Comment by KK—Thursday, January 24, 2008, 8:50 a.m. PST

Then it escalated:

We are about to lose our mortgage because my fiancée is now unemployed due to the strike. Her TV show was put on hiatus and now might not be brought back to finish shooting. She is wardrobe and a union member. The WGA is a bunch of selfish reactionaries and should not have gone on strike before think-ing things through. So many people from so many departments are suffering because of greedy writers who are already making money hand over fist if they are successful. Shame on you, writers. Shame.

Comment by R. Chips—Wednesday, February 6, 2008

Someone responded thus:

To all of the BTLers who are losing their homes, struggling to feed their children and lying on their deathbeds because they don't have medical coverage, I deliver a new concept: FINAN-CIAL PLANNING. If you can't survive for two months without losing your home, starving your kids, or dying, I suspect you probably were living beyond your means. I don't see how that's anyone's problem but your own.

Comment by RJDocky—Tuesday, February 5, 2008, 8:12 a.m. PST

And then a little war broke out:

Hope you're welcomed back with open arms by your trifling below-the-line crew. Godspeed.

Comment by Safety Pass—Tuesday, February 5, 2008, 1:38 a.m. PST

You creative-type writers need to agree to a deal. There are a lot of pissed-off crew people waiting to set up your chairs, hang huge rigs over your heads, or watch your cars. Your WGA leaders may have convinced you that striking is great, but they are idiots. You're not going to get everything you want. If you don't work, you don't get paid. Neither does anyone else in the business. Thanks for screwing all of us.

Comment by Grip—Monday, February 4, 2008

The group of exhausted Writers I came to call the Mensheviks and the television showrunners were horrified by this class war among collaborators. It sped things up, toward a deal. The Mensheviks, Excited in the Ardent Fall but Flagging in February, sounded like this:

Deadline Comments Board

Okay, I'm still out there—not every day, not for three hours at a time, but I still go because I still largely believe in what we're fighting for.

But . . . every single person I've talked to on the line is ready for this to be OVER. We're not going to get everything we want.

I'm not willing to sit out for another six months to get a slightly better percentage than what we're being offered now. It's the diehards that are posting on here, and it's the diehards that are willing to stick this out until the entire town goes to hell. The rest of us, the WORKING writers, know that we're getting fucked. But if we're gonna get fucked anyway, let's get fucked now and get it over with. Me, I just want to get back to work; enough is enough.

Comment by Seriously? —Thursday, February 7, 2008

This was not a feature writer's problem. As Marc Norman says, "If it were up to feature writers, we could have stayed out for a year." Interestingly, feature writers had no skin in the Internet game, as the Net had not yet been monetized for the medium. But showrunners like Shonda Rhimes (*Grey's Anatomy, Private Practice*), who would be among the earliest recipients of online streaming profits should negotiations succeed, were under pressure. They have large crews who are like family and themselves have families. They have been working together for years, and keeping them in work is an enormous responsibility. All of these people were now out of work, and that was a huge burden weighing down all the showrunners. Feature writers are singletons, as Norman says, and make decisions that affect only themselves. So after Christmas, the pressure was on from the showrunners, as well as from other forces.

The DGA had begun quiet conversations with the Moguls in December, which is likely one of the reasons that the Moguls had broken off talks. The Moguls had felt all along that they would have a better time talking turkey with the directors. Their numbers on what online streaming profits could someday be were far from those projected by the WGA, and little could be done to reconcile them. The chemistry and trust between the two teams started badly and never improved. As a very smart neocon feature writer pointed out to me, there may have been some actual value or truth in the Moguls' point of view—in *this* negotiation—but they had so squandered their moral authority through years of systemic lying (see, for example, the Art Buchwald case*, or creative accounting with Writers' net points†) that none of his colleagues believed *anything* the Moguls said.

According to Marc Norman, the Moguls told the WGA in 1988, "People have to go out and buy a DVD player! Nobody's going to do that! We don't know whether there's revenue here, so let's just put it on hold, and if it works down the road, we'll figure something out."

I can hear them now. "DVD, ShmeeVD!" In the meantime, the market accrued huge profits that accounted for a profit margin the studios would never relinquish. (And we now know why!) Thus, the appropriately dubious response from the Writers. And this well-earned skepticism led to wacky posts like this:

Deadline Comments Board

Correct me if I'm wrong, but Internet ad revenues are $40 billion this year and expected to double in three years. Writers know this too.

Comment by PJ—Writer—Monday, February 4, 2008, 7:35 p.m. PST

The Bolshevik/Let's Stay Out 'til June and Menshevik/Let's Make a Deal factions started to split around mid-January, after the holiday vacation. It was hard to keep up the energy unless picketing was your job, being on the committee was your job or you were

---

* *Buchwald v. Paramount,* 1990 Cal. App. LEXIS 634, was a breach-of-contract lawsuit filed and decided in California in which humorist and writer Art Buchwald alleged that Paramount Pictures stole his script idea and turned it into the 1988 movie *Coming to America.* Buchwald won the lawsuit and was awarded damages, then accepted a settlement from Paramount before any appeal took place.

† Profits.

an angry person with union issues (or just issues). Younger Writers were looking for leadership.

There was a faction of successful working Writers on the negotiating committee—the aforementioned Let's Stay Out 'til June faction—who could afford to stay out, and they were spokesmen and leaders of the committee. They wanted to take a strong, roosterlike line, protecting the younger chickens, if I can extend the metaphor without insult. Ironically, many of them were feature writers who as yet had nothing to gain in the Internet game, but who did understand the power game.

Says Marc, who, in his gentle, soft-spoken, literary manner, is very unroosterlike, "I won't participate in any of the Internet benefits. It was always more of a theoretical than a money-in-the-pockets issue. More for future generations."

They were the "respect" guys. They had a lot of Writers looking up to them and didn't want to get screwed like in the last strike. Even if they weren't around for the last strike, they had heard about it and felt that it was their responsibility to not let it happen again. It was the "we won't get fooled again" faction. Their solidarity was tremendous, but unfortunately, the numbers they bandied among their troops were errant.

But despite their motivations, the Let's Stay Out 'til June guys were becoming increasingly isolated.

Deadline Comments Board

Fuck it. We're staying out till June.
   Comment by ScreenVet—Monday, February 4, 2008, 7:02 p.m. PST

In January, the DGA started to negotiate with the Moguls in earnest and in the open, and everything heated up. That undermined the WGA's leverage. The Writers, according to various members of the negotiating committee, tried to get Michael Apted, head of the DGA, to "be more ambitious in the DGA's demands," and not to "roll over like they always do." The DGA didn't want to strike, they wanted to make a deal, and this frustrated the WGA. The Writers tried to buck the Directors up with their ambition and brio, and with their bigger numbers, which were, needless to say, different than the DGA's.

Another factor was bearing down on the negotiations: The Oscar deadline was February 7, and no one, but *no one,* wanted the Oscars canceled. The Oscars are the peak of the movie year, its raison d'être. It was bad enough that the Golden Globes had been canceled. That showed that the Moguls were tough; and anyway, the Globes don't belong to the community, nor were they then vital to the revenue of the studios. Enough was enough. The stars had had it, the agents had had it and even the studios had had it. But writers and actors wouldn't cross the picket line for the Oscars. Even though nobody had figured out how Leno, Jon Stewart and Letterman kept working through the strike ("double talk," per Norman), the Oscars were too high-profile to scab.

All these pressures, the DGA negotiating with the Moguls, a looming February 7 Oscar date, the showrunners' pressure inside the guild, the flagging morale—even feature writers wanted or needed to work again, to say nothing of the furious crew—led to enormous angst on each side.

Then came the final intercession of some of the biggest TV and feature agents from the Association of Talent Agents (ATA), who could talk to both sides. They were friendly with the talent and with the Moguls; they could help to bridge the trust gap. Agencies were in critical condition. They were bleeding money; some of the smaller ones were threatened with closure, and many of the bigger ones had laid off staff. Everyone was off expense account, living on the edge. The ATA sent a few mega-agents from their Agents Negotiating Committee into the fray—Bryan Lourd (again), negotiating on behalf of the big feature writers, and Rick Rosen of WME.

Together with Peter Chernin and showrunners Shawn Ryan and Laeta Kalogridis (who was close to David Young), they all helped the dialogue.

There were conversations around the clock in January. The DGA closed a satisfactory deal with the Moguls on the seventeenth. Verrone knew that that would be the template for any final deal with the Writers; the Moguls would go no further. Finke reported that the hardest part of the last few weeks was getting Verrone to recognize how far off his data was from reality. But now we know why—fool me once, and all that.

Verrone and Young would have a hard job getting their own guys to accept the diminished terms of the deal, given the inflated expectations of their early formulas. But the pressure was on, and Verrone questioned how long he could hold his shaky coalition of feature and television writers in place. Writers wanted to go back to work.

On January 22, word leaked that Fox chairman Peter Chernin had told his friends at the Super Bowl that the strike was over, and the news spread like the wildfires that had kicked off the Ardent Fall. Verrone and Young took the offer to their membership on January 24 and recommended it.

As is clear from Verrone's quote from his final meeting at the Shrine Auditorium, he was bloody but unbowed in February. He knew he'd gotten the best deal he possibly could, and now his job was to sustain the guild's morale. He called out to the exhausted throngs: "Seven multinational conglomerates can fight back really hard. Who knew? But they thought we wouldn't strike, and we did. They thought we wouldn't last, and we did. They thought we wouldn't win. And we did."

But there was the expected flack on Nikki's comment board from the Let's Stay Out 'til June faction about accepting what was, essentially, the DGA deal. I think the WGA bought their own propaganda and fought mightily to right the real wrongs of the past.

Unmanaged expectations were the guild's self-created enemies. To wit:

Deadline Comments Board

Please leaders, do not piss on my leg and tell me that it's raining with a deal that resembles the DGA deal.

Comment by My Vote—Monday, February 4, 2008, 7:01 p.m. PST

At first, Nikki didn't like the deal the membership approved, by 93 percent vote, days after Verrone's speech. This prompted one of my favorite posts: "From what I hear, it is both incremental and excremental."

A Writer responded to the chorus:

Deadline Comments Board

To all you people already frothing at the mouth about "this shitty deal" and "we stay out till June!"—we haven't even seen the deal yet! What is the matter with you? Go and lie down for a couple of hours. I, meanwhile, hereby make a solemn vow to myself to try my best to stay away from this admittedly addictive but ultimately unhelpful, provocative site. Bye.

Comment by Paul—Monday, February 4, 2008, 9:09 p.m. PST

The DGA and the WGA got essentially the same terms, with perhaps some minor differences I will get back to you on once I get my law degree. The thorny new media issue was postponed for three years, as the thorniest issues in a negotiation often are. It will be revisited one day.

The bitterness of the strike, as well as some of its darker implications, appears to have sunk in to the WGA. Few seemed to want to repeat the past, so they voted in Chris Keyser (*Party of Five,*

Lone Star) over Patric Verrone in the WGA leadership elections of 2011. You could read the undercurrent during the election. Keyser didn't explicitly say, "I'm the anti-Verrone candidate," and yet, he wasn't Verrone. The strike, the recession and the Great Contraction scared or tamed everyone, for good or for ill.

I sat with the congenial and insightful Keyser at a chic Santa Monica coffee shop, and we looked back on the whole thing. He said a good part of his job was to try to understand and help prolong the life span of the Writer in the poststrike world. It was fascinating.

"How do we make a living?" he began. "Not just the one percent; how do we make sure the middle class of writers is able to move through a career? Not just a moment, but a whole career. How do we make the writing profession viable?"

I admired his long view. He didn't sound like a firebrand, so I asked him his philosophy on striking.

"I believe no union can be powerful unless it has a viable strike threat." He added, "I ran by saying it's okay to talk first before you strike."

I then asked him about the thorny question, how he viewed the pursuit of a market whose value hadn't yet been calculated. He could see I viewed it with some skepticism, but he opened my eyes to the union's strategy by saying something both simple and profound.

"Once we know exactly how much a market is going to be worth," he said, "it's much more difficult to get concessions. At the moment when the companies know completely and exactly how lucrative the market is, it becomes a much more difficult conversation. It's much more likely for us to have some leeway beforehand.

"For example, once it was clear what DVDs were worth, we could never change that formula. It was *never* going to change. The issue is, you can't be too late, and you can't be too early—so what is that perfect time?"

Insiders say that the key issue of the next negotiation won't even be the Net, but the health and welfare and pension plans that crusader Frances Marion fought so hard for. It is said that they are in terrible shape, a state from which only the hideous Moguls can help bail them out. These bread-and-butter issues may take priority next fire season and push the Internet back under the burning rug.

The strike officially ended on February 9, and the Oscars were held at the Beverly Hilton on February 12. Like refugees emerging from bombed-out buildings after months of shelling, we donned our finery and headed out to the muted festivities.

During this somewhat hysterical time for all of us, I was prepping *The Invention of Lying* with my son and tending to my mother, who was dying in Florida. This entailed escaping from Paramount's creepily silent Potemkin village to scout and cast on location with the hilarious Ricky Gervais, then hopping on a plane to West Palm Beach, where it was not so funny.

My mom struggled to be her best when I arrived, and I did the same to lift her spirits. She was a gifted teacher, all about her mind (she could recite the English kings backward), and it suddenly wasn't working anymore. My father was devastated. At the hospital she would only speak French. (She didn't make it easy.) But my visits made her very happy, as hard as it was for me to see her this way. It was all that I could do to just help my parents have a better weekend than those they'd recently been having. Then I flew back to Lowell, Massachusetts, where I immersed myself in preproduction details and petty fights with a difficult financier. My mother died a month after the strike ended, and shooting started soon after that, on April 14.

THE TIPPING POINT

The aftermath of the strike started playing out as I was blithely shooting away in Lowell. It was, in Malcolm Gladwell's term, the tipping point that commenced the New Abnormal. How did the strike propel the new business model in the direction it was already going, just more quickly and drastically?

It is not good to leave Moguls with time on their hands. And during the strike they had way too much time on their hands to spend with clever business affairs execs, international marketing execs and accountants—all getting scowled at as they passed through the gates—modeling numbers in their cloistered offices.

Suddenly, without having to be in the reactive, competitive posture they are always in—responding to spec scripts, listening to pitches, reading scripts, making offers, making deals, packaging their slates, being competitive for material with other Moguls, making decisions about what movies to put into production—they had time to strategize.

I don't think they were wondering how to bust the union forever. Hollywood is and always will be a union town. I think they were trying to figure out how to stay in business during the recession without the DVD cushion. Hollywood is not a state run by a right-wing legislature and governor; it is a feudal ecosystem. I think what they were wondering instead was, where would the bulk of new profits come from? What were the most reliably growing revenue streams? And unlike the Writers, they didn't see the rainbow in the new media, but in the international market. They had to cut fat and determine how their costs would be prioritized. The Writers were the first to go; because of force majeure, their deals had begun to be suspended anyway. They were lessening their overhead. It felt good in a recession. More deals were soon coming up for renewal.

Should those deals be renewed poststrike? Of course, for the networks, yes. The showrunners and writers were critical for their business, as TV is a writer's medium. Their deals would be renewed at the television studios and networks. But in the meantime, reality television had made dangerous inroads into prime-time territory. Networks and agencies would emerge from the strike with huge reality divisions to rival their scripted divisions.

But what about the studios? What were *movie studio* writers' deals for? To hear what they wanted to make? Who cares? The studios knew by now that they needed to make internationally driven blockbusters that spawned franchises, which would continue to spawn awareness and perform overseas. Therefore, it was now more the Moguls' job to tell Writers what the studios' mandate was and then hire Writers to make their production and release dates. Of course, they'd always done this to some extent, but now they could focus on it and cut the fat—i.e., anything without preawareness or not bound for franchise territory. There would be no more Writers or unnecessary producers (the next to go) whose job it was to generate original material, independent of this mandate. No more bloated inventory of excess development, untargeted for the bull's-eye.

This is what I've come to recognize as my extrasensory paranoia, and it works retroactively as well as reactively.

"Look," they must have said to themselves. "We can generate our own material. Why not? We already know what we want. Franchises! Awareness! Titles! Let's hold on to franchise-generating producers and find those with cofinancing money." To be sure, some of the more secure and stable studios held on to their producers and made them part of their franchise machinery, notably Warner Bros. But most cut back drastically on these deals. And why not? Without franchises, cofinancing money or deep ties to the studio, producers and writers could be hired only when needed! So studios let many producers' deals expire after the strike. The strike allowed them to save money. There was a recession, and their resources had to be spent on the ever-inflating costs of marketing tentpoles.

It's the model we emerged with, and the timing allowed studios to streamline a process in the direction they were already traveling.

This contraction inside the contraction made it cost-effective. The end of the strike and all the changes it wrought made for the end of the Old Abnormal.

But force majeure and learning to live without writers and producers generating original material brought on a new level of development autonomy for studios. No more unnecessary pitches. No more weekly bidding for scripts. No more agency-driven, speculative writers' market. No more producer-driven ideas. One manager told me, "Suddenly we couldn't get anyone to read a script on a Friday if we tried." We had woken up in the New Abnormal.

I arrived home from production of *Invention* and returned to Paramount for the last time. The writing was on the wall. I got a call from Bryan Lourd, my feature agent, who only calls with either very, very good news or very, very bad news. At this time in the biz, there was no very good news for producers without franchises. Brad Grey, though not my adversary by any means, was not Sherry Lansing. He had his own priorities. The consoling yet pained tone in Bryan's voice was clear. Paramount was not renewing my deal.

For thirty years I had always been what we called "re-upped"— that is, a negotiation on my next contract would be initiated months before it came due, so the issue never came up except when you talked to your lawyer or agent about what great new stuff you got (or tried to get) in your new deal. Now, postrecession, post-strike, post–making only two movies in almost eight years, Bryan's voice said everything.

Would I go to another movie studio? There were very few, if any, new deals at movie studios for nonfranchise "nonfinancing" creative producers and makers of romantic comedies. Bryan didn't even have to tell me. I hadn't made a franchise kind of picture since Jodie Foster went to the center of the galaxy in *Contact*.

I had some very bad nights, nights of self-recrimination and hindsight—woulda, shoulda, coulda. What if I'd thought of making a deal with a movie star? They had become a smart new breed of producers with the leverage to get movies made, who were in production when their partners were. Or what if I'd found a director to partner with, as so many smart, forward-thinking ex-agents and managers had done? And what of these managers who were becoming producers and controlling the talent and seeming to make us old-school producers obsolete? Why hadn't I thought of that? But all this second-guessing was useless; I'd done my best, what I knew how to do, and couldn't torture myself over it. There was too much slack to pick up, too many other people who would be happy to take my place. Nora Ephron and I had a saying we'd repeat to each other when either of us had a flop: "Take another swing at the bat!" Then we'd paste big smiles on our faces and start strategizing. That's what the game is all about: longevity.

I would still make movies, but what I'd been thinking for a while is that I would be moving to a new medium as well, one I would have to learn, where pitches still abounded: television. It seemed that more and more what I was missing in movies— making stuff up, creating original ideas—was the coin of the realm in TV. And television's boundaries were expanding as the movie business's were contracting.

I would have to start watching more television, that's for sure—and not just cable. It was time to have a long talk with my television-oriented brother. I was headed to a new deal at a TV studio. I had been on movie lots for more than twenty-five years, and for the first time, I was to be housed on a different kind of lot. It was kind of sad, and kind of scary, but I had to shake that off very fast. There was no time for nostalgia. I had to fly with the times and learn a complicated new language. A new business, really, with different seasons and time slots, and drama and comedy rules, and millions of things I'd have to learn in three months, or three seasons.

But the good news was that it was all about writing and writers.

I could make up ideas again. And there was much better news than that: As movies had been getting dumber, television had been getting smarter. As movies constricted their parameters, television's parameters were growing exponentially. HBO and cable had helped push what was possible, and longtime TV writers picked up the mantle and ran into brilliant uncharted territory. Feature writers felt the creative action happening in TV, and an exodus began. There was a blooming, booming business in this business— a way out of Egypt into a tempting, changing new land.

THE DIASPORA

The Golden Age of Television

At the premiere of Showtime's 2011 series *Homeland,* President Obama's favorite show as well as everybody else's I know, my eighty-seven-year-old father and my brother, Rick, had a conversation about the rapidly changing creative primacy of television and movies that hit the bull's-eye.

The series, the first to be green-lit under Showtime's new president, David Nevins, stars movie actress Claire Danes as a neurotic and brilliant CIA agent who has a very complicated relationship with a returning American POW, who she's convinced has been turned by the Al Qaeda terrorists who captured him. It won the Golden Globes for Best Television Series—Drama, Best Performance by an Actor in a Television Series—Drama for Damian Lewis and Best Performance by an Actress in a Television Series—Drama for Claire Danes. Nine months later *Homeland* stunned the town by sweeping the 2012 Emmys in its first season. It again won for its lead actor (Lewis), actress (Danes), writing (Alex Gansa, Howard Gordon and Gideon Raff) and beat *Mad Men,* the odds-on favorite, to win Showtime's first Outstanding Drama Series Emmy.

Our family had a special rooting interest, as Rick found and represented the original Israeli series on which *Homeland* was based and packaged it with his clients, *24* showrunners Howard Gordon and Alex Gansa. Gordon brought in WME director Michael Cuesta. WME then packaged their actress Claire Danes, and Rick sold the series to Showtime. It was his dearest project in his long career.

Rick is the calmest person in our family, a natural leader who is grounded and very sane. When he was young, my parents would brag about his baseball prowess by claiming he had hit ten home runs that week, and he would correct them by saying he'd hit only six. One of his many virtues is that he can outwait an Israeli and an insult. After the screening, Dad and Rick had a conversation that Rick remembers like this:

"At the end of the pilot, which lasted approximately fifty to fifty-two minutes, something like that, Dad turned to me and said, 'That's it?'

"And I said, 'What do you mean?'

"He said, 'That's all? I want to see more!'

"I said, 'Well, it's over; that was just one episode.'

"Then he said, 'Well, why don't you show more?'

"'We're just showing the pilot, the first episode.'

"And he said, 'You know something, you should make a movie of this; it's too good for television.'

"I answered back, 'You know, Dad, I don't know if you realize it, but you just insulted me.'

"And then he couldn't stop talking about it the whole way home in the car, how he was going to start watching it. I explained that if it was on too late for him at nine o'clock, we could record it on his DVR, but that was too complicated a conversation. But he really was engrossed in it. It was great. You hear him talking about it all the time now. He loves it."

I asked Rick what this meant. We both knew that Dad only watched MSNBC, sports and the Sunday news programs, and he had a regular movie habit.

"His perception is, good things go in the movies, television is crap."

That attitude has been changing, if slowly, in my Dad's set. But among the knowing in pop culture and in the industry, it is a different universe than the one our dad was born into, or the one I entered when I went to my first Golden Globes awards and realized how Movie People looked at Television People in the Old Abnormal.

I vividly remember sitting there at our round table on the ballroom floor with a huge, dumb smile plastered on my face, with nominees Tom Hanks and Meg Ryan and my great friend writer-director Nora Ephron in what seemed like the middle of the universe. We were there for *Sleepless in Seattle*. Everywhere I turned there was another boldface name getting buzzed on the mediocre champagne, laughing, bussing cheeks and working tables.

Suddenly, I looked up and noticed a parallel universe on a semicircular tier above us, with rows and rows of people talking and bussing cheeks and working tables just like we were and getting buzzed on the same bad champagne.

"Who are they?" I asked someone at my table.

"They are Television People," I was told.

These days, if you look upstairs at the Golden Globes, Movie People are sitting upstairs with Television People, and downstairs, Television People are sitting with Movie People; they have merged. Distinctions are moot. In 2011, Mila Kunis—the hot-as-can-be movie star of *Ted, Friends with Benefits* and *Forgetting Sarah Marshall,* among others about to be released—who broke in the seminal hit *That '70s Show,** sat downstairs for her supporting-actress nomination as Natalie Portman's nemesis in the ballet/horror film *Black Swan;* Michelle Williams of *Dawson's Creek* fame sat nearby for her best-actress nomination for *My Week with Mari-*

---

* Which also broke Ashton Kutcher and ran for eight years, from 1998 to 2006.

lyn. Upstairs, Jeremy Irons sat for his nomination for Showtime's *The Borgias,* waving to his agent down below; nearby was Oscar perennial Kate Winslet, nominated for best actress in a miniseries for *Mildred Pierce* on HBO. She could chat with eventual winner for a comedy Laura Dern (*Enlightened*) or Jessica Lange for best actress in a series (*American Horror Story*); this goes on and on. In the same year, TV star Melissa McCarthy (*Mike and Molly*) was nominated for an Oscar for best supporting actress in *Bridesmaids.*

James Wolcott commented in *Vanity Fair*'s television issue in May 2012: "There's always one pill present . . . who takes pride in disclaiming that he or she never watches television . . . pity these poor castaways. They must sit there with glassy, uncomprehending eyes while the rest of us tongue-flap about the latest installment of a favorite series down to the last crumb, like Proust scholars."

I wondered when this began and why I was so slow to notice at first, so I went to talk with Gail Berman, who had run Paramount just as the convergence between movie talent and television talent was becoming clear. She had been hired away from her successful five-year stint as president of the Fox network, where she'd put everything from *American Idol* to *24* to *House* on the air. It was obvious that Gail would have seen all of this coming.

I found her sitting happily in her new office in the fancy Lantana complex in Santa Monica, where she's partnered with Lloyd Braun in a "multiplatform content" company. Over her desk was a watercolor painting of Paramount, signed by an artist named "Meany." We found this hilarious.

I asked her if she had noticed any television prejudice among movie people when she ran Paramount. The question was a bit disingenuous; I knew she had stumbled into a surprising amount of TV snobbery, given that there had been such a long line of notable studio heads recruited from television networks before her: Frank Price, who ran Columbia for years, came from CBS and Universal TV; Barry Diller had come to Paramount from ABC with Michael

Eisner, who later ran Disney for decades; there was NBC's legendary boy wonder Brandon Tartikoff, who'd been hired at Paramount in the nineties; and even Peter Chernin, who was Gail's boss at the Fox network before he ran the studio.

I had been surprised by the attitude, because I'd assumed at the time that her success in TV was the very reason she had been hired.

"You know," she said, slowing down for this answer, "I think feature people have a tendency to look at things myopically, as though television were some sort of foreign business that used other sorts of means of enticing people to work in it or that didn't have a creative process. And it was hurtful, but also really fascinating and amusing on some level. I would talk to people and they would purposefully say, 'I never watch TV.' I would say, 'You don't? Geez, Louise, what do you do?' It was amusing to me. If you're not watching TV, you're missing out on a lot of stuff going on! The twenty-four-hour news cycle? The incredible writing? It's where everything is headed."

One of the things Gail did during her tenure was hire J. J. Abrams to reinvigorate the *Star Trek* franchise. How televisionizing is that?

"Going to J.J. was a natural for me," says Gail. "He was already in the movie business, having done *Mission: Impossible* while I was there, and I just knew he would hit it out of the park. J.J. is a storyteller. That's his intention: to do it across platforms, regardless of the medium."

"When did you first start seeing feature writers in TV? When did all this blending start?"

"At Fox, I used to meet with various feature people who would come in and sit with their arms crossed and say, 'I'm told I can make some money here,' and we'd say, 'Not here you can't, time to go'—people like that who had a chip on their shoulder about TV. But this is all history."

"But the writers' strike was a huge part of the deluge, right?"

"It started before the writers' strike," Gail answered. "But there was still a taint around it at that time. Back between 2000 and 2005, we enticed Paul Attanasio (*Donnie Brasco, Quiz Show*) to come on board."

Paul Attanasio was the trailblazer for successful feature writers crossing over. He was an ex–*Washington Post* reporter and was famously hired for expensive (often up to $250K a week!) production rewrites and polishes because of his ability to write smart and witty banter. He was the first big feature writer I remember crossing over, writing on *House,* and he soon brought many feature drama writers into the writers' room along with him.

Gail knew all: "Paul came in very early on, and certainly working with him on *House* was—"

"So that was you!" I exclaimed, interrupting her.

"Yes," Gail answered. "I did that while I was at Fox; it was a fantastic thing. He had done a show prior to that [with Gail's partner, Lloyd Braun] at ABC, actually, called *Gideon's Crossing,* so he was an example of somebody who was beginning to cross comfortably between both worlds. It certainly didn't diminish him in the feature business, and he was sought after in the television business."

"Is there now essentially a mash of the two businesses?" I asked her. "The end of the separation between the two businesses' talent pools as we know them? Or is this a temporary occurrence because the movie business is currently such a disaster?"

"In my opinion, there's nothing temporary about it," Gail said. "It is the wave of the future. From an artist's point of view, the point is being able to tell stories and get their message out. And as companies make fewer and fewer movies, that's very hard to do. So the question is, can you tell your story in other places where things are happening? So instead of looking at it in a negative way, like, oh, the movie business is so horrible, woe is me . . . to be able to say, 'Okay, I'm a storyteller, I'm an artist; I want to tell stories, and if I can't do that over there, I might have an opportunity to do it over here.' And that to me is how people should be looking at it."

I left Gail's office wondering, Is everyone going to do television now?

One Sunday afternoon, Rick and I were watching an Eagles-Giants game. During a commercial, I taped this conversation:

RICK: Who doesn't do television now? Everybody does it. Anybody who says they won't do it is out of the business. Right? You tell me, who says they won't do it?

LYNDA: Will Smith?

RICK: Will Smith brought us a television show with a log line [*Hawthorne,* a nursing series on TNT]. We sold it, because they put Jada [Pinkett Smith, Will's wife] in it, and once you put Jada in it, it becomes Will Smith's company, Overbrook. Once it becomes Overbrook, twenty people come into your life. So maybe the biggest movie stars in the world—maybe they don't have to do it. But by the way, Brad Pitt is doing a miniseries at HBO with Edward Norton. They're doing *Lewis and Clark* as a miniseries.

LYNDA: I bet George will end up doing TV.

RICK: Well, he came out of TV.

LYNDA: Of course he came out of TV.

RICK: He did ten busted pilots before he did *ER.* I mean, George Clooney, didn't he—

LYNDA: He did something. He did that live one-hour thing with [producer] Laura Ziskin after he was a movie star.

RICK: Right, exactly. Based on *Fail Safe.* He wouldn't do a show for HBO?

LYNDA: If it was political? Please, of course he would.

RICK: He did an HBO series.

LYNDA: *K Street!* A series about lobbyists.

    (We laugh.)

LYNDA: Of course, Angelina's not going to do TV.

RICK: Right, but she doesn't have to. She's doing something at Lifetime, I think. I think she's directing something.

LYNDA: You know, there probably isn't anybody. Sandy [Bullock]? Nope, Sandy did. She did something with George Lopez. And I submitted a Texas show to her last year.

RICK: Who says "I don't do TV" in this day and age? I don't know. I mean, if HBO brings you something great, are you going to say, "No, I won't do it"?

LYNDA: And now Scott Rudin has two HBO series. [Note: Scott's deal was canceled; we'll see about that.]

RICK: And David Fincher [*Social Network, The Girl with the Dragon Tattoo*] is doing *House of Lords* on Netflix.

LYNDA: Yes, Netflix looks like it's going to be the home for the A-list movie directors. There's no one not doing TV.*

How did this happen? Do actors follow the writing? The opportunities? Women certainly follow the parts! Rick and I talked about how they cast Claire Danes in *Homeland*. "You show an actor material; they respond to the character, to the material, to the writing," Rick said. "If you're a thirty-five-year-old woman, where are you going to get a part like Laura Linney [*The Big C* on Showtime] and Claire are getting in television?"

"Or," I added, "Laura Dern is producing for herself with *Enlightenment*." The paucity of quality parts for women in features made the question rhetorical.

I asked Rick if he had a hard time getting the top feature writers to do series these days.

"Oh, they're eager and excited to do it now. They have been for more than five years. Eighteen years ago, Endeavor† was founded

---

* Redford has not done television, though I tried to get him.

† The agency he and his WME partners first founded via ICM.

on the premise that there was no such thing as a strict feature writer or a strict television writer. Everyone does both. We have people like Aaron Sorkin, who goes from medium to medium. He writes a play (*A Few Good Men*); he writes a television series (*West Wing*); he writes a movie (*The Social Network*). He's a writer. And many of our successful television writers all came out of features, like Josh Schwartz; he was initially a feature writer, and then he did *The O.C.* and *Gossip Girl* and other shows. Writers write, and putting them in a box, which is what used to happen, is unhealthy."

Now it's fully transitive. Movies want TV writers for comedy rewrites and more; TV likes feature writers. Mitch Hurwitz of *Arrested Development* fame (now being restarted on Netflix) did a rewrite of a script that was meant to be my directorial debut— about girlfriends from college reconnecting over a weekend gone haywire—but sadly, after a momentary *Bridesmaids* bump, it went nowhere fast. Jonathan Nolan (called Jonah), with whom I was working on a big project for Paramount and who was also the writer of the *Batman* franchise, launched himself from tentpole city into television (*Person of Interest* on CBS), stunning everyone, especially me. He had just gotten his first pilot picked up, while I was awaiting the fate of my major tentpole in features. Drama writers are moving to television in droves. It's like an oasis where they can write characters and not set pieces. Drama is a whole department in television, not a reason to be rejected. And since the onslaught of *tentpole über alles,* dramatic films have been mainly relegated to the indie side of the market.

From the vantage point of four years in television, it's clear that the great writing in TV isn't due to the influx of feature writers. The greatest shows from the start of this era were born from network stalwarts like David Chase, whose *Sopranos* changed the landscape forever, but who was a writer for years on *Remington Steel.* A journalist turned TV writer, David Simon, wrote *The Wire.* I wept like I did for Anna Karenina over seasons two and

My son, Oly Obst, now a manager at 3Arts and also my confidant and best friend, on the set of *Invention of Lying*, starring Ricky Gervais and Jen Garner. As a mom, it was a great source of pride and excitement to me that we were producing this together. For Oly, it was working with your mother.

Peter Chernin, a great studio head, beloved by Wall Street, low-key and understated but as savvy with scripts as he was with numbers. Chernin enjoyed a reign that saw him green-light the two biggest grossing films in history—one of which was *Titanic*, for which he was called an idiot by most at the time—and experienced the economic model of the industry transforming beneath him.

Sue Kroll, Warner Bros. Pictures President (Worldwide Marketing), is considered among the most innovative creative marketing executives in Hollywood. She has spearheaded many of the biggest campaigns for original movies in Hollywood by promoting the filmmakers and the concepts. If that strategy keeps succeeding, movies other than sequels can break through.

Kevin Goetz, marketing guru to studios and producers alike, practices his wizardry with test audiences. He asks a focus group what it thinks about what to cut, where the ending goes wrong, what would make them recommend the film to their friends. Their answers can make or break a picture.

Jim Gianopulos (*right*), now Chairman of Fox, then head of International, and James Cameron (*left*), director, surround Leonardo DiCaprio as they enjoy the record-breaking international success of *Titanic*. Gianopulos pushed the frontiers of the emerging markets in Russia by helping Cameron keep an almost impossible promise, and reaching out to some folks he'd worked with on the movie who'd never seen a theater before. That kind of reach helped make *Titanic* the most successful picture of all time until *Avatar*.

The closest thing Hollywood has/had to a queen, Sherry Lansing reigned from 1992 to 2004 with an abundance of class and charm. She made choices with her brain and gut and then cut the budget to a number she'd fought to the bone with her partner, Jon Dolgen. Their strategy worked until the town changed. She was loyal to her friends, didn't have enemies and never fired someone before Christmas.

The very chic John Goldwyn in front of the very chic Walt Disney Concert Hall. He was Head of Production for Paramount from 1991 to 2003. He brought me in under Sherry's guidance and was a mentor and friend. Then Paramount became a place of strain for him, as his life began to change.

Donald De Line, then President of Paramount, in the happiest of times. He was my horse in the race for Goldwyn's job, and I think Sherry picked him because she got that "kick your shoes off" feeling from him. Plus, everyone loved him. But that didn't keep him from being fired, followed by a bad week of all the execs crying in my bungalow.

Gail Berman, formerly President of Entertainment for Fox Broad-casting Company, was recruited to be President of Paramount Pictures while Donald De Line was in London. She was selected by Brad Grey because of her great American taste (*24*, *Malcolm in the Middle*, *House*, *American Idol*), but she ultimately found the pace of the picture business too slow, and they ultimately found her wanting.

Patric Verrone, the fiery, idealistic coleader of the WGA, held his troops in an organized array throughout the painful strike, which was no small feat. He kept the press on his side, kept the soccer moms honking the studios in support and kept the pressure on for four long months as the tough-minded studios played hardball. They vilified him all they could, but he held firm to his principles as many factions battled it out privately while venting on the Internet.

Chris Keyser, cocreator of *Party of Five*, was elected as a more moderate candidate in the post-strike 2011 WGA election. He is devising new strategies to get to the promised land of digital revenues.

Rick Rosen, my brother, head of television and founding partner of WME, with his friend and client Howard Gordon, writer/producer of *Homeland*, as it won the Emmy, September 23, 2012. The show he found in Israel and repackaged has now won the Golden Globe for best dramatic series twice, as well as the Emmy for its first season.

Conan O'Brien always makes Rick laugh. That's one reason he's a favorite among his clients. Here the two are with Jeff Ross, who runs Conan's company.

The *Hot In Cleveland* gang on the night they were taping an episode with Mary Tyler Moore, who doesn't remember she was my boss for one terrible year. The beautiful blonde next to Mary is the showrunner, Suzanne Martin, who is responsible for the jokes and the show's longevity. That's Valerie Bertinelli, on Mary's left, Jane Leeves to her left, Betty White, of course, to Suzanne's right, Wendy Malick to Betty's left, with my partner, executive producer Todd Milliner, and assorted TV Land executives.

Jonathan Nolan, successful tentpole and indie screenwriter of the Batman franchise and cowriter of *Memento* and *The Prestige*, decided to write for television. A year later, here he is on the set of his new top-rated CBS hit, *Person of Interest*. He could have done anything he wanted in features, but he chose TV. He wanted to play more.

Michael Lynton, walking arm in arm with his partner, Amy Pascal. The two are known for their intelligence and good taste. For every *Moneyball*, *Social Network*, or *Zero Dark Thirty*, there is a *Spider-Man*, *Transylvania,* or *Ghostbusters*. They are tight on the budgets of the movies they love and can react quickly to changing demographics and trends.

With Nora Ephron at an event I made her go to in New York City where I was getting an award for chicks in flix (she was really tired of these). Later she told me she was very happy she came, which was a great relief. And now I have a treasure trove of pictures from what I didn't know was the last year we'd have together.

three of *Damages,* written by longtime television writers and former playwrights Glenn Kessler, Todd Kessler and Daniel Zelman.
Mad Men's illustrious creator, Matt Weiner, still struggles to make
his first feature, and *Homeland*'s Howard Gordon came from network hit *24. Breaking Bad* was the brainchild of Vince Gilligan,
who had grown up on *The X-Files,* a breakthrough Fox show.
Television became great via its own writers pushing boundaries
as outlets like HBO made it possible, creating a loop of reactions,
from Fox courting the youth demographic outward to the hungrier
and more ambitious networks. Those writers knew where to push
and had the relationships and trust to transform the envelope as the
media universe changed. TV became an oasis for starved feature
writers, tired of writing set pieces or tiny tadpoles for free. They
are starved for the opportunity to write juicy, flawed characters—
mothers having affairs or dying of cancer, crack-dealing teachers,
all the permanent no-nos of the movies.

Their feature credits and prestige lend credibility to these
projects, which helps them get made. Big feature directors are
also doing lots of television as they look for work between stalled
movies. (My favorite network series, *Revenge,* had its pilot shot by
director Phillip Noyce, of *Clear and Present Danger, Rabbit-Proof
Fence, Salt* and *Patriot Games* fame.) The television business is in
constant motion: The networks have to air something, and there
are more and more cable and online outlets blooming every day.
Everyone knows that a hit series is a gold mine.

An apocryphal Hollywood saying goes: "A hit movie gets you
a great table at Morton's; a hit series gets you a house in Malibu."

Or, as Rick said this weekend when we chatted about why I
should get into the television business, "It's like what famous bank
robber Willie Sutton said when they asked him why he robbed
banks: 'It's where the money is!'"

Certainly the agencies and corporations have learned this,
as television rakes in a huge proportion of the entertainment

conglomerates' revenues compared to film, a total reversal of the old norm. Now the writers, managers and producers are getting wise.

All of this is dependent, of course, on getting a series on the air. And that is dependent on figuring out what a series is, something I would learn on the job while watching a lot of television.

TRYING TO LEARN THE GAME

My team and I unpacked our boxes from location in Boston after wrapping *The Invention of Lying* in June of 2008, year of the Catastrophe. We moved into our new bungalow at Paramount TV, which we treated like our old bungalow at the Paramount motion picture studio. We decorated it with all our wonderful things, only to discover it was really half a bungalow. We were sharing it with another producer "pod." Fortunately, it turned out that all of our bungalow-mates were happy with our antique Texas chandelier and furniture. But we discovered that we weren't supposed to be redecorating our bungalow. Apparently, television offices are supposed to be hellholes in which everyone writes twenty-four hours a day.

And so, early one morning as we were moving in, the personnel police arrived and took down our chandelier, movie posters and antique coatrack, much to my executive Rachel Abarbanell's shock. Rachel has been with me for seven years and has evolved to become my trusty president of production, lifesaver and chief of everything.

She had organized our move impeccably; she wanted me to be excited when I walked into the new office to begin this new facet of our careers. She called me at home in dismay. "Our Texas chandelier and movie posters are coming down!"

Our bungalow-mates told the personnel police, "But we need

a coatrack!" (It was usually eighty-seven degrees in the Valley.) It didn't matter, because we weren't supposed to have a decorated office.

I discovered this when I visited other television offices. They turned out to be frantic production offices thrown together with interchangeable office-catalog furniture; everyone in them is too tired and busy to look up to notice a chandelier. In other offices, people are keeping their heads down in case their shows get canceled. Each office has cycled through five shows in six years, so they are not homey spots where you entertain movie stars and highly sought-after hoo-hahs. "But we're still doing movies too," we tried to explain to the personnel police. They didn't want to hear that, since Paramount was paying us to do television.

It was the most interesting possible time to be learning TV. I had made a miniseries called *The '60s* for NBC years before, and it had been a blast—it was even nominated for an Emmy—but that was essentially making a long movie. It was not playing the television game by any stretch. Now there was so much to learn, it was unbelievable. Everything was "The Package"; "The Season"; "The Showrunner." I had only a vague sense of what these all-important terms really meant.

Who my agent was was critically important. I'd been repped by CAA (Creative Artists Agency) throughout my film career. Well, too bad for me; I had to switch to WME. This is not a business whose rules were made to be broken. How many pages were in a script? There should be 121 in a feature; 57 in an hour-long drama. Fascinating. A page a minute. How many acts? Three in a feature; five, I discovered, in a TV pilot. (For commercial breaks!) And what on earth was a cold open? Or a teaser? Just learning the language would take a few seasons. And figuring out what seasons were would take a few seasons.

I arrived at my Studio City office and sat in my chair, twirled a bit and tried to figure out where to begin. Rick had tipped me off that movie producers tend to fare better in drama "one hours" than comedy "half hours," so I figured that would be my departure point. I twirled in my chair, read the paper, read Kirkus book reviews, trolled the Internet, twirled some more and started calling writers. But something big was bothering me. A bit embarrassed, I called Rick.

"Is Rick there? It's his sister. Again."

"I am so, so sorry to bother you so soon," I said, once he picked up, "and I promise I won't call all the time; I'll get the hang of it quickly. But I forgot to ask you one really important question. I promise this is it. What is the difference between a television show and a movie?"

Rick laughed. "Good question, Lynnie. Better late than never. When I talk to feature writers and producers, I tell them that the main difference is that when you pitch a movie you're pitching something that ultimately ends. In a television pitch, you're really pitching characters and essentially what the show is about. You have to give the network a sense of where the show is going and how it will live on. This is broadcast television, so they have to imagine how it can go on for a hundred episodes. So think about that. I love you and I have a meeting."

I sat in my chair and pondered. One hundred episodes. What could that possibly mean?

Our job at the Paramount studio was to feed Paramount's two main networks, CBS and the CW, both run by Les Moonves. Paramount TV was their main supplier, and that allowed us to simply concentrate on the clear sensibilities of those two network buyers.* This seemed easy. On the other hand, I had no idea whatsoever how to generate a hundred episodes of anything.

CBS has been the number-one network continuously since

---

* The studios pitch their shows to the networks. The studios also finance the shows for the networks, and therefore reap the profits from syndication. The broadcast networks—CBS, ABC, NBC, Fox, and the CW—only receive advertising revenues.

2005, with the exception of 2008, when it lost to Fox. Moonves has achieved that dominance by building a slate of successful procedural franchises, comedies and reality shows over his tenure since 1995, first fighting to break the back of NBC's vaunted Thursday-night comedy block in the nineties (*Friends, Seinfeld, Mad About You, Will and Grace, 3rd Rock from the Sun, Frasier,* etc.), and then heading off the threat of Fox's powerhouse *American Idol*—the national star-making competition that spawned so many clones—with the solidity of his schedule. Featuring perennial favorites like *CSI, NCIS, Criminal Minds, The Mentalist, Mike and Molly, How I Met Your Mother* and *Two and a Half Men,* his track record in picking hits is remarkable.

He is a patriarch surrounded by brilliant women he empowers, such as Nina Tassler, his longtime number two at CBS. His scheduling and programming prowess has worked longer than should be possible in a fracturing network universe. Not only has cable siphoned off some of the huge network audience, but now even online streaming engines like Amazon, Netflix, Hulu, Facebook and YouTube are getting into original programming and further fragmenting what was, when I was growing up, a three-network universe. But CBS holds on to more than 11.75 million viewers nightly in prime time against all odds, thanks to this programming and scheduling wizard at its helm.

CBS largely means dramatic procedurals, mostly police and legal series, in which the main story is "closed"—i.e., completed in one episode—like their phenomenally successful franchises *CSI* and *NCIS,* which can reboot in every city, and have, or likely will (*CSI: NY, CSI: Miami,* ad infinitum). I thought and thought and came up with an idea. An old CBS procedural, *Cagney and Lacey,* served as my template, and I updated it with an article I found in the *LA Weekly* about the two women running L.A.'s downtown police department, called the Central Division. Downtown L.A., renovated to include the Staples Center, Walt Disney Concert

Hall and fancy new co-ops all mixed with L.A.'s skid row, was an incendiary blend, requiring sociology as well as cop instincts. The terrific ladies had both. I did the fun and compulsory ride-along with cops that producers do. Cleverly, we called it *Central Division*. Under the supervision of the execs at Paramount TV and my agents at WME, we found a showrunner who had worked on *CSI* whom CBS was excited to work with, and introduced her to the fabulous married-with-children cops.

It looked like we had the right showrunner, and a show that was right up CBS's alley. CBS bought the pitch. It turned out that there were three sets of notes—mine, the studio's (Paramount TV) and the network's. Guess which one the writer cared about least? I'd never done a procedural before, nor did I know where the act breaks were supposed to go. But we worked on the script all pilot season and delivered an exceedingly mediocre product. But it was so close to what CBS was looking for that we managed to make it "on the bubble." I had to ask an agent at WME what this meant. It turns out that it means you were neither rejected nor selected. It means you're almost picked! You're not dead. You are one of those pilots that could go either way.

At Moonves's other network, the CW, that season, in my never-ending effort to make a career out of *How to Lose a Guy,* I pitched it as a series, which was a natural, since Paramount Pictures already owned it. We got Jenny Bicks of *Sex and the City* and *Men in Trees,* who was, I thought, a perfect writer for the project. We worked really hard with the CW team. But just as we were about to submit the pilot script to the network executives, we got brand-new ideas to add, such as, "I just heard [Katy Perry's] 'I Kissed a Girl' on the radio! Can we come up with a lesbian subplot?" New ideas at this late stage were a bad sign. Maybe they feared the script wasn't edgy enough and needed to be roughed up a bit. We added some same-sex undertones and got on the bubble with that project as well.

Now I was on the bubble with two of my scripts. All I had to do was try to get some casting with *Central Division*. I desperately went through WME's available female stars, trying to make a "package": a producer, a showrunner and a star all from the same agency, the home run of the business. (For the agency, at least!)

I went after Ashley Judd. When it fell through, I went after Ashley Judd again. But honestly, who was I kidding? I knew Ashley. I'd made a romantic comedy with her and Hugh Jackman called *Someone Like You,* about a heartbroken woman who was trying to figure out why she was dumped. If she were to do TV (I was one season too early), she would never wear a cop's uniform! She needed wardrobe. I went after Ashley Judd again the next season, with a show that never even made the bubble but had much better wardrobe.

However, as I was flailing and thinking I was failing, unbeknown to me, I was also sort of succeeding. I had pitched a reinvention of *The Golden Girls* to a hilarious showrunner, Suzanne Martin (*Frasier*). She is a beautiful blond bombshell of a gal with whom I clicked the moment she walked into our bungalow.

I had cooked up a fantasy straight from my life: What if three "besties" of a certain age—so unappreciated in La La Land, where gorgeous thirtysomethings couldn't get dates because guys their age were cruising for twentysomethings—suddenly made an emergency landing in a plane in Cleveland. On the layover, all the men there appreciated them in ways that they hadn't been appreciated in years, and suddenly they felt sexy again! They decided to stay in Cleveland and move in together, and they learned the joys and deprivations of life in the middle of the country—sort of like me in Texas, but more on the nose.

Suzanne immediately responded to it—and also wanted to update *The Golden Girls*—so she made up a fabulous pilot story on the spot, and we called it *Hot in Cleveland*. We pitched it to Paramount TV and then CBS. At the CBS comedy division, as we pitched our hearts out, they looked at us like we were from Pluto.

"Older women? Seriously?!"

I had no idea what you were allowed to do, what they were looking for, what was *in,* what was out. All I kept hearing was that the sitcom was dead, besides of course *Two and a Half Men,* which you apparently can't kill with a stick, a drug-induced implosion, a lawsuit or a bludgeon. (And then we knew that apparently anything can be saved by Ashton Kutcher.)

Most important, this was just before the 2009 debut of *Modern Family,* the award-winning ABC comedy about three related families that redefine what "family" means in the new millennium. This breakthrough show reinvented the comedy wheel with the single-camera half-hour model, spawning a subgenre of successful new sitcoms. "Single camera" means it's shot off the stage with one camera, like a feature, or like a drama is shot for TV, without either a laugh track or a live audience, as we do on *Hot in Cleveland.* At this point, in 2009–10, dozens of sitcoms had been flopping since *Friends,* and nothing seemed to click.

CBS knows what is right for CBS—better than any other network knows what is right for it. Our little show was meant for another home, which was just being born. It helped create another network.

HOW MY (EVENTUAL) CO-EXECUTIVE PRODUCER PITCHED ON THE FLY, SOLD IT IN A PARKING LOT AND HELPED CREATE A NEW NETWORK

(The parking-lot pitch is still alive somewhere)

Todd Milliner is an infectiously adorable TV producer whom I'd never met until we became co–exec producers on *Hot in Cleveland*. He and his partner, Sean Hayes—whom I'd seen thousands of times on television playing Jack in *Will & Grace,* but also had never met—went on to sell Suzanne's pitch by accident. We were having dinner before a taping one night in Studio City when he told me the story of how he and Sean parking-lot-pitched *Hot in Cleveland* and helped launch the previously unknown cable station TV Land. It is now going on its fourth year.

"Sean and I were meeting with TV Land, which had only done syndicated shows and reality shows. They were meeting with us for a potential nonscripted series—we don't generally do that—and after the meeting, we were on the way to the parking lot, and we said, 'Well . . . there's this one idea . . .'

"Suzanne Martin had come in and told us very generally what the idea was, and we fell in love with it. So we told them about it on the fly, and before we got to the parking lot, they bought it. We never even pitched it!

"We got back and called Suzanne's agent, because Suzanne was editing a movie that she'd made. Her agent, Richard Weitz, called her and said, 'Sean sold your show to TV Land.'

"She said, 'Great! What's TV Land?'

"I said, 'That's exactly what I said.'"

"Nobody had ever heard of this network," I said, "and yet it became a hit, and sold to syndication in its first year! How could this happen?" I asked Sean.

"We had a lot of convergence," Sean answered. "First of all, Betty White had just started to peak with *SNL* drafting her to host and her hit Super Bowl commercial. We got weirdly lucky with that. She was a guest star on the first episode. We didn't think she was part of the ensemble. And then these other ladies we had met with— Jane Leeves and Wendie Malick—we didn't do any other casting sessions; we saw no one else. These were the ladies. We knew we wanted real actors who were looking for a way to start their next chapter too, just like the show. Thematically, it all fit for them."

I added, "The casting was great for TV Land's syndication hook too."

Todd agreed. "Jane Leeves is in syndication with *Frasier,* and Wendy Malick is in syndication with *Just Shoot Me!* And Valerie Bertinelli is classic in *One Day at a Time*."

"It happened so quickly," I said to Todd. "I couldn't believe how quickly the show took off, and how much TV Land got behind it. Did it shock anybody there when it happened so quickly?"

Todd laughed, remembering the day I was talking about.

"Oh, yeah. When we got the numbers for the first episode, I was walking out in the street and literally almost got hit by a car. We thought we'd be lucky, but that car almost killed me! And the numbers [4.8 million viewers—making network history as TV Land's highest-rated and most-watched telecast ever] almost gave me a heart attack!" (By comparison, HBO's *Game of Thrones* season one finale had 4.2 million viewers.)

"We made headlines in the trades and on Deadline. No one could believe the numbers. They were solid cable hit numbers."

I added: "And no one had any idea where in the world TV Land was on the dial! There is no dial anymore. Doesn't it prove in some way that if an audience wants to find a show, it doesn't matter where it is, because they will find it?"

He said, "Especially with DVRs. If only I could explain them to my dad."

"Me too," I said, and smiled.

There were a lot of great things about Paramount and CBS, but it was virtually impossible to get a show on the network because its schedule was so successful that it had no room. Also, I was barely qualified to take a shot, as I hadn't figured how to make a successful police, medical or legal procedural that could generate one hundred episodes. And, worse, I couldn't work in cable there.

Cable wasn't a priority for Les Moonves's empire at that time,* so if I could create something that was good, I'd need more outlets to pitch to. I had sci-fi ideas that would never fit into the CW's or CBS's wheelhouse, and ideas inspired by my time in Texas that may not fit anywhere but were gut shots, so I wanted to give them a try. It was time to move on.

While I (or, really, my agent) went looking for a new home where I might partake of the golden age of cable, I heard on the street that my favorite movie writer, Jonah Nolan, had pitched a series to CBS that they loved, and it had gotten picked up. Jonah? In TV? That proved it! Everyone! And what would come of my potential tentpole?

I wasn't surprised CBS had bitten on an idea of his; he was one of the most exciting collaborators I'd ever had. But why was Jonah moving to the small screen when he was king of the tentpole as the cowriter of the *Dark Knight* franchise? He was not exactly suffering movie business despair! He could do anything in features that he wanted to. I had to go see him. I knew the reasons behind his choice would shed light on what Wolcott was calling the golden age of television. Not only that—he had taken one swing at bat and had made the hardest schedule of all to crack, CBS's.

The thing about Jonah is that everything he touches turns to gold. His short story was the basis of his brother Christopher

---

* Showtime is part of the CBS empire, and with the current phenomenal success of *Homeland* and the cable financial model, he is said to be much more interested in it now.

Nolan's award-winning film *Memento.* Jonah's first franchise film was *The Dark Knight,* and his first TV show made the CBS schedule Thursday night at ten. Perhaps I could learn something from Jonah that might prepare me for next season. He would have had to master the procedural trick for *Person of Interest,* his new show, and figured out how to get a hundred episodes out of the premise of his show. I would listen carefully to what he had to say about what drove him from features to television and what television taught him about story.

JONAH IN THE TUBE

Jonah is the American Nolan, while Christopher, the spectacular director and his brother and collaborator, grew up in England. Jonah grew up in Chicago, went to Georgetown University and looks like a college football hero, bordering on Tom Brady. Hunky, funny, curious and self-deprecating, Jonah can seem too good to be true—but he's true blue.

By the time we got together in his makeshift production office near Warner Bros. (*This* is what a television office is supposed to look like, I said to myself), my three bubbles had burst and he'd had his first pitch picked up to series. He was basically living in this space now, in what he called "the tube." I loved the phrase, and asked him to explain.

"The first time I heard it," he said, "my partner, Greg Plageman, and I were spending a month in New York, shooting the pilot. We ran into a showrunner friend of his. He saw the two of us coming back from a day on set, frozen solid, probably looking pretty pathetic. He was there on a project, but he wasn't actively shooting anything.

"'Oh, you guys are in "the tube,"' he said.

"'What do you mean by "the tube"?' I asked.

"'A network TV show is like a tube,' he said. 'You go into it, and you don't come out of it again until it's canceled or you get fired.'"

I loved the term and longed for the horrible feeling he'd described.

Jonah continued, "And that's still, to this point, the best description I've heard for a television show. It's a tube—you really are in it. There's no time for friends, there's no time for family, there's no time for anything."

He looked exhilarated and exhausted at the same time; I was amazed he had found time to talk.

"How did you get to this point?" I asked. "What gravitational force led you into the tube when you could have just kept writing blockbusters?"

"I know for myself," he said, "the attraction is that working on these big spectacle films, which is great fun and some of the work that I'm proudest of . . . it's a little like singing the national anthem in a baseball stadium. Right? You don't know you're out of tune until about eight seconds later. You never get the feedback. I cowrote *The Dark Knight,* the first draft, in fall of 2005. Didn't see a frame of film until the first assembly in early 2008."

I shook my head, knowing Christopher Nolan was known as the fastest A-plus-list director in town.

"We're talking two and a half years later. For that scale of film, that was literally the fastest turnaround possible. Usually, you'd be stuck in development hell; average turnaround would be five years. I've got a project I've been working on for, at this point, eight, nine, ten years.

"In television," Jonah went on, "you have the opposite problem. Maybe you don't have the time you would like to have to polish it as much as you want. But you can't be precious, because it's going to be on the air in three weeks. We rewrote a scene for the third episode of the show: We had the sets, the actors, we issued the pages and I saw it two and a half weeks later—as opposed to two and a half years later! For me, the fun of it is watching it with the audience."

"So it was the immediacy that hooked you?"

"That's a part of it," Jonah continued. "The beginning of my career was Chris making *Memento,* a taut psychological thriller about a man struggling with memory loss as he seeks vengeance on his wife's killer.

"I don't know how you'd make that film now . . . They don't know how to market them, and in a sense that's rational; the films that are now being made come at the expense of these dramatic films, which, frankly, were the entry point for me."

"It's going back to your roots?" I asked.

"In part. You know the tragedy of film is that there are some pretty classic films that exist only in someone's desk drawer. And that is tragic. You know? Truly. With television, again, it's the opposite problem. It's 'What do you got? You got a script somewhere? You got a page? Let's have it! Because we need twenty-four of these things. We need one next week.' And I love that."

I smiled as he continued. "Television is all about how much story do you have, because I want eighty episodes, a hundred episodes, and then the business model makes sense. So you have to have one hundred hours of story—and that's a spectacular problem to have! The fun of writing for me is creating moments—some write for character; some write for story; I write for moments. I love story and character, but for me, writing is a delivery device for moments. You've got no time, you've got no money, and so it's this insatiable appetite. It's a black hole. It's 'Whaddaya got?' Story, character, ideas? You know, what's the idea you've been hanging on to for *five years*? Because we're just going to throw it into the pot and try to make it work. I love the fact that television gives you the opportunity to create as many moments as you've got the imagination and capacity to create."

"So this is how you generate a hundred episodes?" I asked.

"One of the nice things about a procedural is it's not a one-off. It's a world. You've created a self-propelled mechanism."

This was spectacular. I was getting a sense of the writers' room, of what went on inside and how fast the ideas shot out—using every story and moment in your head in service of the premise of the show. Spitballing what you had and cross-pollinating it with the engine of the show.

"It's fascinating, Jonah," I said, "because most people talk about television being a writer's medium from a *control* point of view. But what I am hearing from you is that it's a writer's medium from an *inventive* point of view."

"Yeah!"

One thing I learn over and over in this business is that control, when it works, is never what you think it is.

"It's more 'the writers are in control,' because the writers are responsible for the narrative continuing to unfold. If moments don't continue to unfold, then there's no show."

"Whereas my writer friends want to be producers," I said, "because they're waiting for the moment they can cast their best friends."

Jonah laughed. "I have hired exactly zero people, from a list of a hundred friends. Look," he went on, "the control is a pain in the ass. Look at my arrangement with Chris: He does all the hard stuff, and I get to go write. He gets to write too, but he has all this other stuff that he has to do. And so the second I started doing the TV show, we were five, six weeks into it, I called him up and I said, 'Thank you for the last ten years of me not having to worry about this *bullshit*.'"

I asked Jonah why he decided to do network instead of cable.

He thought for a second, then answered, "My mom was a flight attendant for forty-plus years, and her superpower was to check into a hotel, anywhere in the world, and within five minutes find an episode of *Law & Order* on TV. The power and pleasure of that franchise was undeniable. You knew just what to expect, and yet every episode was different and compelling. That is shooting out a hundred episodes, a hundred times.

"I decided I wanted to do a pretty old-fashioned network television show that was essentially a procedural, but that benefited from the influence of these amazing serialized shows that are on the air. I think everyone knows now that the audience expects some return on their investment. They expect that these characters they're looking at will have an arc, a big one, above and beyond the individual episodes. And so I wanted to do a TV show a little more like the ones that I was actually watching when I was a kid. When you talk about shows like *Hill Street Blues,* you talk about shows that deliver when you have an hour to spare and you want to see a complete story, to be taken on a journey. That's the challenge of network television, to be able to tell a complete story. And at the same time, it's a laboratory for character."

I asked if he thought television was going to continue to attract writers of his caliber.

"We are clearly in the golden age of television," Jonah said. "You can look at shows like *The Wire* [the HBO series written by a former police reporter, set in Baltimore] or *Breaking Bad* [Vince Gilligan's show about a chemistry teacher with lung cancer turned crystal meth dealer]. They are legitimately the best things anyone has ever put on TV. Something amazing happened, and you had all these storytellers migrate over to television. There is a hole in the feature business." He started to laugh. "Roughly the size of . . . television!"

And I had slipped right through.

ONWARD TO SONY, JEWISH SOLDIERETTES

Armed with Jonah's insights, I had a better grip on the question of what made one hundred episodes: a world that could be a self-propelled mechanism, filled with great characters and fed by moments—and sustained by a room of writers offering "whatever they got!"

We made a deal at Sony. Rick said that in selecting the studio, he tried to find the one farthest from my house. He did a wonderful job, because it's an hour's drive from Silver Lake to Culver City, longer at rush hour (which is constant). But it was a brilliant choice, because, as opposed to Paramount TV, Sony does not have a primary relationship with a network, and therefore its mandate is to sell to everyone. It has a renowned creative history (*Seinfeld, Breaking Bad, Damages, All in the Family, Married . . . with Children,* among many others). Its independence makes it very attractive to writer-producers who aren't limited to a single network buyer when creating their shows. They run the gamut of Net and cable as potential buyers, making the range of creative options for the artist as broad as possible, because each buyer has a different audience and sensibility. I was to engage in this broadest of possible creative mandates. The team was fantastic, supportive and smart, so the only one who could screw this up was me.

I met a delightful writer from Texas, Jordan Budde, with whom I bonded immediately, and we decided to develop a show that takes place in the Hill Country outside Austin, where I had my home. He loved this area also (an affection we share with almost no buyers at any known networks or outlets, including, amazingly, CMT—Country Music Television). We created a family drama–cum–procedural about two battling sisters, then stacked up the odds against us: We made the main character a judge instead of a lawyer, in addition to making the setting rural. But NBC bit, and Sony was thrilled, so we wrote the absolute best version of a Texas judge procedural—a premise with two core strikes against it—that anyone could.

That year Robert Greenblatt, who had been responsible for Showtime's great programming successes from *Weeds,* about a mom who moonlights as a pot dealer, to *The Big C,* was named president of NBC/Universal, which had been in last place for eight years; nothing had been working on its schedule except *The Voice,* which was yet another *American Idol* clone, though by now the biggest.

The entire creative community was thrilled about the move. It indicated to many the growing convergence of sensibilities between networks and cable—as far as was possible, given FCC (Federal Communications Commission) rules on broadcast television. Writers for the broadcast networks are governed by the FCC, and are constantly battling their rules and frustrated by their language constraints. No four-letter words, no inhaling in the Clintonian sense (exhaling is okay); nothing that could be considered obscene was allowed on broadcast television. The ten o'clock slot is the most coveted one because the rules are somewhat relaxed at that time, but it still can't compete with the anything-goes freedom of pay television. But the networks have been getting edgier thanks to the growing influence of the successful cable programming with which they have to compete at Emmy Season (to their great and constant frustration). Greenblatt would shake things up at the network, it was assumed, and *Smash,* a Showtime project he was bringing with him to NBC, with Spielberg at the helm, was already rumored to be exactly that.

We turned in a script that I, as well as Sony and the execs I had pitched it to, adored. I was in Texas when the decision was being made, trying not to call Rick too often or look at every place I went as a potential location. The studio was calling—should I try for Ashley Judd again? At these moments everyone does a full-court press on the network and the agency for casting. But with one phone call it was dead: This show about a Texas judge abandoned by her gay husband wasn't what the sophisticated Broadway buff now running NBC was looking for.

I sent off a sci-fi piece to AMC with a great writer from *Breaking Bad,* and it won this thing they call a "bake-off" (really, like Betty Crocker). But that year they didn't reward the winner with a pilot deal, they just continued developing us for another year and started a renegotiation of their deal with Sony. That was very disappointing, to say the least. With a showrunner from *Friends* I went out with a scripted take on the Miss America beauty pageant. This was the year after all the period pieces had been picked up, and by the time we were ready to pitch, *Playboy,* about bunnies and their mates in the sixties, was tanking on NBC, and *Pan Am,* about stewardesses in the sixties, was looking iffy on ABC. I couldn't help but think we went out with the pitch too late. I needed to get the timing right the next season. I would have to attack the networks like a field marshal. We put a calendar up on the wall. I had to think backward.

CBS, NBC, ABC, Fox and the CW all ran on a strict yearly schedule. They have upfront in May, when they expose their new shows to advertisers and announce their schedules to the aforementioned advertisers, producer-writers and agents (and each other). They buy pitches and scripts from June to early October. They have all their pilots written between September and December or the beginning of January. They pick up all of their shows in January (the madness of all these pilots casting at once cannot be overstated). Then they shoot in February and March, to go to postproduction in April. Then they decide what's going on the air at the end of April or in early May. Then the whole process starts all over again. I had been late with *Miss America* the previous year at Sony, and I had to internalize the calendar to make sure that didn't happen again. But there were nuances to the calendar that I still had to master. And for these I would need, well, a master.

THE BUYING SEASONS

I zeroed back in on Gail Berman. Lord knows I couldn't bother Rick again. I had to ask Gail about the seasons, since the year before they had smashed me in the head, even though I thought I had a good running start.

"I'm back," I said. "I need some advice. The seasons."

"Yes?" She leaned in.

"They come at you very quickly," I complained.

She looked at me sympathetically. "There used to be a break. At least, everyone tells me there used to be a break, but I don't really remember there being one."

She didn't seem as stressed out about this as I was.

I said, "Every time I think I'm ready, it's like, 'Oh, no, the buying window already passed.' 'Okay, well, you're late on the network.' 'Wait a second. I just got my ideas together, and comedy is closing? And then cable is open? Now hold on . . .' Like when—"

She interrupted my pathetic babbling. "I always say the same thing: I'd like to be finished selling by Labor Day. And every year the deadline gets pushed earlier. It's weird."

Oh, God, I thought. I'm already late. And nobody at my agency wanted to tell me. I pressed on. "Is that what I should remember? Be finished by Labor Day?"

"That's what I always tell everybody," she reiterated. "That's the rule in my head. It doesn't always work at this company, but the goal is to be done by then."

Kissing good-bye all future hopes of visiting my New York friends in the Hamptons, I said, "So you can't go away for the summer?"

"Not if you want to sell; you have to be finished selling by Labor Day. Most people look at me and say, 'What are you talking about? You can sell through October.' But I always thought you had your best shot by getting in early, before they had everything else set up. Even your more out-there ideas might get set up if you do it early. So Labor Day is always a good deadline."

The bad news absorbed, I asked, "When you can still wear white?"

Gail laughed out loud. She loved this, since we obey no clothing laws in California and this bonded us as secret East Coasters.

"Right!" she said. "While you're wearing white, you can sell. Once you have to take the white off, you're done!"

Then she explained why, and I knew I would never make this mistake again.

"It is seasonal because material gets old quickly, unlike in the movie business."

I added, "And they seem to know what they want before they start."

"They think they know, and then the season starts and something catches on, and then *that's* the thing they want. There is a little bit of a buying flux around the end of October, when they start to say, 'Well, this seems to be sticking, so we'll need a companion piece for that.' So you have to know what's working to finish out the selling season. It's a wonderful business. It moves."

The mid-season flux. It was like a Zen koan. This was the kind of nuance only experience could teach! Looking for that companion piece to *New Girl,* this year's big hit? How about *New Boy*! A guy moves in with two girl roommates.

Already pitched. Nextino.

Next at the speed of a neutrino.

I asked Gail if the feature business felt slow after being in television.

She found the question comical. "It was stunning to me. It was the biggest change for me. It was *so* slow. I thought, Well, we're on track here, and then that track just stalled. And somehow everyone was quite comfortable with that. I was out of that rhythm. That rhythm was off for me. I was expecting that script on such and such a day, give or take a couple of weeks. The script literally never came during my entire tenure." She burst out laughing in retrospect. "Things like that were crazy to me."

"But," I said, realizing that I'd missed the hot spot of the network buying season, "there's fast, and then there's *fast*. One season's over, you get started for cable and they're already booked."

She smiled. "Remember, no white. You'll get it next year."

SPEED JUNKIES: FROM NEXT TO NEXTINO

First of all, during pitch season (which is essentially always, since most of cable is open full-time, but here I'm talking about network pitch season) everyone is racing all around L.A., going from pitch to pitch, every hour on the hour. The networks are located as far away from each other as they possibly can be, from West L.A. to the deep Valley, with only CBS in between. They are devilishly scheduled in sequence so that only Indy 500 race car drivers can make them, and they all take place on the same day with no concern for the seller's point of departure or driving ability. This accounts for the heart-thumping danger of the whole thing. Can you get there on time? How fast can you go without getting a ticket and missing the meeting? What alternative is there to the permanent Carmageddon on the 405? Will you scare your team into thinking you will hold up the pitch? Are you the one who will walk in late, after most people are already there? If so, the network will start the meeting without you if you're not the showrunner.

In the end, you get there, after being sent to a back parking lot, which further delays your arrival and forces you to sprint to the meeting and arrive out of breath and disheveled. In the network waiting room, eleven bigger pitches with comedy stars attached await, and the network president himself comes out to visit with them. How can you make them laugh after that? Sweat forms on the brow of your writer. It's all part of the game.

SO THIS YEAR 2012

Having gotten absolutely nothing on the air the previous year, I was determined to get it right in 2012. I studied the calendar. I hadn't scheduled any trips over the summer. I studied my IPs (intellectual properties, or books, as they're called in other cities) in *Kirkus* and watched TV like I was a cross between a slacker and Alessandra Stanley, television reviewer for the *New York Times.* I discovered a network show that I got hooked on like crack— *Revenge,* on ABC (which, as it turns out, was based on *The Count of Monte Cristo*). I spent months reviewing every classic novel I had ever read or not read for plot ideas. Emily Thorne, the heroine of *Revenge,* was a kick-ass female lead, pretending to be someone she wasn't in order to avenge her father's death, even daring to marry into the family who murdered him so she could exact her punishment. I became a student of how it generated and rapidly burned up story. I had to be ready by the time the industry returned from the "upfronts"—still sort of mysterious to me, as I hadn't yet earned my ticket there by winning a slot on a network schedule. Every May there's a huge hoopla when everyone who matters in television is in New York attending the upfronts. Equally as important, the time slots and full schedule are announced, throwing everything into turmoil when old shows are moved and new shows get fantastic or terrible time slots. Then the execs come home and start staffing the selected shows with writers, and the whole season starts over again with June pitches.

Sony had a new head of drama, Suzanne Patmore-Gibbs, and everyone told me I would love working with her. We were both alumni of Pomona College, she a lit major, and the whole thing seemed almost too good to be true. It was an exciting hire for Sony, as Suzanne had just been head of drama at ABC, where she had developed many of their hits, including—as it turned out—*Revenge*!

To prepare for our first meeting, I met with a very talented friend who had also had a hand in bringing *Revenge* to life, Patrick Moran. Moran, the boyfriend of my writer Jordan Budde, who created my Texas procedural *Emily Swan,* was the smart, natty and charming senior vice president and head of creative development for ABC Studios. He had been a Fox executive on *Glee,* and is known to work wonderfully with writers. He joined ABC as head of drama, and two years later was promoted to senior vice president of the studio in charge of drama and comedy. I was thrilled when he agreed to give me his take on the genesis of *Revenge* and help get me ready for my new season.

We sat in his office at ABC on a rare slow day; the upfronts were going on in New York, and for a brief moment the decisions were out of our hands.

Patrick's priority is to provide shows to his own network, but he has made a great case to his network president, Paul Lee, that he can attract better writers to his studio if the writers he makes deals with feel they can sell their ideas to other networks as well. His studio makes huge profits for Disney by selling their shows overseas and to cable, hoping for syndication dollars. This is where the money is in television, as networks can only make advertising dollars.

He said, "I'd been wanting to do an updated *Count of Monte Cristo* for a long time, and just hadn't been able to get it to work."

I later read that Paul Lee also wanted to update *The Count,* and his deputy Suzanne told me she did as well. This was obviously an idea waiting to pop. The question was, who could break it?

Patrick continued: "And then, when I came here, I wanted very much to work with Mike Kelley [*Swingtown*], who had a deal at ABC. He was working on something else that he loved too, but that ultimately didn't work for various reasons. I pitched this *Monte Cristo* idea to him, but he turned me down. He didn't respond to it at all. I pitched it again, and he still didn't respond. The producers he was working with [Wyck Godfrey and Marty Bowen, of the *Twilight* franchise] were excited about doing a show set in the Hamptons and kept at him until he finally relented and said he'd give it a try, though without any commitments. This was very late in the season, around October."

October! My God! No one can get anything on in October— unless, of course, you're the main supplier to the ABC network.

"And then, after working on it for a while," Patrick continued, "suddenly it started to click for Mike."

"What was it that clicked?" I asked.

Patrick thought for a moment. "It was Emily's revenge, her single-minded determination to redeem her father at all costs. The madness of it was clicking in the writing. Mike was enjoying it."

And so was I, along with so many other women I knew.

"Casting was the key," Patrick added. "If the heroine had been a bit older, she'd lose sympathy; any younger, she'd be insane. They cast her perfectly, with an actress, Emily VanCamp, who had a following from the long-running series *Brothers and Sisters*." Patrick went on, "Madeleine Stowe was a dream 'get.' She wasn't afraid of the part, as many other actresses were."

"She's divine," I said. "This is the best thing she's done since *Last of the Mohicans*."

"You *are* a fan," Patrick said.

• • •

Of course, what Patrick didn't know is that the president of my company, Rachel Abarbanell, had been enduring versions of *Revenge* for six months. Heroine as blighted orphan, à la *Jane Eyre*. Heroine as abandoned-at-birth aristocrat (a loosely updated take on *Anastasia*) showing up at her real family's current estate, only to be thrown out by her siblings. My drama meeting with Sony was two weeks away. The upfronts were ending, and I was reading Deadline Hollywood to get the last of the pilot pickups when Rachel suddenly burst through my door.

"Read the log line of *Notorious,* which NBC just put on its schedule," she cried.

"You read it," I said.

"A female detective goes undercover in the home of the rich family for whom her mother was a maid to solve the murder of the daughter who was once her best friend."

"It's a *Revenge,*" I said in despair. "I'm too late. Who is the producer?"

"Gail Berman," she said.

I started to laugh. I was one full buying season behind. "Well, at least if I get beat by a season, it's by a master."

Onward. Nextino.

Still, I had my *Revenge,* which was so ridiculously complicated that it had taken me all season to develop, and by the time my fabulous writer and I were ready, ABC was filled to the brim with soaps. I was saved by a fresh and funny procedural from *Dexter* showrunner Manny Coto, a kind of *Moneyball* meets *Homicide* that he called *The Defectives.* Even though ABC had hung out a sign at the beginning of the season that said NO PROCEDURALS, by that time they were so loaded up with *Revenge*-a-likes that they needed a procedural again, so they bit. Manny turned in a terrific script, and we crossed our fingers and waited to hear. They didn't pick it up. We were crestfallen. He was a wonderful collaborator, and the show would have been so much fun.

Then, out of the blue, a spec pilot from a first-time writer named Cameron Porsandeh, who had done a thousand interesting things in his life besides write TV, was submitted to me by WME. It was about a very scary man-made virus that runs amok in an outlaw lab in the Arctic. After a little work, I brought it to Sony and they bought it, attaching a major showrunner, Ron Moore (*Battlestar Galactica*), with whom they had a deal. We were going to go out competitively with the pilot when SyFy offered a rare pilot-to-series order (meaning they were committing to a thirteen-episode series, not contingent on seeing the pilot first). Blackjack! I was getting something on the air this fall, albeit from left field.

At dinner one night with Patrick and Jordan at the Chateau Marmont, I shared my good fortune. Patrick gave me lots of advice—for instance, we should delay our production to make sure we wouldn't be casting at the same time as the networks and competing for the same pool of actors. At one point I asked him how to keep a show like ours going—a show without a precinct, a hospital or a spaceship chasing Cylons, in which the bad guy keeps mutating. As ever, he had fascinating things to say, and used *Revenge* as a departure point for our discussion.

Patrick explained that *Revenge* was the soap descendent of a different kind of show called the "Brightly Burning Show." The model was different from that of a normal show in that it was not picked up because it could obviously generate a hundred episodes. It was called a brightly burning show because it burned through story so fast and generated a lot of heat. He pinpointed *24* as the prime example of this genre. Perhaps our show too could be a brightly burning show, and if we hit the bull's-eye with story, we could burn just as bright and fast as the virus could consume the facility.

"I remember when *24* launched I was working at UPN [United Paramount Network] at the time," Patrick said. "My boss thought it was ridiculous. He said, 'How is that ever going to work? They'll be lucky to get through a season.'

"I said, 'But that's what's fun about *24*—how can they up this?' And that's what made for water-cooler talk and compulsive viewing.

"At that time the business shifted slightly, and that show became such an asset to the studio because the DVD sales were enormous. The success of those early adrenaline shows coincided with the success of the DVD market, which has since gone away," Patrick recalled.

Boy, did that sound familiar.

"People were buying DVDs and watching them in these marathon sittings. They burn through five or six episodes at a time. Suddenly a different paradigm was born. The question was not only can you keep the series going for seven years, but also what is the value for the series outside of that? So we talked about shows that would burn very bright and very fast. You think about them slightly differently. The network was no longer hung up on having to sustain it for a hundred episodes if you could create a sensation behind a show."

Digital outlets are now starting to make a huge financial impact on critically acclaimed shows with cultural cachet and devoted followings, but with a fraction of the viewers that a traditional hit once had. AMC's *Mad Men* sold exclusive online streaming rights to Netflix as a way for Netflix to garner more subscribers. Netflix paid $75 million for those rights; that's $1 million an episode. This is a whole new universe for hotly burning cable shows.

Nextino. Just as I learn something, it changes.

But here's the other crucial thing I learned, not for my network meetings but for the business: These shows are streaming online now, and the studios that create them are making online deals with all kinds of new providers. In general, they are not yet generating as much profit as DVDs did, but the studios are starting to make some profits on exclusive sales of their shows to venues like Netflix. TV writers are starting to see that Internet profit model they were looking for.

The profit models are changing because the platforms are changing. These shows that sell new platforms generate buzz.

Patrick says, "If a show seems to hold people's attention—even if it feels like it might burn fast but bright—if it pops, it's still meaningful, because it helps you to cut through the clutter."

Ahh, getting the signal through the noise. And, to come full circle, we return to the way the movie business thinks.

If an idea pops, if it gets through the clutter, then the television studios will find a way to monetize it, even if it doesn't follow the network model of one hundred episodes for syndication. Nothing has yet come out to replace the DVD bundle for those marathon sittings, but the *appetite* for shows we watch in that manner has been created, and we watch them now on our tablets (and maybe soon on our phones) without it yet making up for what was once significant revenue. Packaging multiple seasons of beloved "hot-burning series" and selling them online will be a business, especially as we find a foolproof firewall from piracy and a cloud for storage. Then it will be something worth WGA striking for. And you can be sure it will be worth the AMPTP fighting to hold on to as well.

Every day, new venues for creating original programming emerge: Amazon, Hulu, Apple, Google, Netflix, YouTube, Facebook, Microsoft and many more are all creating new scripted and reality shows for your computers or devices, or to be distributed on their own platforms. And these are just the well-known corporate players. Facebook is becoming a distributor for TV and films. Funny or Die, a venue born during the strike that creates product for its own Web site, just formed a strategic partnership with Turner Broadcasting System (TBS and Adult Swim). It also just created its own experiment in iPad publishing: *The Occasional,* a new iPad magazine. Soon webisodes moving to cable will be as common as cable being watched on the Web.

The icing on the cake of this changing menu was applied in 2012, when Microsoft lured Nancy Tellem, longtime number two to Les Moonves at CBS and among the most highly respected network executives in the business, to head its digital and media production studio, overseeing the launch of new "interactive and linear content" to turn its Xbox gaming console into a leading entertainment platform. That means you will be watching exclusive series, which she knows how to develop as well as anyone, on your (or your child's) Xbox. It is to be a destination as well for interactive movies and music. Xbox is aiming to be a total entertainment experience, and has the means, talent and distribution channel into every household with a boy to do it.

I had to turn my television into a computer this week because I sold a show to Amazon and I want to be able to watch it. The speed of change is alarming, exciting—you're panicking and galloping along with a headless horseman looking for a buck that's hidden in the house like the matzo at Passover. Everyone is looking to replace the revenue that once came from DVDs.

Someone will soon be making money on the Net somewhere. At the very least, it means work for writers, more niche programming, and more opportunities for a multitude of voices. Each venue is looking for an identity to single itself out. With so many alternative venues, so many shots for every idea, they can drown each other out. No wonder ideas have to pop.

Nextino.

After my drama meeting, I met with Sony's head of international television. That's an arena where profits are being made, as TV shows are sold (and cofinanced) overseas to various markets, though it's not driving what gets produced. Hopefully, our SyFy series will do well for Sony overseas. For years our shows have been seen in syndication off network in America and around the world. It is a huge revenue stream for the financiers of the shows, the studios. Now, in the way we are buying foreign formats like *Homeland* (Israel) and *American Idol* (Britain) to remake as ours, the rest of the world is also now buying our formats and remaking them in indigenous versions, as they do with our movies: Turkey has its own *Desperate Housewives;* Sony has remade *Married . . . with Children* a dozen times around the world; *Gossip Girl* is getting an international do-over; and on and on. All this is a new source of vital international revenue. It's beginning to sound very much like one giant global entertainment ecosystem, transforming like Gaia, the living earth, in response to attacks on its existence.

But television is thriving, outpacing movies in profits on a scale that no one would have believed twenty years ago, when the movie divisions of entertainment companies were their profit engines and television was treated as a stepchild. Now movie divisions look like the specialty-art divisions of their respective entertainment conglomerates, and the two media have reversed positions. For example, at Time Warner, the movie division made $600 million in profits last year, and the television division $5.5 billion (see chart). It's a similar ratio at the other entertainment conglomerates, where movie divisions generate revenue in the hundreds of millions while the TV divisions generate billions. It's a different world than the one my dad was born into, or the one I joined during the Old Abnormal. It is clear which bank Willie Sutton has chosen to rob.

PROFITS AT A GLANCE		
	Movies	**TV**
Viacom	$341 M	$3.85 B
Disney	$618 M	$6.15 B
Time Warner	$600 M	$5.05 B
News Corp.	$927 M	$3.67 B
NBCU	$27 M	$3.318 B
Total	**$2.513 B**	**$22.038 B**

Source: thewrap.com.

My conversation with Rick, below, explains the source of these enormous profits.

BILLION-DOLLAR BABIES: TELEVISION

I was, of course, inclined to do cable when I started television. It was the most movielike and had the most creative freedom. Most of the writers I first had access to wanted to do cable too. I loved *Mad Men, Breaking Bad* and *Big Love,* and now, of course, *Homeland.* I was thinking movie-think. But subtly I felt my studio, Sony, and my agency pushing me toward network-think. Not being entirely stupid, I gradually got the joke. Network was the bull's-eye. Cable might make the most money for its carriers, but network makes the most money for its producers.

This is how it works: Studios finance and own the shows that they sell to cable and the networks. Cablers like HBO and AMC finance their own shows, but they like to share the risk, so they buy from studios too.

Studios sell to networks and cable stations* and make their money through the successful run of the shows and through selling the syndication rights domestically and internationally. WME and the other television agencies get packaging fees on each episode. We producers have our deals—a fee for each episode and a portion of the profits, depending on our track record—negotiated up front as we sell the pitch to the studio or the network directly through our agent.

As I came to understand all this, it became clear why the networks all eventually started their own studios. They needed rating points for advertising, which is where they make their money.† By owning their own studios, the networks can develop the shows that they think will work on air and get them the rating points they need. Plus, if they own the studios that make the shows, they can earn money even when the shows are syndicated to other networks. The studio-network conglomerates are positioned to make money at every level. I asked Rick to describe how television's

---

* These relationships are forged by ownership. Conglomerates own the networks and the studios—i.e., Universal Media Studios (NBC) is owned by General Electric, ABC Studios (ABC) by the Walt Disney Company, 20th Century Fox Television (Fox) by News Corp., CBS Television Studios (CBS/CW/Showtime) by CBS Corporation, Sony Pictures Television (unaffiliated with a network) by Sony Corp. and Warner Bros. Television (unaffiliated with a network) by Time Warner.

† This is why it is so crucial for advertisers to update how they use the Nielsen rating system, which measures how many households are watching a given show at a given time. Measurements are presented either in relation to total televisions in actual use—the share—or how many households are watching the given program—the rating. The problem is that fewer and fewer people are actually watching their favorite TV shows when the shows are actually programmed on the networks' nightly schedules. Since the advent of TiVo and other digital recording devices, people "binge watch," or just record their favorite shows and watch them when they damn well please. And although Nielsen has developed a measurement for digital video recording—which promises to have a huge impact on television ratings—advertisers have resisted using it as a component in their ad pricing. This has made hot new shows that are widely recorded less valuable than they should be to the networks. This is archaic, unfair and costing the networks tons of cash.

Billion-Dollar Babies amass so much wealth for their studio owners (and showrunners).

RICK: In the television pyramid, the most valuable commodity is a multicamera sitcom that can be played off the network [on local affiliates] at six o'clock and eleven o'clock: *Friends, Malcolm in the Middle, Two and a Half Men,* etc.

LYNDA: What makes them so valuable? That they can be syndicated domestically?

RICK: Yes, and internationally. And they can play on the stations at two different times, early and late night.

LYNDA: Give me examples.

RICK: It's *Big Bang,* it's *Two and a Half Men*—these are each billion-dollar babies. And it goes on for ten to fifteen years. The money just keeps coming in. Listen; when we merged with William Morris, I saw that there was still money coming in from *I Love Lucy* from all around the world. Now, it's not millions of dollars, but it's still hundreds of thousands of dollars coming from a show made over fifty years ago. These shows are still playing all over the world in large and small territories, in tiny territories in Africa and Asia.

LYNDA: Interesting. [Dawn comes to Mohammed.] Those kinds of domestic hits that play in syndication are your billion-dollar babies.

RICK: Not mine, but the studio's. We get our commission.

LYNDA: And the studio gets *all* that money?

RICK: Except what they pay to participants, after they recoup their cost.

LYNDA: Why doesn't ABC buy only from ABC Studios, and CBS from their studios, etc.?

RICK: Because most new shows fail. The networks don't want to take all the risk, so they spread it around by buying from other studio providers.

LYNDA: So how do networks make money?

RICK: Networks derive their revenue from advertising. That's it. And the big disparity, the big fight between broadcast and cable, is that there is a dual revenue stream in cable. In other words, the cable networks—even basic cable, like Lifetime—have dual revenue streams: subscription [per-person subscription fees] and advertising. HBO doesn't make advertising money, but Lifetime, for example, makes money from advertising *and* from subscriptions.

LYNDA: I never felt bad for networks before.

RICK: Don't. The top-rated network—CBS—is taking in a lot of money in advertising now. The advertising market is healthier now than it was after the financial collapse of 2008. And what I find interesting is that despite the proliferation of all the new platforms, from Netflix to YouTube to whatever new digital platforms, traditional television is still a very healthy business.

LYNDA: That's a relief. So I won't throw them a benefit or anything.

DOES THE FUTURE HAVE A FUTURE?

At the height of the Old Abnormal, when the pace was frantic and the toll in the trenches was punishing (but often fun), I wrote about the Hollywood grind in my book *Hello, He Lied*.

> A wild free-for-all has gripped the business like a gang war. The agents who try to impress and sign the stars that open the movies, the studios that need to open their movies, and we producers who need them to make the movies, are all climbing over one another for a start date . . . We are all competing in a frantic frenzy of bidding worse than the hottest auction because a bloated and expensive movie is better than no movie at all. So we fight over the stars and they win until the movie is a disaster and brings down the studio . . . The cycle is swelling to a crescendo no one fully understands. We simply know that the race is on and that we're panting for a pause that will never come . . .

Ten years later, the pause came. It arrived in the form of a brutal recession and market crash colliding with a horribly timed writers' strike. This was the very moment the DVD revenues that allowed this escalating industry-wide fever to peak disappeared.

We knew it was insane, but since we were all abnormal in the first place, caught up in a struggle to succeed in a town built on overnight success and daily doom, we didn't realize we were essentially living in Miami in the middle of the housing boom, buying strips of beachfront property adjacent to unfinished condos sight unseen. We were all in this disaster together, and when the bell rang, there was, unbelievably, no more credit available to our formerly sacrosanct studios for about two years. It was much, much worse than changing into Blue and Red and Yellow teams. It was worse than anything we could have dreamed up in our horror-filled imaginations. It was, in a way, a total realignment of all teams. And everyone was now forced to take the studios' side. Big agents who had been setting $20 million–plus fees for actors saw those actors replaced by less expensive unknowns. The studios set the fees, the mandates and the pace.

Could we have dreamed that the music would stop? That spec sales would disappear for years? That pitches would virtually die out for just as long? That big stars would lose so much cachet? That the way we put pictures together would change from an age-old "outside-in" model (from the talent to the agents to the studios) to an "inside-out" model (from the studios to the agents to the talent)?

When the music stopped, there were new classes of haves and have-nots, just like in the rest of America after the crash, membership of which depended on your immediate situation. Did you have a reliable, ongoing franchise like *Spider-Man*? Were you at a stable studio like Warner Bros., where they were not suspending deals? Was your BFF the head of the studio, like mine was for a time? Did you have a partner who was a movie star who could open movies or an A-list or at least bankable director? Did you have a personal bank account or a hedge fund or a rich and Romney-like Sugar Daddy who could sustain you through the freeze? Or were you a one-off, having to make it on wits alone? If so, you were likely to be standing, not sitting, when the music stopped.

Wherever you were standing or sitting, it was still harder to make pictures because there was less money in the system. I was standing, but my legs were wobbly and in order to survive, I would have to get even stronger than I had believed possible in the old days, when all that was required was to push an increasingly unwieldy boulder up Mt. Studio.

The box office itself, despite the heavy breathing every weekend, has stayed remarkably stable over time. Despite some hugely expensive flops, the 2012 summer box office was up 14 percent at the season's midpoint over 2011, partially due to the phenomenal success of *The Avengers* and *Ted.* But the numbers fell in late summer in the wake of the Aurora, Colorado, shooting in a theater showing *The Dark Knight Rises.* Not only were *TDKR*'s numbers depressed over the course of a few weeks, but analysts saw the numbers go down in general for evening attendance at theaters all over the country.* By the end of the summer of 2012, the box office tally was $4.2 billion, down 2.7 percent from the previous summer, very likely because of the anomalous underperformance of *The Dark Knight Rises* and other evening showings of all movies after the tragedy in Colorado.

However, the industry had a very strong January-to-April period in 2012, so that on aggregate, 2012 surpassed the previous year. *The Hunger Games* is largely responsible for the surge. In general, the year made some studios look very good because of their fresh choices: a new female-based franchise in *The Hunger Games* from Lionsgate and a raunchy original comedy, *Ted,* created by Seth MacFarlane—who is becoming a franchise himself—from Universal.

But what you see over time is that despite some ups and downs, the aggregate summer domestic box office number has risen slowly but steadily over the last ten years. Some years it is down a hundred million, and other years it is up a hundred

---

* The overall loss number for *TDKR* is estimated to be about $10 to $30 million domestically. In fact, industry-wide nighttime business didn't recover from the national trauma until the release of *Taken 2* in mid-October of that year.

million, which means the domestic audience is not abandoning the malls, at least not over the summer.

So why the moaning, agonizing dread every weekend? There are a number of things to be unpacked from these positive trends. The domestic audience is volatile and unpredictable; they seek fresh ideas while the international market seeks familiar. Besides costs due to inflation, the production costs of movies have swelled as they seek to please an international audience that sees bigger as better—and bigger is now $150 to $200 million. Where do the studios go from there? Perhaps more worrisome, the cost of marketing these movies has increased to the point that it keeps the heads of studios up at night; the old formula—half of production costs—is still touted, though it is not thought to be credible. Those numbers are likely to be much higher now, but we don't know for sure because they are never released by the studios. While the business has survived its DVD crisis by opening all these new markets abroad, the cost of doing so is astronomical and rising. Even many successful movies that rack up big numbers will basically only break even, given their production and marketing costs. The question is, can the business survive and sustain itself with its level of *profitability,* as opposed to box office gross?

We have been through an ice age in the entertainment business, and while television has been the beneficiary of the movies' distress, there are recent box office signs that the ice may be receding, leaving the ground rugged and, one hopes, fertile. A remarkable cockroach-like ability to survive has shown itself over the course of the disaster. Will we have gotten smarter? Will we find new ways to get original movies out there without spending hundreds of millions of dollars? Will Hollywood remain a land of massive tentpoles that leave tadpoles gasping for breath and struggling for room to play each week? What will be next?

There are clues that some filmmakers, producers and studios are starting to sort out. Audiences are telling them loudly and clearly what they like and what they don't. Some big IPs are work-ing: *Hunger Games* fever swept the nation for a month in 2012, delivering its young adult audience exactly what it wanted. *The Avengers* (featuring six iconic Marvel superheroes) was an interna-tional phenomenon, now the third-biggest movie of all time, after *Titanic* and *Avatar*.

But some big tentpoles crashed to the ground with a loud thud, even some based on big titles with preawareness: *Green Lantern, Cowboys and Aliens, John Carter** and *Battleship* (based loosely on the Hasbro game) all basically bombed during the writing of this book. It became clear that not all comic-book heroes will do. A cer-tain exhaustion is setting in. The cost of each tentpole picture, even the moderately successful ones, is being minutely analyzed online and in the boardrooms. Perhaps as a result, the 2013 releases had among them the most varied set of films Hollywood had made for years. It was an unusually exciting year, a rebound perhaps—a ten-tative reaction to the drought of original offerings even the studios had been suffering through.

THE DEMISE OF THE CHICK IN HOLLYWOOD HAS BEEN FOILED AGAIN

Fascinating things have occurred, however, almost by mistake. When 2012 began, it was the worst time for female-oriented projects in the business, perhaps in history. The industry's focus on franchises had driven female-starring projects into virtual dormancy. But with the phenomenal success of two franchises written by female authors and featuring female central characters, embraced by both the books' female fan base and two other quad-rants, lower male and upper female, both *Twilight* and *The Hunger*

---

* Shorn of its *of Mars* IP title by marketing.

Games made international stars out of their leads, Kristen Stewart[*] and Jennifer Lawrence, respectively.

Moreover, that success made the idea of a female-based franchise a reality: "We believe there is enormous opportunity for female leads," Lionsgate vice chairman Michael Burns said at a producers' conference in June 2012. His studio had released both films and had recently announced itself to be in "the Jennifer Lawrence business." At the same conference, *Hunger Games* producer and former Disney president Nina Jacobson argued, "The future of Hollywood franchises is female; I think Hollywood was just too stupid to figure that out for a while."

There was disagreement on this from some of the fanboy producers, but that there was a conversation on the subject at all was stunning in and of itself. Jacobson further pointed out that women had become the breadwinners in the family. It was like a political debate. *Go, Nina!* I thought as I read this. A year ago, if anyone had said that the future of Hollywood franchises is female, they might have been sent to the funny farm. It's all a big, open conversation, but at least girls are in it now when they weren't a year ago. That's a sea change, accomplished within a year.

THE STATE OF SEQUELITIS

There are interesting and optimistic clues to be found even in sequelitis: In the near and immediate future, our highly paid studio assembly-line sequel creators can anticipate ferocious creative competition. Now that franchises are built more and more on adaptations of big books that have already been serialized far into the future by talented novelists (as the *Harry Potter* series was in

---

[*] In 2012, Kristen Stewart was the highest-paid female star in the world, with $34 million earned from May 2011 to May 2012, surpassing Angelina Jolie and Sandra Bullock.

the past), the studio factory will be challenged. These sagas, with characters the audience already knows and with complicated story lines, are building audiences' hunger for serialized drama. The more these movies and our excellent television serializations are syndicated around the world, the higher the bar will be raised internationally—as it has been here—for the story quality of our sequels. Special effects and 3D will not dazzle on their own merits forever; novelty wears out in the face of exposure to excellence. Sequels will just have to get better and cost less if they are to survive far into the future.

I got some excellent perspective from Keith Simanton of the terrific Web search engine BoxOfficeMojo.com, who pointed out to me that in the sometimes idealized days of the studio system—1947, for example—the classic *It's a Wonderful Life* was only the seventeenth most successful movie. What was the most successful? *Al Jolson Sings Again,* the sequel to *Al Jolson Sings.* We have always made sequels. If America or the world loves something, we give them more; that has always been the rule. (And it has given us brilliant sequels like *The Godfather II.*) The issue is how many, for how much, and what else?

FAUX IPS

What I find most interesting is what is being bought as I write this in the summer of 2012. The movies coming out now were bought at the height of the New Abnormal IP frenzy, before this intense wave of very expensive tentpoles began to stop making financial sense. By the way, I hate that in Hollywood we call them IPs. Is calling them books somehow diminishing? The IP imprimatur inflates their intrinsic value to the status of games and toys. I think this is pathetic. We have relied on books to fuel our best movies since the beginning of film. We have no more reliable a source for quality material.

In certain places during the frenzy of the New Abnormal, taste and discrimination were abandoned altogether. Titles and game libraries were being bought willy-nilly merely because someone somewhere in the building had heard of them. Warner Bros. already owned the DC catalog and Disney bought Marvel, and everyone else had comic-book envy. In the absence of a catalog (and, of course, any pitches), producers set up brand-new comic books and graphic novels at studios as though they were IPs. They'd find young artists to turn some made-up superhero story into a comic book or graphic novel. *CrushMan! RobotGuy!* (These are my inane versions, obviously.) Then they would sell this new character to a studio as though it had already been sold in your neighborhood comic-book store as an established brand, though the exec was fully in on the gimmick. Buying the story without the fake comic book would have required confidence in the story itself on the part of the buyer.

Now all those scripts are coming in, and the heads of marketing are saying, "Who are these characters? I've never heard of them." The story has to be good on its own in order to succeed, as it had to have been from the outset. You can fool a development executive with pretend marketing, but you can't fool marketing. And you can't fool the audience. The same goes for the new nutty subgenre, the mash-up: *Cowboys and Aliens* (Seriously, Tonto, there's someone sucking your blood!); *Abraham Lincoln: Vampire Hunter*.

They may make fun books, but when you have to look at the mash-up on a huge screen, I contend that it looks silly. Hey, what is that giant-squid alien doing with that cowboy? There's our president, Abe Lincoln, who emancipated the slaves, chasing down vampires. It sounds like a huge idea in a pitch room because it sounds fresh; people haven't heard it before. But there is a reason no one has heard of it: It's ridiculous. (And it flopped, all around the world.)

I think this faux-IP/mash-up madness expresses the height of the delirium of post-Contraction preawareness terror on the part of producers and execs. It is not about the doughnut—i.e., the story; it is about the hole—i.e., trying to invent awareness of the idea. These products are not to be confused with original movies, as they are one-sheet-based efforts. Awareness is either intrinsic—for example, with Kleenex, Snow White, Jell-O, Spider-Man, Superman, Batman; you grew up with it—or marketing creates it. It's not the job of the writer-producer. Our job is the story.

WHAT'S NEXT, PAPA HEGEL?

When I was an undergraduate, I fell under the thrall of nineteenth-century German philosopher Georg Wilhelm Friedrich Hegel, who thought that the cycle of history was driven by what he called the dialectic. Most people who fall under Hegel's spell abandon this grand system shortly thereafter, as it is widely thought to be incoherent (he's a horrible writer) by academics other than Marxists, but I see the dialectic stubbornly at work in the movie business.

In dialectical movement, a thesis/antithesis situation occurs. For example, Thesis A: The DVD market collapses due to piracy, and our profit cushion collapses. In reaction, there is Antithesis B: We pursue international markets and revenue with mad vigor, making bigger and bigger movies (including movies based on undeserving properties), driving up costs beyond reason and squeezing other domestically oriented and original movies out of the market, creating occasional hits but many more expensive flops and movies that barely break even because of the costs of production and marketing. Then synthesis of A and B occurs, equaling C: The failures create more careful discernment as to what should and should not be made; a new fiscal model is born that may allow for more originals; new ideas about what works in both domestic and international markets emerge.

We are now seeing producers, writers and studios figure out the synthesis of the wild reactions to the Great Contraction. Some promising signs are emerging, like lichens after a forest fire. *Green Lantern* producer Donald De Line returned to Paramount (from whence he had been fired) to make an edgy $27 million heist movie called *Pain & Gain* with *Transformers* director Michael Bay, starring Mark Wahlberg. This move is very post–New Abnormal. Trust me when I say that all of the studio heads had seen the overseas grosses on *The Best Exotic Marigold Hotel* ($110 million) before it opened wide here with an Oscar campaign. They noted that it was not geared to Mud Pies but to the upper, upper, upper quadrant, who are alive, actually, and going out to the theater. There are movies that can be made by studios for the domestic audience that will appeal to the international audience as well, and that aren't sequels or based on games or previously known characters.

I was simultaneously wild with jealousy and inspired when I read of Peter Chernin's new comedy about two female cops, created by hilarious *Parks and Recreation* writer Katie Dippold, starring Sandra Bullock and Melissa McCarthy. It's an original script, written by a TV writer. Sandy is huge overseas, and Melissa has that big *Bridesmaids* bump. All of the lessons about making a female comedy that can play here and abroad are assembled in this package. That's thinking. It's not brain surgery, it's not *Jules and Jim,* but it's using what we've learned to create comedy, which at the beginning of the cycle looked endangered. That's why the business is not cyclical but dialectical. Because as new movies open up new territories to new genres and stars that hadn't performed internationally before, the path is cleared for more new stars and movies to open overseas. Comedies like *The Hangover* and *Bridesmaids* and now *Family Guy* auteur Seth MacFarlane's *Ted*—the phenomenally popular 2012 comedy about a man, his girlfriend and his foul-mouthed talking teddy bear that surpassed half a billion dollars gross worldwide—are opening doors for a multitude of stars who are now known internationally. Our dumb jokes are starting to travel.

The studios' notion of preawareness is starting to evolve as well. Classic tales from the Bible, an old Hollywood staple, are being pursued as if the Bible were a recently discovered trove of Marvel comic books. Spielberg is flirting with a Moses epic, Warner is doing *Pontius Pilate,* Darren Aronofsky (*Black Swan*) is directing *Noah* and *Showgirls* and *Basic Instinct* director Paul Verhoeven is attempting another Jesus epic, written by *Pulp Fiction* scripter Roger Avary. Recognizable titles are single-named things, be they caped crusaders or real ones. At least some grown-ups will want to see these heroes take on the Bible's built-in bad guys. And it should play in Peoria.

Maybe it means there is a glimmer of possibility that an aperture is opening that was once thought permanently closed. In October 2011, more speculative scripts were sold to the studios than in the previous five years. Competitive pitches sold this year more than twice! (This used to happen every week.) This is either a Really Big Thing, the start of another pendulum swing, or an anomaly. Let's see how many of these scripts get made. It is still too early to tell. There are female franchises. But female comedies? One gauge will be when I try to package my next chick flick and pretend it's not a romantic comedy, a genre that is temporarily dormant or dead. We will see. So much has changed in a year that the actresses agents used to want for the project will be off their list, and they will go after Jennifer Lawrence, whom the studios never would have considered a year ago. She will be unavailable.

Right now, as I finish this book, my life seems more cyclical than dialectical. Have I moved forward from where I was when I finished my last book, more than ten years ago? Or have I made a gigantic loop? Kierkegaard said that trying to live your life by

Hegel was like trying to get around Copenhagen with a map of Denmark. So it's hard to tell.

At the time, in 1998, I was uncertain about the fate of *Contact* and was considering a directing debut. Now, here I am, again looking into a black box when it comes to the fate of my most important features, and again considering a directing debut. How is that possible? It seems like it all took place in another universe—far, far away, as Luke Skywalker would say. *Plus ça change, plus c'est la même chose.*

A painful drama was playing out as I finished that book, which I'd wanted to resolve for the ending, as well as for my general state of mind. I had been working on *Contact* for twelve years on and off, and was close to being able to announce that George Miller would direct and give out our long-delayed start date. But then my beloved director got himself summarily removed from the picture by refusing to pick a release date. Before you could say Christmas, 1999 (the date Warner Bros. wanted him to commit to), Bob Zemeckis was at the helm, and I was in despair. Yes, it would eventually be made brilliantly; and yes, I would be executive producer, and all my hard work on the script would be preserved; but that all came long after.

As for my directing, that went nowhere. No one optioned the wonderful Meg Wolitzer novel *Friends for Life* that I wanted to direct. It was by the same author whose first novel, *This Is Your Life,* had been adapted by Nora Ephron for her feature debut, which I had produced. I had Nora's full support; she would executive produce. But the movie world was much less friendly toward female comedies then than it is now, to say nothing of female directing debuts. I just dropped the whole idea and concentrated on producing movies.

I am currently developing a romantic comedy, the now moribund genre that was my former bread and butter, with my two favorite tadpole producers, Tatiana Kelly and Jim Young—the producers who made five movies in 2011 and got one into Sundance and bought by CBS Films. They've optioned a popular British novel and want to make a traditional, if offbeat, romantic comedy on a microbudget. I was their girl. Oly introduced us. The script had potential; the idea was charming.

Now, every time I read a new draft, I hear Nora from over my shoulder: "It doesn't matter if it's commercial. It doesn't matter if it's a hit. It has to be good. You have to be proud of it." We were so in love with *This Is My Life*. It didn't matter that it made about $4.98 at the box office; we can watch it now and still be happy with it. Nora could have cast a big star, but she chose Julie Kavner—of Marge Simpson fame—because she was funny, and because she wouldn't have to spend her whole debut worrying about a diva's demands as she learned to direct, even if it might have opened the movie to bigger numbers.

This Is My Life was about being a career mom—a story we both lived, with our sons on set and in the film (trees 1, 2 and 3 in a school play scene). Nothing in the movie I am going to direct yet has the kind of essential truths that movie had. And the one thing I am sensing from the dialectic in the market zeitgeist is that women's movies have to change. They have to get messier—no auto-resolves in the third act, as this one currently has—and realer, as Nora's was twenty-five years ago. I can't do this movie until it registers in the right key for this next generation of romantic comedies. I am going to have to persuade my indie producers, who hired me because I was mainstream, to make this movie more indie.

As in 1998, my biggest feature is still in flux. Who knows when it will be resolved? Thank heaven for television, where there's always action, or about to be action. Suddenly I realized that my evolution into a television producer, having learned a new part of the business at the wobbliest moment of my feature career, is exactly what makes my life not cynical but dialectical. I moved into a new medium, which is sending Rachel and me to Montreal with just enough money to eat poutine and make a potentially terrifying and really cool science-fiction series. Series breed series, and action breeds action. So who knows where we go from here. All we know is that box Rachel keeps packed for location, full of outerware and extra skin product, is finally going somewhere! We are scouting, casting, perhaps not the movie we meant to be making, but a very long series of little movies nonetheless. Recognizing that the movie business was the entertainment business that wasn't moving fast enough to fill my creative and financial coffers was an impetus to grow, and that has taken me and so many of my colleagues into a larger world. Denmark, not Copenhagen.

So I may not have a third-act movie victory to report right now. But the great news about series television is there is no third-act resolve. There's always another episode, a shot for another season. I have found the escape velocity from the doom of the $100 million start-up machine. There are things to do between tentpoles. I must say I've seen some intrepid, human, non-franchise-controlling feature producers keep it going during the New Abnormal, and hats off to them. But not this control freak. This one has had to learn patience, ingenuity, cordiality and to take on multiple tasks in other media in order to keep her from utterly losing her mind during the wait for the big moments to happen. The same thing goes for picking a director; one cannot rush the moments of decision, because they only come when they come.

But as I finish this book there is something that feels very different from ten years ago, and it's not just the hard truths of the New Abnormal. I have gotten a strong sense of what is going on in this mad, mad, mad, mad world. All the time I have been writing, I have also been working my "buck slip"—a piece of rectangular stationery that lists all of the projects that a producer has in inventory. I've been keeping alive the ideas and scripts I thought could survive through the rough patches of the New Abnormal, and trying to drive those films forward. It was starting to look like maybe one or two might get made, now that the market was taking a positive turn. Hopefully it will happen in my lifetime, as I like to say. Maybe next year it will be a feature. Two are close. The box packed at the office with our essentials is now stamped CANADA.

Woman plans and God laughs. But things look good. Somehow next year feels like the one I've been planning for (though I say this every year). Frankly, Crazy Pollyanna is the only tenable posture you can maintain in this business, otherwise you just give up or give in. I always say attrition kills more producers, directors, writers and agents than combat.

When Oscar Season 2012 came along, it was a 180-degree turn to the studios from the indie-driven year before. There was a fancy offering from almost every studio that fit the Venn diagram of potential commercial plus Academy Award quality. Sony had Kathryn Bigelow's controversial film about the hunt for Osama bin Laden, *Zero Dark Thirty;* Warner Bros. had Ben Affleck's *Argo* and Christopher Nolan's *The Dark Knight Rises;* Universal had the adaptation of the evergreen theatrical musical *Les Misérables;* MGM had Sam Mendes's smash James Bond offering, *Skyfall;* Paramount had Robert Zemeckis's redemptive *Flight;* Fox had Ang Lee's adaptation of *Life of Pi;* and Disney/DreamWorks had Spielberg's *Lincoln.* That's literally one for each. Amazing.

That's a lot of quick reaction to a market that is indicating its desire for more original and adult fare. I think the studios are responding to the unexpectedly successful runs of the hit Academy Award winners of recent years (*The King's Speech, The Social Network, Moneyball, The Help*). What they are doing is very smart: They are exploiting their best assets—director relationships and access to good material—in service of both the audience and the bottom line. The good news about attention-deficit-disorder executives with bouncing knees is that they don't sit still very long in the face of compelling counterevidence. Will they act on the right principles this year? The studios had a lousy summer in 2012, but a great spring and fall, and the biggest Christmas ever. Is this rebound the reaction to the great mistakes made after the Great Contraction? What will that mean for 2013's summer tentpoles?

Ah, Hamlet, that is the question. We cannot judge the business by what happens during Oscar Season. It's like judging your own work behavior only by the times your boss is in the room.

THE FUTURE OF THE BIZ

Is God laughing at the movie business? With all our bad karma and bad-faith deals, comparing what we do to brain surgery and war, is it possible we have so disgusted God that He decided to test us like Job? To make all of the money grabbers suddenly find they were in a business that couldn't make money? Or in which, as my grandmother used to say, "you couldn't make a living, you could only get rich"? Is there still a business in the business, as Oly would say, or a future in the business that we have traditionally, and now horribly, drawn our children into?

I wanted to talk with Michael Lynton, chairman of Sony Pictures. I knew he would have fascinating insights into where we were headed. A politically and culturally active member of the L.A. community, Lynton, like Peter Chernin, came out of publishing in New York, and his intellectual reach is wide and rich. I sat down with him, a very modest man with a bare yet elegant office in the Irving Thalberg Building, where he and his partner, Amy Pascal, work.

"Are the glory days gone?" I asked him. "The days when we had a cushion that allowed us to make movies in the middle, that weren't either tentpoles or tadpoles?"

He was quick to reply. "There was so much money swilling around in the system in 2006 and 2007, when you could afford to make enormous mistakes because of the safety net of the DVD business. That gave the false illusion that you could get by."

The good old days as false illusion, I thought sadly.

"I'm a little reminded," he went on, "in a funny sort of way, of the Netherlands." Lynton was born in Holland. "In the seventies, when we had offshore oil, we had eighteen percent unemployment. But we didn't have to fix what was structurally wrong with the economy, because we had so much money coming in from something that cost so little to produce, we could afford all these social services."

I said, "Like Norway."

"Norway is a good case in point," he continued. "You didn't really have to have underneath it all an economy that was actually functioning. In a funny sort of way, I don't think this is an unhealthy thing. I think it's going to get everybody's head straight as to what things probably *should* cost. You're more experienced than I am at making movies, at how much it *should* cost to produce a movie."

Less than they are making them for, that's for sure, I thought.

"I'm Jewish," he said. "But I come from a Calvinist Dutch background, and my basic feeling about things is that people perform better when there's less. I'm saying something that's not new, but we see it in our everyday life. The one thing human beings do not do well with is abundance."

"They go cuckoo," I said.

"It's self-destructive," he added. "We eat too much when there's too much food in front of us, we drink too much when there's too much liquor in front of us, we spend too much when there's too much money in front of us. Abundance is simply something that we are not genetically geared for." He was bringing this around to a philosophy for his studio. "But there's incredible ingenuity and innovation available to people when all of a sudden you say to them, 'Here's a number. What can you do?'"

I said, "They do better."

I'd lived it with Terry Gilliam on *The Fisher King,* who, while working under the constraints of a limited budget for the first time, did some of the finest work of his career. Unlimited budgets make for a lack of precise decision-making. Necessity is the mother of invention, and all that.

"So that's how you and Amy green-light the tough ones like *Moneyball?*" Amy worked on *Moneyball* for seven years before it was green-lit. Because baseball is inherently American and the business was becoming increasingly internationally oriented, she had to keep improving the script and modeling the budget downward while holding on to its most important element, its star, Brad Pitt. She had to cut the budget without compromising the quality of the picture or she could lose him, and thus the chance of making the film, a character piece that had to attract more than just baseball fans.

"One of the things that's brilliant about Amy is that she has a remarkable ability to want to change who she is and how she does business, and the minute she spotted the change in the world order, she was responsive to that."

"It's not easy to have come into the business when Amy and I did," I said, "and then have to totally change the way you work. The paradigm shifted in the middle of her reign."

"That is what gives Amy longevity," he said.

"So is it going to get better, this contraction?" I asked. "Like the bouncing universe, will it contract and then expand again?" I felt like I was asking Stephen Hawking about the fate of it all.

Michael answered, "Will we look back and say, 'Oh my goodness, 2006 to 2007 was a glory moment for the movie industry, when there was more money in the industry than there ever was before or after'?"

"Or will ever be?"

"Yes, probably," he answered, not sadly. "Those years may look a little bit in retrospect like the movie industry probably looked in the thirties, when there was no competition, there was no television and you could churn out . . . God knows how many movies they were churning out in 1930; you could probably tell me thirty-nine. There was always a new double feature in the theaters, and everybody was going to the movies every week. I have no doubt that that time will not be seen again."

I felt glum, yet Michael looked fine and went right on. "I think there's going to be plenty of money in the system from all these new avenues we haven't yet discovered to keep making movies. If we say we're currently all making around twenty, then it's probably going to be closer to fifteen or sixteen, which isn't a bad thing. It means that the weekends get less crowded and movies get to live longer in the movie theaters. I think everything is going to be more modest in terms of how movies are made. I think we all, executives included, will live a little bit more modestly, which is not a bad thing either. I have every confidence that this is going to get itself figured out."

The thought of the movie biz princes living modestly almost made me giggle. Oh, screw it, who cared how everyone else lived as long as good movies got made. So I asked him the big question.

"And what of all these sequels and superheroes and the like? Will they conquer all?"

"I think at a certain point," he laughed, "enough is enough. Throwing fireballs and running around in tights." And then he added, "Except Spider-Man, of course." From his mouth to God's ears.

Of course in this case, God is the audience, despite what Adorno might say. He didn't know about the Internet. Marketing may try to tell you what you want to see, but if you hear it's a stinker, you'll refuse to go. That has become clear. The audience has made the specialty market flourish like mad this year, going to little tadpoles like Wes Anderson's *Moonrise Kingdom*—a wonderfully reviewed tadpole about two awkward twelve-year-olds who run away together—and *The Best Exotic Marigold Hotel,* about a trip to India gone wonderfully awry, starring Dev Patel (from *Slumdog Millionaire*), Judi Dench, Tom Wilkinson and Maggie Smith. *Marigold* has made over $117 million worldwide and cost only $10 million pre-Oscars, without any prior awareness and marketing outside of word of mouth. The audience crowned the Oscar winner about the stuttering king, *The King's Speech.* It helped *The Help*—based on a book about black domestic workers in the South in the sixties and their white teen champion—become the fifth most profitable movie vis-à-vis budget to box office of 2011. These successful tadpoles make a case to the studios—and not just to their classics divisions—about their profitability and reinforce the notion of the "audience's confounding craving for something different."

At times like these—when there is some uncertainty as to what movies to make—the industry can be a mirror of the audience's taste, and the best creative execs are receptive to the wishes of the most fervent moviegoers out there. If we can reduce the costs of marketing these movies, more can be made. Perhaps the Internet, our piratical nemesis, our entrepreneurial enemy in the first round of our failed congressional regulations, ultimately holds the answer to our hard marketing-cost issues. As online campaigns become more and more effective, perhaps they can help not just the movie's fan base but also the larger general base for opening weekends. And perhaps we can be part of the solution to their unknown advertising capabilities. He that taketh away sometimes giveth back.

VIOLENT PHASE TRANSITIONS: THE ONLY WAY HOLLYWOOD IS UNLIKE HELL AND MORE LIKE THE HEAVENS

In astrophysics, there are fascinating phenomena called violent phase transitions, wherein things hardly change at all for eons—literally hundreds of millions of years—and then all of a sudden everything changes at once. Of course, unseen gravitational forces have been building toward that phase change, gases have been swirling faster and faster for ages, dust particles have been condensing, but not in ways anyone would notice (if there were anyone to look). But all that slow swirling movement coalesces in an unexpected moment into a grand celestial catastrophe of creation and destruction. Thus it is in the movie business. Things just go their nutty, merry way for years, unchanging, until we get hit by an asteroid like the DVD collapse, and the dense suck of technological change creates huge gravitational forces that condense and transform and reconstitute all matter in their wake. Gigantic implosions occur, destroying old models. Movie stars open movies! Let's sell a script this weekend! Chick flicks! Disney buys X in competitive bidding! Pitches are dead. Drama is dead. You can't sell anything anymore! Spec market over . . . until nothing familiar is left.

Seemingly at random, new explosions and implosions create new matter. In the movie business, with our violent phase transitions, old structures and models are destroyed, but it is ever so clear that new models always evolve to take their place. A new structure of the universe is emerging, barely visible in its outlines but presenting itself on the horizon daily and expanding like the universe.

This new phase of the universe is called "narrowcasting." Tadpoles are the narrowcasts of the movie business. They have a specific targeted audience, like *The Best Exotic Marigold Hotel,* yet they can break out to a wide audience if they work in narrowcast (a tiny release, in a film's case, that then goes into wider release as word spreads, or after an Oscar campaign, as in *The King's Speech* and many others). Anyone can make a movie and get it distributed somewhere online if not in theaters. New theatrical distributors and online distributors are born every day, like stars in a stellar nursery. Distribution and production were the bottlenecks through which the studios used to control moviemaking. Movies were expensive, and only studios had the funds for production. Distribution was limited and controlled by the studios, and nearly impossible for an outsider to penetrate. Digital moviemaking ended this bottleneck in a few milliseconds for both production and now online distribution, where a movie can be discovered by anyone, anywhere.

Soon people will stop looking to their local mall—like teens already have—and go instead to their computer or home entertainment system to find a new movie or television series they've just heard about. With fewer movies, the best of these will eventually make it to the mall too. Instead of relying on studios to make the "show" pieces of the show-business equation, we will increasingly see programming from brand-new and aggressive content providers, trying to establish themselves by trolling the edges and inlets of pop culture. And they have an audience already.

Kids don't bring TVs to college anymore; they bring their tablets or a computer. They are watching twenty-two hours of television a week online. They will likely never return to the malls in the numbers that the industry once relied upon for openings. But they are finding new shows on the Web, created for them by one another. YouTube is spending $100 million on programming to reach them digitally via the traditional content providers—i.e., former film producers. The best ones are smart enough to know or have young enough kids to tell them where to go on Twitter or YouTube or WhoKnowsWhereElse.com to find the online teen stars and sites like Cheezburger (which began life as a site for funny cat videos) and create programming with them. Amazon,

Hulu, Netflix, Funny or Die, Machinima and dozens of start-ups are trolling different niche demographics to satisfy appetites unmet by traditional programmers. Their aim? To burn brightly enough to break through the cacophony of new voices and establish their venues in the pantheon of premier content providers while making new media stars of them and their servers.

What does Papa Hegel have to say about all this? That it's all gravity. All that smallness will give way to bigness: The smaller planetoids will crash into each other and merge; larger planets and even stars will consume them until denser, larger clusters of matter coalesce into powerful galaxies—i.e., media conglomerates again. This is called aggregation. Some massive servers will become Amazonian, perhaps eating up media giants, the way AOL once ate Time Warner. Other, smaller providers will be devoured whole and become healthy subdivisions of entertainment corporations. Some will be lost in the Darwinian power struggle for galactic survival. But the synthesis of this wild and woolly narrowcasting universe and our familiar broadcasting one will be very different from what we feared would happen when we all were suffering from the worst effects of Tinseltown's sequilitis. For the audience, the writers and the producers alike, there will be many more alternatives to watch, write and produce than when the New Abnormal began to resist fresh ideas.

Audience members will suddenly be able to find things so suited to their idiosyncratic tastes that it will be as if they had placed an order on a menu. From country to country, as the Net blurs all boundaries, we will learn each other's jokes and love stories—without 3D or special effects. Soon Net films and series will be made and made better by a generation that learned the alphabet on an iPad. And this generation, brought up by the best four-quadrant movies ever, movies like *The Lion King, Toy Story, Madagascar, WALL-E* and *Brave*—many made by Pixar, some musicals, all original, requiring years to develop—will have a lot to say about what they need as teens, weaned as they were on the best of the best.

The industry will not and should not give up on getting this generation into the malls as they did the last one, before losing it to the lure of the Net's delights. The movie business has a huge job ahead of retooling itself creatively for the new domestic market to come, and the less innocent international market of the future. Necessity is the mother of invention, and all that. There is a gigantic market of technologically sophisticated media juniors out there with the means of production and distribution already in their hands. They will be trolling the Web for media-content providers, with each wondering about the other in equal measure, "Whattya got? Whattya got?"

THE NEWS OF OUR DEATH HAS BEEN GREATLY EXAGGERATED

The unlikely finale to the saga of Hollywood's now infamous summer of 2013 could be summed up by one of my mother's favorite quotes from Mark Twain: "The news of my death has been greatly exaggerated." It would take a wise man like him to unravel the conundrum that was the controversial year this book came out. Soon after its release (by fortuitous coincidence, as it turned out, for the book tour), five studio tentpoles flopped and Steven Spielberg pronounced the studio model on the precipice of doom. During a USC conference, he told a stunned audience, "I think . . . an implosion in the film industry is inevitable, whereby a half dozen or so $250 million movies flop at the box office and alter the industry forever."

Also present was George Lucas, who agreed. This declaration, made by the nearly godlike sages who virtually invented the blockbuster, while the industry was in the wake of sequential mega-flops, brought on an international watch for the imminent collapse of the American studio system. There was certainly a lot to talk about!

However, by the time the full year's accounting was tabulated, 2013 had squeaked by 2012 as the biggest in history. This was thanks to ever-rising ticket prices and wildly successful pre-established franchises. Again, all the moaning and keening led to a wash. The huge winners were: *The Hobbit: The Desolation of Smaug* (on its penultimate installment), *Fast & Furious 6* (whose gorgeous star, God and speed took from us while shooting *Fast &*

Furious 7), *Iron Man 3*, *Man Of Steel* and the sequels to *Despicable Me* and *The Hunger Games*, and even the prequel to *The Wizard of Oz*, *Oz the Great and Powerful*. The performances of these movies were so dominant domestically and internationally that most of the studios could absorb the losses of August 2013. The lesson of August is a harder story, in that all the original tentpoles bombed.

So it was the best of times and the worst of times, as the known entities soared across the world while the studios' efforts to launch new franchises in the summer (the primary business objective of the New Abnormal) failed miserably.

It was the bombs that sounded the loudest. The cacophony drowned out any other news the summer also brought: comedy was alive; *The Heat* was over-performing with its female leads as cops. The audience was dying to laugh, but everyone just wanted to talk flops.

The summer's bummer sounded alarms around the world. Everywhere I went and everyone I spoke with asked if the sky was falling. Had the studios lost their touch? Why did *The Lone Ranger* fail? Would Disney collapse? In fact, Disney had its best year ever at $3 billion in profits with *Iron Man 3*, *Monsters University* (the prequel to the 2001 *Monsters, Inc.*) and even *Oz the Great and Powerful*. Later that year, it blasted its winter rivals with the phenomenally successful *Frozen*, one of the only original hits of the year to be clearly sequelizable. A preteen feminist tale warning girls off falling for the first lad/cad who comes a courting, this breakthrough hit was the Christmas gift that kept on giving. A billion-dollar baby by March, *Frozen* is now the biggest-grossing animated movie of all time. Because of this success, Disney could handle the $160 million *Lone Ranger* write-off and the departure of Jerry Bruckheimer back to Paramount.

Sony's two summer flops led to the interference of a Wall Street mogul interloper who tried to destabilize the administration. He was asking for more "Spidey-type" tent-poles. They were responsible for two of the five flops that summer, and this investor had decided that someone had to pay. The Sony bosses in Japan resisted his entreaties and heads were saved. Sony agreed to invest more in TV, cut their overhead, and they are clearly looking for tentpole-type personnel to bring to the lot, along with more ways to exploit Spidey. In the meantime, Sony had a great November of profitable original films for Oscar time, like *Captain Phillips* ($216 million worldwide so far) and *American Hustle* ($127 million domestically and going strong at Oscar time). It also reduced the number of movies it would make in its summer 2014 season. Is this good? Who knows? Who needs Wall Street people—who embody the saying "a little bit of info is a dangerous thing"—telling studios what to make? That is not good, for sure.

Universal survived its flops, *47 Ronin* (Christmas) and *R.I.P.D.* (summer), via *Fast & Furious 6*, some successful comedies, and its incredibly profitable *Despicable Me 2* ($76 million to produce), but they ended up changing their entire company anyway. Who won? Who lost? Who made what? Who knows?

Paramount, my one time paramour, went from top in market share (the portion of the entire market controlled by a single studio) when I wrote this book, to last in market share as I write this epilogue in 2013. This is partly a result of Paramount releasing fewer movies. Now it's touting a new strategy of profitability: earnings vs. expenditures, the former strategy of the Dolgen-Lansing administration it boldly replaced. The more things change, the more they stay the same.

Warner Bros. was number one in market share with *Gravity*, the *Hobbit* trilogy, *The Great Gatsby*, *The Hangover Part III* and *Man of Steel*. Regardless, there was a Vesuvian-scale eruption there, long brewing at the famously stable studio, a power struggle for the chairman spot long held by CEO Barry Meyer. The top contenders: Bruce Rosenblum, the head of its wildly successful television division; Jeff Rabinov, the head of its wildly successful movie division; and Kevin Tsujihara, 17-year veteran of the studio, who worked his way up to become head of its forward thinking home entertainment division, which, significantly, includes digital.

Above them, in a powerful and smarting blow to the powers that were—and as a prime example of the direction the movie business is traveling (discussed in the last chapter)—is the chairman, Kevin Tsujihara, who was head of the digital division. Digital is where the money is being mined in the future of the coalescing business.

As for China, there's always a mogul who represents the cutting edge of a particular space, and without a doubt, the man of the year for "the China space" was Wang Jianlin of the Dalian Wanda Group. A real estate mogul, who the state encourages as a mega-developer of mega-condo complexes, he is also the owner of the largest movie chain in China—and that's major real estate! In 2012, he bought the US distributor AMC Entertainment (not the cable net) for $2.6 billion and immediately became a vital international player. This year, he feted a who's who of Hollywood—including Leonardo DiCaprio, Harvey Weinstein, John Travolta, Nicole Kidman, and other on- and offscreen luminaries of his $8.2 billion Qingdao Oriental Movie Metropolis complex—to hear the facility's plans to fill out the complex's 10,000 square meters with studios, a film museum, movie theaters, resort hotels, and other "cultural tourism" projects.

This fantabulous Chinese mogul also announced his plan to bring in over fifty domestic production companies to the complex in order to make one hundred films and TV shows per year, with another thirty foreign movies expected to be made in China. This sent everyone into a tizzy. He then unveiled plans for another multibillion-dollar studio complex to rival Disney China near Shanghai. The American hotshots were duly dazzled. He had moxie, money and connections on high. Tinseltown emissaries got on board. "The future of the development of the world film market is right here in China," the company announced in a statement. Then, for good measure, Wanda donated $20 million to the Academy of Motion Picture Arts and Sciences for its film museum, with the stipulation that the name Wanda appear on the building somewhere. What? No parking space?

Can they buy, bully or party their way in? Do they want all the way in? The irony is that this year indigenous Chinese films won seven of the ten top spots in the Chinese market (second largest in the world and growing fast). Local markets open and tastes change as the provincials want local stories. A romantic comedy and a thriller, both suited to Chinese sensibilities, beat our entries (those that made the tight quota that is). Only *Iron Man 3*, *Gravity* and *Pacific Rim* broke the list. Is this bad for those US producers trying so hard to get co-productions off the ground? Ironically, no. If the Chinese succeed in harvesting their own product, they might let more of ours in, or stop blacklisting the best dates for our biggest entries. *Despicable Me 2* will reach China six months after its domestic release. The wolves are at each other's doorsteps, smiling, trying to do business. Even so, 2013 was—according to DMG's Dan Mintz, the most successful American player in the co-production scene—"a game-changer . . . It's like those time-lapse movies of glaciers melting over 100,000 years."

Meanwhile, TV is in a constant state of shuffle and change. Executives at networks are threatening to end seasons and buy year-round like the cable networks do. This hasn't happened yet but will at any moment, threatening to eviscerate the one solid piece of knowledge I have gleaned. Is this good? I have no idea. It is exciting and scary.

Breaking Bad went off the air to the sound of a nation addicted going cold turkey. What will take its place? I was gutted when ABC, my go-to network for fun on the *Revenge* and Shonda Rhimes (*Scandal*) front, bought and promoted *Agents of S.H.I.E.L.D.* from Marvel as its biggest show last season. "Oh my God," I thought. "The networks are turning into the studios looking for pre-awareness." I considered jumping into Silver Lake next to my house but reconsidered and watched. I thought it would be very hard for even Joss Whedon to deliver Marvel movie-level effects and expectations on a weekly TV schedule, especially given how busy he is making the *Avengers* sequel. But it was *Blacklist* on NBC—a mild take on

Silence of the Lambs, yet a classic procedural—that became the hit of the season. "What movies can I remake?" I asked myself in a moment of extreme lack of originality. "One of my own," I answered! And now Ridley Scott and I are finally going to make *Hot Zone*— the movie I was unable to make for fifteen years as a feature—into a limited series, the new, hot term for a miniseries. A miniseries can lead to what we call a "back door" series, a limited effort that if wildly successful, could lead to a regular series.

What's on Amazon? Who knows? What will happen this year on Netflix's fabulous series *Orange Is the New Black*? *House of Cards*? What new treats do Showtime and HBO have in store? Netflix has such audacity and money that during our precious November this year it trumped ABC foursquare and ordered a four series deal with Marvel, including properties Daredevil, Luke Cage, Jessica Jones, and Iron Fist. I didn't even know Marvel had that many available titles. Did Disney let them go? Were they hiding in a vault or under a mushroom on some faraway planet? How many more are there? Will this dilute the Marvel brand? Will Netflix be able to produce weekly episodes of feature-level quality? Will no one care? Will they give these four series Fincher's vast budget for *House of Cards*? Sheesh. Everything is merging again and losing its distinct flavor. Netflix, I thought I knew thee.

Nextino. The zeitgeist is ticking away more quickly these days, and you have to stop binge watching for a minute to figure out what to sell to whom.

Oh, and the weirdest thing: Nikki Finke got herself fired from the website she invented for constantly fighting with her boss, Jay Penske. This is no fun for anyone except her rival Sharon Waxman, who first posted it. Furthermore, now there are no more comments on the no-longer-snarky *Deadline* website. No one cares. There are no more cowering executives afraid to be outed for being mean-phone-throwers or for lesser crimes. Now there are no scoops. No sides being divided along class lines, or above or below lines. Now in our reporting there is only the sound of one hand clapping: the publicity department's.

In the wake of the fascinating saga of 2013, let's not bury the lede. The audience spoke in August and told the studios what it did *not* want to see. It said: *I am weary of seeing the same cities blown up, the lack of interesting human stories, and the overly familiar plotlines and set pieces I get instead of thoughtful twists and turns. Make movies for me or I won't go. I'd rather laugh, and you've exhausted me with sameness.* (This is just how philosopher Theodore Adorno predicted the audience would feel in scene four of my book!) The audience said: *Give me something I've never seen. Wow me. I don't want this over-produced predictable noise anymore.* How the studios will process this information remains to be seen. They are likely to be more careful with anything other than comedies and the biggest properties.

After that telling and consequential summer, October brought the first great original blockbuster: *Gravity*, with George Clooney and Sandra Bullock in a real space adventure. It had exactly what the audience craved: an experience it had never had. It orbited out of the stratosphere and into blockbuster territory. It wasn't even trying to be a franchise, just a movie. But it invented a technology for its story that you had to go to the movies to see, and it was even better in 3D or IMAX. Then came November.

We will always have November; the month the Academy gave us when it extended its former five Best Picture nominations to ten. At five, a studio's best fare rarely made the cut and the indies always beat them out for Best Picture. It's very nerve wracking for a studio head to be at the Oscars all dressed up with no Best Picture nominations for your whole lot. And then, even if you have one, you're likely to lose to some tiny indie. So (as I see it, anyway) the Academy expanded the category to ten nominations and gave the studios a vested interest to get in the game. Even a nomination is worth millions in free advertising and increased box office sales! This in turn has given us a reliable month of originals when the summer—and more often the rest of the year—is an exercise in sequels. I sometimes think that the best November movies could not generate a sequel even if they were offered a green light, three thousand theaters and an unlimited budget. *American Hustle 2? 24 Years a Slave? Nebraska Again? Anti-Gravity?* No, actually, that works.

The ultimate test of the meaning of the catastrophic summer of 2013—and the fate of the franchise model—will be summer 2015. There will be no expensive originals in this battle of the super-duper franchises taking form now—no one will make that mistake for a long time. Instead, the studio's biggest all-time pre-awareness players will take each other on each weekend from May to August. Lining up with these components will be *Batman* vs. *Superman* vs. *The Avengers* vs. *Fast & Furious 7* vs. *The Terminator* vs. *Fantastic Four 3D* vs. *The Hunger Games: Mockingjay, Part 2* vs. *Star Wars* vs. *Mission Impossible* vs. *James Bond*. And this is only a partial list. Our movie solar system will get so dense with giant planets in the summer of 2015 that they can't help but crash into each other. Which will survive the initial weekend head-on orbit? Which will crash into smithereens, obliterating another launch?

It seems obvious that the movies that come out in May will have the best chance given our history of sequel fatigue. But will we be immune to sequel fatigue if that sequel is *Star Wars* or *James Bond*? Nonetheless, there will be a lot of jockeying, arm twisting and racing to post for those early slots.

Will this be the biggest summer of all time or will it be a late Rome–like disaster? How can that many movies, on three thousand screens each weekend, hold them and still make room for the blockbuster on the way? How does the model work? How big does each international opening have to be to justify the cost of the movie? Papa Hegel thinks this will be interesting to watch and see.

—Lynda Obst
March 2014

ACKNOWLEDGMENTS

There are so many people who helped me figure out, write and finish this book, and each helped so much that I feel awards are due.

Best Achievement in Keeping Me Going goes to my über-editor, Alice Mayhew. Through lunch after inspiring lunch at Michael's, she egged me on as she helped me sort out what was happening on the left coast. We made each other laugh as I found the plot. She was my champion, my best company and finally my friend. Without her there would be no book. I wrote *to* her—as she said to me, "I am your audience, not Hollywood. Make *me* understand all this."

Best Male Actor Supporting a Female goes to my terrific agent, Sloan Harris. Sloan puts the "literary" in literary agent, through his reading, editing, careful encouragement and brilliant management of the entire process. As a person who married, birthed and is a sister to agents, I know a great one when I find one.

The Best Supporting New York Cast goes to the first-rate editors who surrounded Alice and became indispensable to me: Karyn Marcus and Jonathan Cox.

Back in Los Angeles are the recipients of the Best Local Editors award: Andrea Cagan, whose input on first read and inspiration kept me going, as it did on *Hello, He Lied;* and Rachel Abarbanell, who is the president of my production company and was charged with keeping it going while I hid out and wrote; she turned into an editor—and a gifted one—herself toward the end of the final draft.

To Kiwi Smith, strategic partner in girl power, pledge sister and early reader with constant, wonderful suggestions and support, my continual thanks, and the title committee—a shout-out to my fine, foxy Silver Lake crew.

And my final award is the Sine Qua Non award. The "Without Which, Nothing" award goes to my interviewees. The generosity of the people to whom I spoke at length and who helped me figure out the puzzle cannot be overestimated. Thank you to Peter Chernin, Sherry Lansing, Jim Gianopulos, John Goldwyn, Michael Lynton, Sue Kroll, Gail Berman, Patrick Moran, Kevin Goetz, Jonah Nolan, and especially my brother, Rick Rosen. Not only is he a smart, superb and classy agent with great creative instincts, he is the best, most generous brother imaginable.

All of these industry leaders took significant time out of their absurdly busy schedules to talk to me for this book. They didn't do it for me (except maybe Rick) but for the love of what they do—this crazy, difficult, constantly changing business. They want the world to understand how the whole puzzle actually works, and how hard they try to make good movies and TV shows.

SOURCES

SCENE ONE: THE NEW ABNORMAL

Aljean Harmetz, quoting Laura Ziskin in the *Hollywood Reporter.* "Laura Ziskin, Producer of 'Spider-Man' and 'Pretty Woman' Dies at 61," *New York Times,* June 13, 2011.

Oly Obst, comments in discussion with author, 2011.

Kevin Goetz, comments in discussion with author, 2011.

SCENE TWO: THE GREAT CONTRACTION

Peter Chernin, interview with author, November 2011.

Cassian Elwes, comments in discussion with author, July 2011.

SCENE THREE: HAVE YOUR POPCORN WITH SOME CHOPSTICKS

Jim Gianopulos, interview with author, September 12, 2012.

Richard Verrier, Ben Fritz, and Sergei Loiko, "Coming Soon to a Theater Near Yuri," *Los Angeles Times,* June 25, 2011.

Sanford Panitch, interview with author, September 15, 2011.

Michael Cieply, "In China Movie Pact, More 3D, Less Reality," *New York Times,* February 19, 2012.

Rachel Abrams, "China's Film Quota Cracked," *Variety,* February 20, 2012.

Clifford Coonan, quoting Zhang Hongsen, vice head of SARFT's Film Bureau, "China Clears 'Dark Knight,' Spidey Showdown," *Variety,* July 19, 2012.

Nikki Finke, "Thomas Tull Forms Legendary East Ltd: Marks Formal Entry into Chinese Film Market," Deadline Hollywood, June 8, 2011.

Steven Zeitchik and Jonathan Landreth, "Hollywood Gripped by Pressure System from China," *Los Angeles Times,* June 12, 2012.

SCENE FOUR: CREATING PREAWARENESS

Vincent Bruzzese, comments in discussion with author, 2011.

Sue Kroll, comments in discussion with author, August 19, 2009.

SCENE FIVE: FROM PARAMOUNT TO PARANOIA

John Goldwyn, interview with author, March 27, 2009.

Sherry Lansing, interview with author, October 11, 2011.

Donald De Line, comments in discussion with author, August 12, 2012.

SCENE SIX: THE CATASTROPHE

Rick Rosen, comments in discussion with author, 2011.

Marc Norman, interview with author, August 18, 2011.

Patric Verrone, comments in discussion with author, October 24, 2012.

Robert Evans, *The Kid Stays in the Picture* (Beverly Hills, CA: New Millennium Press, 2002).

Nikki Finke, quoting an insider, "Exclusive: Talks Day #3 'Stalemated,'" Deadline Hollywood, November 29, 2007.

Chris Keyser, interview with author, December 7, 2011.

SCENE SEVEN: THE DIASPORA

Rick Rosen, comments in discussion with author, 2011.

James Wolcott, "Prime Time's Graduation," *Vanity Fair,* May 2012.

Gail Berman, interview with author, September 15, 2011.

Todd Milliner, interview with author, October 3, 2011.

Jonathan Nolan, interview with author, January 4, 2012.

Patrick Moran, interview with author, June 24, 2011.

SCENE EIGHT: DOES THE FUTURE HAVE A FUTURE?

Jonathan Nolan, interview with author, January 4, 2012.

Michael Lynton, interview with author, December 16, 2011.

PHOTO CREDITS

1. Licensed By: Warner Bros. Entertainment Inc. All Rights Reserved.
2. Photo by Kevin Winter/Getty Images
3. Courtesy of Sue Kroll
4. Courtesy of Kevin Goetz
5. Courtesy of Jim Gianopulos
6. Photo by Eric Charbonneau / BEImages
7. Courtesy of John Goldwyn
8. Photo by Eric Charbonneau / BEImages
9. Courtesy of Gail Berman
10. Photo by Leroy Hamilton
11. Photo by Michael Jones
12. Courtesy of Rick Rosen and Howard Gordon
13. Courtesy of WME
14. Photo by Mike Yarish—© 2012 Viacom International Inc. Courtesy of TV Land
15. Photo: John P. Filo/CBS © 2011 CBS Broadcasting Inc. All Rights Reserved.
16. Photo by Jamie Rector / www.jamierector.com
17. Photo by Susan Baker

INDEX

Abandon, 119–24
Abarbanell, Rachel, 206, 230, 253
ABC Studios, 223, 228
Abduction, 26
About Schmidt, 92
Abraham Lincoln: Vampire Hunter,
    61, 247
Abrams, J. J., 156–57, 200
Accused, The, 110
Adorno, Theodor, 105, 258
Adult Swim, 234
Affleck, Ben, 6, 7, 15, 82, 254
Aftershock, 71
aggregation, 262
Alias, 156
Alice in Wonderland, 5, 67
Al Jolson Sings, 246
All in the Family, 221
Almost Famous, 125
alternate venues, 233–34
Amazing Spider-Man, The, 5, 9, 70, 72,
    241, 258
Amazon, 39, 209, 233, 234, 261
AMC Entertainment, 69, 236–37
American-Arab Anti-Discrimination
    Committee, 114–16
American Horror Story, 199
American Idol, 150, 199, 209, 222, 235
AMPTP (Alliance of Motion Picture
    and Television Producers)
    [aka Moguls], 163, 233
  see also writers' strike

Anastasia, 230
Anderson, Paul Thomas, 92, 159
Anderson, Wes, 258
"Angry Birds," 5
Angus, Thongs and Perfect Snogging,
    157, 159
animation, 3, 129
Annaud, Jean-Jacques, 75
AOL, 262
Apatow, Judd, 8
Apple, 233
Apple Pie quadrant, 87–88, 90, 99
Apted, Michael, 185
Arbitrage, 45
Argo, 6, 16, 82, 254
Aronofsky, Darren, 92, 250
Arrested Development, 204
Assassin's Creed, 5
Association of Talent Agents (ATA),
    186–87
Attanasio, Paul, 201
Aurora, Colorado, shooting, 242
Avary, Roger, 250
Avatar, 48, 51, 63, 67, 71, 75–76, 89,
    244
Avengers, The, 5, 110, 242, 244
Aviv, Oren, 104
Awards Season, 29–30

Bachelorette, 45
Bad Teacher, 21
Bardem, Javier, 62

Basic Instinct, 250

Bateman, Jason, 34

Batman franchise, 5, 6, 47, 204

Battleship, 5, 244

Battlestar Galactica, 231

Bay, Michael, 249

Beasts of the Southern Wild, 45

Beatty, Warren, 133n

Bend It Like Beckham, 157

Bening, Annette, 114, 115

Berman, Gail, 146–48, 150–52,
    156–58, 199–202, 224–26, 230

Berry Pie quadrant, 87, 90, 99

Bertinelli, Valerie, 214

Besson, Luc, 26

Best Exotic Marigold Hotel, The, 152,
    249, 259, 260

Beverly Hills Cop, 109

Bible, 250

Bicks, Jenny, 210

bidding wars, 23

Biden, Joe, 67

Bieber, Justin, 45

Big Bang, 238

Big C, The, 203, 222

Big Chill, The, 10

Bigelow, Kathryn, 7, 47, 254

Big Love, 236

Black Swan, 16, 123, 198, 250

Blair Witch Project, The, 99

Blake, Jeff, 86, 103

Blocker (production exec), 131–32,
    139, 141, 144, 145–46, 148

Body of Lies, 149

Bonaventura, Lorenzo di, 138

Bond, James, 19, 254

Borgias, The, 199

Bourne Ultimatum, The, 146

Bowen, Marty, 229

box office, stability of, 242–43

BoxOfficeMojo.com, 246

Boyle, Danny, 66

Branagh, Kenneth, 8

Bratt, Benjamin, 124

Braun, Lloyd, 199, 201

Brave, 262

Braveheart, 3

Brazil, 9

Breaking Bad, 205, 220, 221, 223, 236

Brewer, Craig, 145

Bridesmaids, 13–18, 33, 204, 249
    and buzz, 15
    and chick flicks, 8, 9, 16, 17–18
    opening, 15, 18, 100
    and Oscar nominations, 199
    overperformance of, 18, 58, 98–99
    and quadrants, 88, 98–99
    and risk-taking, 11
    tracking numbers, 8–9, 13–14, 18

Brillstein-Grey Entertainment,
    143

broadcast television, FCC rules for,
    222

Brothers and Sisters, 229

Bruckheimer, Jerry, 109

Bruzzese, Vinny, 83, 98, 99, 102,
    104–5

BSkyB, 52n

Buchwald, Art, 184

Budde, Jordan, 221, 228, 231

Bullock, Sandra, 53, 61–62, 203, 245n,
    249

Burns, Michael, 245

Butler, The, 42

buzz, 14–15, 84, 101–2

CAA (Creative Artists Agency), 69,
    124, 133, 137, 138, 152, 154, 207

cable TV, 215, 219, 236–37, 239

Cagney and Lacey, 209

Call of Duty, 5

Cameron, James, 7, 48–49, 51, 54–55,
    130

Camp, Colleen, 136

Campbell, Joseph, 108

Can You Keep a Secret?, 131, 139, 141,
    151–53

Captain America, 5

Cars, 11, 89

Casablanca, 105

CBS, 208–10, 211–12, 215, 223, 239, 252

Central Division, 209–12

CGI, 3, 129

Chadha, Gurinder, 157

Chan, Jackie, 101

Chase, David, 204

Cheezburger, 261

Chen Guangcheng, 70

Chernin, Peter, 34–40, 255
   and Fox, 34–36, 52, 106–7, 117, 200
   as producer, 52, 249
   and Titanic, 48–50
   and writers' strike, 186, 187

chick projects, 8–9, 15–17, 244–45, 251–52

China:
   coproduction deals in, 69–74, 75
   as fickle friends, 72–74
   film market in, 56–57, 64, 65, 69–76, 77
   government regulations, 74–76
   piracy in, 68
   and sequels, 76–78
   and 3D, 57, 67–68
   Xi Jinping's U.S. visit, 67, 72, 73–74

China Film Group, 72

chops (acting talent), 21–22

Christo, 84

Clash of the Titans, 79, 85

Clear and Present Danger, 205

Clios (advertising awards), 82

Clooney, George, 6, 7, 23, 92, 124, 133n, 202

Clue, 60

Coen brothers, 159

Columbia Pictures, 112

Columbus, Chris, 120

Comic-Con, 28–29

Connelly, Jennifer, 133n

Connick, Harry, Jr., 53

Contact, 193, 251

"Cookie," 139–41, 146, 148, 150, 151, 153, 157–58

Cooper, Bradley, 43

Coopers, Mini, 138

Costner, Kevin, 9

Coto, Manny, 230–31

Count of Monte Cristo, The, 227, 228–29

Cowboys & Aliens, 61, 244, 247

Creative Artists Agency (CAA), 69, 124, 133, 137, 138, 152, 154, 207

creative destruction, 111

creativity, waning, 33

Criminal Minds, 209

Crouching Tiger, Hidden Dragon, 102

Crowe, Cameron, 125

Cruise, Tom, 109, 151, 154–56

Cruz, Penélope, 18, 62

CSI, 209, 210

Cuesta, Michael, 197

Curious Case of Benjamin Button, The, 104

CW network, 208, 210, 215, 223

Damages, 205, 221

Damon, Matt, 80, 81

Danes, Claire, 196–97, 203

Daniel, Sean, 118

Daniels, Lee, 42

Dark Knight franchise, 5, 27, 63, 69, 70, 72, 84, 215, 216, 217, 242, 254

Dauman, Philippe, 155

Davidson, Eben, 137

Dawson's Creek, 198

Days of Thunder, 109

DC Comics, 146, 247

Deadline Hollywood, 28

DeadlineHollywoodDaily.com, 169–70

Defectives, 230

Definite Interest Intensity (DII), 99–100, 101, 102

De Line, Donald:
  and Paramount, 137, 138–39,
    140–41, 142, 143, 145–50, 249
  and Warner Bros., 149
Dench, Dame Judi, 259
Deng, Wendi, 74–75
Departed, The, 47, 67
Depp, Johnny, 59–60
Dern, Laura, 199, 203
Descendants, The, 92, 104
Desperate Housewives, 235
Devil Wears Prada, The, 88
Dexter, 230
DGA (Directors Guild of America),
    164, 167–68, 180, 183, 185–88
dialectical movement, 248–49
Diaz, Cameron, 21
digital production, 43–45, 232, 261
Dippold, Katie, 249
Disney Studios, 4, 65, 110, 200, 247,
    254
Diving Bell and the Butterfly, The, 153
DMG Entertainment, 73
Dodd, Chris, 67–68
Dolgen, Jon:
  and DVD rights, 2–3, 127
  and Paramount, 2–3, 5, 109, 110,
    117, 127–29, 130, 131, 133, 143,
    150
  and Viacom, 5, 129, 142
Donnie Brasco, 201
Douglas, Michael, 109
Downey, Robert, Jr., 133n
DreamWorks Studios, 47, 74, 89, 143,
    160, 254
Driving Miss Daisy, 10
DVD rights:
  keeping, 2–3, 127
  and Old Abnormal, 36, 37, 40, 232,
    233, 240, 256
  piracy of, 68
  replacing the revenue from, 39, 40,
    50, 57, 106, 234, 260

slipping sales of, 11, 37–40, 191,
    232, 240
and technology, 38–39, 57
and writers' strike, 163, 174, 189, 191

Eat Pray Love, 86
Eisner, Michael, 200
Elwes, Cassian, 41–42, 43
Emily Swan, 228
Endeavor, 203–4
Endgame, 73
Enlightened, 199, 203
Ephron, Nora, 120, 131–32, 194, 198,
    251, 252
Evans, Robert, 126, 174

Facebook, 86, 209, 233
Fail Safe, 202
Family Guy, 249
Fast and the Furious, 12, 33, 129
Fast Five, 8, 11, 33
Fatal Attraction, 109, 110
FCC (Federal Communications
    Commission), 222
Felicity, 156
Few Good Men, A, 204
Field of Dreams, 9
Field, Todd, 133n
50 Cent, 145
Fifty Shades of Grey, 5
Fighter, The, 16, 159
Fincher, David, 21, 86, 104, 203
Finke, Nikki, 169–70, 174–76, 180,
    187–88
Fisher King, The, 9, 10, 257
Flashdance, 23
Flight, 254
Flying Tigers, 71
Ford, Tom, 133n
Forgetting Sarah Marshall, 198
Forrest Gump, 3, 9
Foster, Jodie, 62, 110, 193
Founding of a Party, The, 71

Fowkes, Richard, 144
Fox:
  author's departure from, 106–7,
    112–13, 117
  and Cameron, 48
  and Chernin, 34–36, 52, 106–7,
    117, 200
  international presence of, 4, 65–66,
    74
  and market share, 209
  and Oscar season, 254
  Searchlight, 92, 104
  yearly schedule of, 223
Fox 2000 (Little Fox), 47
Fox Broadcasting Company, 36
Fox Filmed Entertainment, 51–53
Fox International Productions (FIP),
  63, 64, 71
franchises, 5, 8, 12, 18–19, 46, 192,
  220, 245, 250
Frasier, 209, 211, 214
Freston, Tom, 141–44, 145, 148, 150,
  154–56, 159
Friedkin, Billy, 142
Friedman, Rob, 138, 142, 143, 145
Friends, 209, 212, 223, 238
Friends for Life, 251
Friends with Benefits, 198
Fringe, 156
Funny or Die, 233–34, 262

Gabler, Elizabeth, 47
Gaghan, Steve, 119–20, 121–22
Game of Thrones, 214
Gansa, Alex, 196–97
Garfield, Andrew, 5
Garner, Jennifer, 46, 80
Gelfond, Richard, 71
Germany, film market in, 62, 65
Gervais, Ricky, 46, 80, 190
Get Rich or Die Tryin', 145
Gianopulos, Jim, 51–53, 54–56, 58,
  59, 62, 63, 64, 74, 77–78, 106

Gibson, Mel, 3
Gideon's Crossing, 201
Gigli, 15
G.I. Joe, 5, 111
Gilliam, Terry, 9, 257
Gilligan, Vince, 205, 220
Girl with the Dragon Tattoo, The, 203
Gladwell, Malcolm, 190
Glee, 228
Glory, 24
Godfather, The, 126–27, 246
Godfrey, Wyck, 229
Goetz, Kevin, 14, 18–19, 90
Golden Girls, The, 211
Golden Globes, 186, 198–99
Goldwyn, John:
  on craftsmanship, 130–31
  as head of production, 134–35
  leaving Paramount, 137, 139
  and Paramount, 109, 110, 113–17,
    120, 124–26, 129, 130–31, 133–37
Goldwyn, Samuel, 113
Gone with the Wind, 92–94
Goodman, Adam, 160
Google, 233
Gordon, Howard, 196–97, 205
Gordon, Larry, 146, 148
Gossip Girl, 204, 235
Graduate, The, 10
Grant, Hugh, 140
Great Contraction, 37–38, 41, 43,
  46–47, 106, 189
Greenblatt, Robert, 222
Greengrass, Paul, 146
Green Lantern, 5, 82, 149, 244, 249
Green Zone, 146
Grey, Brad:
  and author's contract, 193
  and Berman, 148, 150, 158
  and Brillstein-Grey, 143
  and De Line, 138, 147–48
  and Freston, 143, 145, 156
  and Lesher, 159–60

Grey, Brad (*continued*)
  as Paramount chairman, 57, 108–9,
    110, 143, 144, 145
  and Redstone, 111, 154
  in Russia, 57
  and Spielberg, 160
Grey's Anatomy, 183

Hangover, The, 11, 16–17, 58, 69, 82,
    85, 100, 249
Hanks, Tom, 3, 88, 153, 198
Harry Potter, 3, 5, 12, 80, 129, 130
Harry Potter sequels, 11, 33, 245
Harwood, Sir Ronald, 153
Hasbro, 5, 12, 60, 244
Hawthorne, 202
Hayes, Sean, 213–14
HBO, 4, 236, 239
Hegel, Georg Wilhelm Friedrich,
    248, 251, 262
Hello, He Lied (Obst), 15, 240
Help, The, 16, 21, 47, 254, 259
Hemsworth, Chris, 18
High Definition (HD), 43–44
Hill, Debra, 60
Hill Street Blues, 220
Hipster (production exec), 120, 131,
    133
history, dialectic-driven, 248
Hoffa, Jimmy, 174
Hoffman, Michael, 124
Hollywood Reporter, 9, 146–47
Holmes, Katie, 124
Homeland, 196–97, 203, 205, 215n,
    235, 236
Hong Kong, financial market in, 70
Hope Floats, 47, 53, 88
Hopper, Hedda, 169
hot-burning series, 233
Hot in Cleveland, 211–12, 213–14
House, 150, 199, 201
House of Cards, 203
Howard, Terrence, 145
How I Met Your Mother, 209

How to Lose a Guy in 10 Days, 2–3, 4,
    88, 99, 101, 124–27, 210
Hudson, Kate, 2–3, 8, 125–27,
    131–32, 140–41, 153
Huffington Post, 28
Hulk, The, 102, 103, 138
Hulu, 209, 233, 262
Hunger Games, 5, 28, 62, 89, 130, 242,
    244–45
Hunnam, Charlie, 124
Hurt Locker, The, 7, 47
Hurwitz, Mitch, 204
Hustle & Flow, 145
Huvane, Kevin, 152

IATSE (International Alliance of
    Theatrical Stage Employees),
    180–83
Ice Age, 76–77
Ice Storm, The, 102
ICM, 126
Identity Thief, 34
Igby Goes Down, 125
I Love Lucy, 238
I Love You, Man, 149
IMAX, 57, 67–68, 71, 74, 76
Inception, 47, 63, 69, 79, 82, 83–85, 99
Indecent Proposal, 109, 110
India:
  Bollywood, 64, 66
  film market in, 56, 59
Informant, The, 80, 81
intellectual property, marketability
    of, 130
international market, 4–5, 12, 23, 74
  comedy not viable in, 58–59
  coproduction deals, 69–74
  distribution offices, 63–66, 69
  emergence of, 51–56
  and IMAX, 67–68, 71, 74, 76
  in New Abnormal, 7, 32, 39, 50,
    51–54
  and Old Abnormal, 150–51
  and P&Ls, 40

and sequels, 76–78
and 3D, 66–68, 106
what doesn't travel, 58–61
women, 61–63
Internet, 258, 259, 262–63
alternative venues, 45, 233–34, 239
profit model, 233
and word of mouth, 99
and writers' strike, 38, 163–64, 165, 166, 185
Invention of Lying, The, 46, 80, 81, 190, 206
iPad publishing, 234
iPhone apps, 5
IPs, 246–48
Ipsos (OTX), 83
Iron Man, 5, 70, 88, 110
Irons, Jeremy, 43, 199
Italian Job, The, 138
It's a Wonderful Life, 246
"It's Hard Out Here for a Pimp," 145
iTunes, 39

Jack and Jill, 103
Jackman, Hugh, 211
Jacobson, Nina, 245
Jaffe, Stanley, 109, 112, 116, 130
Jane Eyre, 230
Japan, film market in, 56, 59, 62
Jesus of Nazareth, 250
Johansson, Scarlett, 133n
John Carter, 14, 244
Johnson, Dwayne "The Rock," 8
Jolie, Angelina, 59–60, 62, 151, 203, 245n
Jovovich, Milla, 62
Judd, Ashley, 211
Jules and Jim, 105, 249
Julie & Julia, 88
Jumanji, 5
Just Shoot Me!, 214

Kaliningrad, *Titanic* shown in, 54–56
Kalogridis, Laeta, 187

Karmazin, Mel, 127–28
Katzenberg, Jeffrey, 174
Kavanaugh, Ryan, 69
Kavner, Julie, 252
Kelley, Mike, 229
Kelly, Tatiana, 43, 252
Kessler, Glenn, 205
Kessler, Todd, 205
Keyser, Chris, 188–89
Kid Stays in the Picture, The, 126, 174
Kierkegaard, Søren, 250
Kilday, Gregg, 146–47
King's Speech, The, 254, 259, 261
Kinsella, Sophie, 131, 152
Kirkpatrick, Nancy, 100–101, 147
Kiss the Girls, 110
Klein, Marc, 171
Korshak, Sidney, 174
Kroll, Sue, 79–81, 83, 84–85
K Street, 202
Kudrow, Lisa, 132
Kunis, Mila, 198
Kutcher, Ashton, 198n, 212

Lange, Jessica, 199
Lansing, Sherry:
and De Line, 138–39, 142, 143, 149–50
foundation of, 136, 142
and Goldwyn, 136, 137
last days at Paramount, 142–44
at Paramount, 2–3, 4, 108–13, 117, 120–21, 124–28, 130, 133–34, 145, 150
and previews, 96
Lara Croft: Tomb Raider, 151
Last of the Mohicans, 229
Lautner, Taylor, 26
Law & Order, 18, 220
LA Weekly, 209
Lawrence, Jennifer, 61, 245, 250
Lee, Ang, 6, 47, 102, 138, 254
Lee, Paul, 228
Leeves, Jane, 214

Legally Blonde, 15, 88
Legendary Pictures, 69
Leno, Jay, 186
Lesher, John, 159–60
Les Misérables, 254
Letterman, David, 186
Lewis, Damian, 196
Lewis and Clark, 202
Libatique, Matthew, 123
Life of Pi, 6, 47, 254
Lifetime TV, 87, 239
"lightning in a bottle," 17
Limato, Ed, 126
Lincoln, 6, 254
Linney, Laura, 203
Lion King, The, 89, 262
Lionsgate Studios, 69, 100–101, 242, 245
Looper, 73, 74, 75
Lopez, George, 203
Lopez, Jennifer, 15
Lost, 156
Lost in Thailand, 73
Louis C.K., 46
Lourd, Bryan, 133, 137–38, 175–76, 186, 193
Love Story, 126
Lucas, George, 11, 44, 108
Lucky Numbers, 132
Lynton, Michael, 255–58

MacFarlane, Seth, 242, 249
Machinima, 262
Mad About You, 209
Madagascar, 89, 262
Mad Men, 196, 205, 232, 236
Magic: The Gathering, 60
Malcolm in the Middle, 150, 238
Malik, Wendie, 214
"Man" movies, 8, 29
Marion, Frances, 174, 190
marketing:
    advertising and publicity, 81, 98
    and audience power, 103–5

and commodity fetishism, 105
costs of, 44, 243
creating buzz, 14–15, 84, 101–2
Definite Interest Intensity (DII), 99–100, 101, 102
and the "everything" number, 95–97
in-house, 82–83
and playability, 103
and preawareness, 79–81, 106
quadrant-think, 86–89, 90, 99
selling *Inception,* 83–85
test previews, 89–94
Married . . . with Children, 221, 235
Martin, Suzanne, 211, 213
Marvel comics, 247
Master, The, 92
Matrix, The, 138
MCA, 174
McAvoy, James, 5
McCarthy, Melissa, 17, 34, 199, 249
McConaughey, Matthew, 2, 125–27
Memento, 216, 218
Mendes, Sam, 254
Men in Trees, 210
Mentalist, The, 209
Meredith (girlfriend), 30–31
Meyer, Stephenie, 100
MGM, 254
Microsoft, 233, 234
Mike and Molly, 17, 199, 209
Mildred Pierce, 199
Miller, George, 251
Milliner, Todd, 213–14
Mirror Mirror, 5, 171
Miss America, 223
Mission: Impossible, 5, 75, 110, 151, 154, 200
Mitchell, Joni, 36
Modern Family, 212
Moguls (AMPTP), *see* writers' strike
Moneyball, 47, 60, 254, 257
Monroe, Marilyn, 62
Monty Python and the Holy Grail, 9

Moonrise Kingdom, 258–59
Moonstruck, 10
Moonves, Les, 128, 142, 208–10, 215, 234
Moore, Rob, 145, 150, 156, 160
Moore, Ron, 231
Moran, Patrick, 228–30, 231–32, 233
Morgan, Kathy, 58, 59
Mortal Kombat, 61
Movie People:
  blending with TV People, 200–206
  and the future, 255–58
  vs. Television People, 198–200
  vs. TV profitability, 235–36
movies:
  based on video games, 60–61
  box office stability, 242–43
  marketing, *see* marketing
  microbudgets, 43, 45
  multiple investors in, 42
  original, 106
  parallel worlds in, 48–49
  pitching ideas for, 12–13, 16, 22–27
  playability of, 103
  Prints and Ads costs, 43–44
  profit margin in, 37, 39, 46, 243
  standardization of, 105
  test previews, 89–94
  tight schedules of, 44
  tracking reports of, 13–14, 28
movie studio heads, 48
  as Moguls, *see* writers' strike
movie studios, 11–12
  artists under contract to, 47–48
  and blockbusters, 192
  indies, 13, 44, 46
  and marketing, *see* marketing
  minimajors (without lots), 69
  P&Ls in, 39–40
  and transition, 241
MRC, 46
MTV, 141–42, 145, 156
Mud Pie quadrant, 88, 90, 99
Mummy, The, 118

Murdoch, Rupert, 36, 52–53, 68
Murphy, Eddie, 109
My Name is Khan, 64
MySpace, 154
Mystic Pizza, 126
My Week with Marilyn, 198–99

narrowcasting, 260–61
National Lampoon's Animal House, 118
National Treasure, 104
NBC, 209, 221, 223
NBC/Universal, 222
NCIS, 209
Neeson, Liam, 26
Netflix, 11, 39, 203, 209, 232, 233, 239, 262
Nevins, David, 196
New Abnormal:
  birth of, 1
  casting in, 20–21, 22
  culture changes of, 19–22, 27
  day in the life: online, 27–29
  formula for, 11–12
  "friending" in, 30–32
  and Great Contraction, 41, 46
  international market in, 7, 32, 39, 50, 51–54
  IP frenzy of, 246–48
  "lightning in a bottle," 17
  movie and TV people blending, 200–206
  movies that wouldn't get made in, 9–10
  and Old Abnormal merge, 29–30
  Old Abnormal vs., 7, 240–42
  at Paramount, 4–5, 110
  pitching in, 25–27
  properties chosen in, 4–5
  sequels in, 5, 11–12, 18, 76–78, 106, 130, 245–46
  tentpoles in, 6
  transitions to, 4, 27, 130–31, 260–63
New Regency Enterprises, 65

News Corp., 34
Nichols, Mike, 133n
Nickelodeon, 157
Nielsen rating system, 237n
Noah, 92, 250
No Country for Old Men, 159
Nolan, Christopher, 7, 130, 219
  and *Batman,* 6, 47
  and *Dark Knight,* 84, 217, 254
  and *Inception,* 47, 79
  and *Memento,* 216, 218
Nolan, Jonathan (Jonah), 204,
  215–20, 221
Norman, Marc, 168, 172, 183, 184–85,
  186
Norton, Ed, 138, 202
Notorious, 230
No Way Out, 9
Noyce, Phillip, 205
Number, The, 94, 95–97
Nyswaner, Ron, 153

Observe and Report, 149
Obst, Oly, 46, 80, 140, 153, 190
Occasional, The, 234
O.C., The, 204
Old Abnormal:
  casting in, 19–20, 21
  "chops" in, 21–22
  craftsmanship in, 130
  death of, 1
  and *Hello, He Lied,* 240
  high-concept model, 16–17, 109–10
  and international, 150–51
  Movie People vs. Television People
    in, 198–200
  and New Abnormal merge,
    29–30
  New Abnormal vs., 7, 240–42
  at Paramount, 2–4, 109, 117
  pitching ideas in, 12–13, 16, 22–27
  transitions from, 4, 27, 130–31,
    260–63

One Day at a Time, 214
One Fine Day, 23, 124
online distribution, 261
online streaming, 163, 232, 233
Oscars:
  dominated by independents, 13
  and writers' strike, 186, 190
Oscar Season, 29–30, 45
  (2012), 45, 254–55
  (2013), 6
OTX (Ipsos), 83, 90, 99
Ouija, 60

Pain & Gain, 249
Paltrow, Gwyneth, 124–25
Pan Am, 223
Panitch, Sanford, 63, 64–65, 66, 73
Paramount Pictures:
  author's contract not renewed by,
    193–95
  author's move to, 108–14, 118
  conservatism of, 2–4, 110, 121,
    127–31, 150
  flops, 127, 133–35
  international franchises, 5, 150–51,
    157
  and market share, 110–11, 129
  networks of, 208
  and New Abnormal, 4–5, 110
  and Old Abnormal, 2–4, 109, 117
  and Oscar season, 254
  reducing the budget, 118, 127–28
  and Scorsese, 47
Paramount TV:
  author's move to, 206–8
  and *Central Division,* 209–12
  schedule of, 215
Paramount Vantage, 159–60
Paranormal Activity, 60, 160
Parker, Ol, 152
Parker Bros., 60
Parks and Recreation, 249
Pascal, Amy, 47, 149, 255, 257

Patel, Dev, 259
Patmore-Gibbs, Suzanne, 228, 229
Patriot Games, 205
Patterson, James, 110
Payne, Alexander, 92
Pecan Pie quadrant, 88, 90
Penn, Sean, 133n
Perry, Katy, 210
Person of Interest, 204, 216
Peters, Christine, 125
Petrie, Donald, 126
Pfeiffer, Michelle, 23, 124
Philadelphia, 153
Pianist, The, 153
piracy, 11, 39, 43, 68, 165, 233
Pirates of the Caribbean, 8, 11, 12, 104
Pitt, Brad, 47, 60, 111, 143, 202, 257
Pixar, 262
Plageman, Greg, 216
Planet of the Apes, 5, 33, 34, 35
Playboy, 223
Ponte, Gideon, 123
Pontius Pilate, 250
Porsandeh, Cameron, 231
Portman, Natalie, 198
preawareness, 12, 35, 78, 79–81, 106, 192, 244, 248, 250
Precious, 42
Pretty Woman, 9
Private Practice, 183
Proposal, The, 88

quadrant-think, 86–89, 90, 98–99
Quaid, Dennis, 43
Quiz Show, 201

Rabbit-Proof Fence, 205
Raff, Gideon, 196
Rahman, Sheik, 115
recession, 38, 189, 192, 240
Redford, Robert, 203n

Redstone, Sumner M., 111, 127–28, 141, 154–56
Relativity Media, 69
Remington Steele, 204
Resnick, Adam, 132
Revenge, 205, 227–28, 230, 231
Rhimes, Shonda, 183
Rich, Blair, 80
Ripa, Kelly, 133n
Rise of the Planet of the Apes, 33, 34, 35
risk aversion, 2–4, 11, 40
Roberts, Emma, 157
Roberts, Julia, 9, 62, 86, 126
Robinov, Jeff, 80, 81
Robinson, Matthew, 46
Romeo and Juliet, 48–49
Rosen, Rick, 147, 150, 207–8
  and *Homeland,* 196–97
  on profitability, 237–39
  on TV-movie blending, 202–4, 205
  and writers' strike, 166, 186
Rothman, Tom, 52
Rudin, Scott, 137, 203
Russia:
  film market in, 65, 67
  Titanic shown in, 54–56
  Transformers shown in, 57
Ryan, Meg, 198
Ryan, Shawn, 186

Saldana, Zoe, 43
Salt, 205
Sandler, Adam, 103
Saturday Night Live (SNL), 15, 214
Schwartz, Josh, 204
Schwarzenegger, Arnold, 173
Scorsese, Martin, 47, 67
Scott, Ridley, 149
Scott, Seann William, 141
Screen Actors Guild (SAG), 167–68
Screen Engine, 90
seasons, 224–26
Seinfeld, 209, 221

Sella, Tony, 104
Selznick, David O., 5, 92–94, 97
Sense and Sensibility, 102
sequel fatigue, 105–6
sequels, 5, 11–12, 18, 33, 76–78, 106, 130, 245–46
Serendipity, 171
Seven Years in Tibet, 75
Sex and the City, 210
Shakespeare in Love, 168
Shalhoub, Tony, 116
Shanghai Knights, 101
Shankman, Adam, 141
Sheridan, Jim, 145
Sherry Lansing Foundation, 136, 142
Showgirls, 250
Showtime, 196–97, 199, 215n, 222
Shrek, 3, 129
Siege, The, 23, 24, 113, 114, 119
Silver Linings Playbook, The, 16
Simanton, Keith, 246
Simon, David, 204
Simon, Ellen, 125
Simpson, Don, 109
Sixties, The, 207
Skyfall, 254
Sky TV, 117
Sleepless in Seattle, 88, 99, 198
Slumdog Millionaire, 66, 104, 259
Smash, 222
Smith, Kiwi, 15, 171
Smith, Maggie, 259
Smith, Pinkett, 202
Smith, Will, 202
Snider, Stacey, 47, 143
Snow Flower and the Secret Fan, 74
Snow White and the Huntsman, 5
Social Network, The, 86, 103–4, 203, 204, 254
Soho House, 29
Someone Like You, 211
Something Borrowed, 8
Something's Gotta Give, 88

Sony Pictures:
    author's deal with, 221–23, 230–31, 235
    and China, 70–71, 72, 73
    international television, 235
    and marketing, 86
    and *Moneyball,* 47
    and Oscar season, 254
Sopranos, 204
Sorkin, Aaron, 104, 204
special effects, 3, 75, 129–31
Spider-Man, 5, 9, 70, 72, 241, 258
Spielberg, Steven, 6, 21, 84, 130, 143, 160, 222, 250, 254
Stanley, Alessandra, 227
Star Trek, 5, 100, 110, 151, 200
Star TV, 4, 52
Star Wars, 11
Steel, Dawn, 23, 65, 112
Steers, Burr, 125
Step-Dude, 140
Stewart, Jon, 186
Stewart, Kristen, 245
Stone, Emma, 5, 21
Stone, Oliver, 133n
Stowe, Madeleine, 229
Streep, Meryl, 61–62
Sucker Punch, 82
Summit Entertainment, 69
Sundance, 45, 145, 252
Superbad, 21
Sutton, Willie, 205, 235
Swingtown, 229
SyFy, 231, 235

tadpoles, 9–10, 41–46, 258–59, 260–61
Taken, 26–27
Tarantino, Quentin, 61
Tartikoff, Brandon, 200
Tassler, Nina, 209
TBS (Turner Broadcasting System), 234
Teamsters Union, 174, 180

technology, 11
  digital shooting, 43–45, 232, 261
  emails, 31–32
  "film program" manipulating
    pixels, 44
  and Great Contraction, 37–38, 41,
    43
  High Definition (HD), 43–44
  IMAX, 57, 67–68, 71, 74, 76
  online streaming, 163, 232, 233
  special effects, 3, 75, 129–31
  3D, 57, 66–68, 76, 106
  and writers' strike, 38–39
Ted, 198, 242, 249–50
television:
  advertising, 228, 237, 239
  author's move to, 194–95
  and the "Brightly Burning Show,"
    231–33
  broadcast, 208, 222
  cable, 215, 219, 236–37, 239
  digital outlets, 232–34
  FCC rules, 222
  golden age of, 220
  international, 235
  network, 216–20, 228, 237, 239
  online streaming, 232–33
  ownership of, 236–39
  packaging fees, 237
  pitch season, 32, 226–27
  profitability of, 205–6, 235–39
  rating points, 237
  reality programming, 165
  seasons, 224–26
  series, 206, 253
  showrunners, 180, 183, 191
  studios, 236–37
  syndication rights, 228, 235, 237, 238
  as writer's medium, 191, 195, 219
Television People:
  blending with Movie People,
    200–206
  vs. Movie People, 198–200

Tellem, Nancy, 234
tentpole movies, 5–7, 12, 18, 23, 35,
  41, 46, 130, 192, 204, 244, 246
That '70s Show, 198
There's Something About Mary, 21
There Will Be Blood, 159
Theron, Charlize, 138
Thing, The, 5
Third Rock from the Sun, 209
This Is My Life, 252
This Is Your Life, 251
Thor, 5, 8, 15, 18, 88
3D, 57, 66–68, 76, 106
Time Warner, 235
Titanic, 3, 48–50, 51, 54–56, 89, 244
Tomb Raider, 61
Top Gun, 109
Toronto Film Festival, 79–80
Tourist, The, 59–60
Town, The, 16
Toy Story, 89, 262
Traffic, 119
Traister, Rebecca, 15
Transformers, 5, 11, 12, 57, 63, 110,
  160, 249
Travolta, John, 132
TriStar, 73
Tull, Thomas, 69, 74
TV Land, 213–14
12 Monkeys, 9
21 and Over, 70
Twentieth-Century Fox Film, 36
24, 150, 199, 205, 231–32
Twilight franchise, 5, 11, 28, 69, 89,
  100–101, 130, 229, 244
Twitter, 261
Two and a Half Men, 209, 212, 238

United 93, 146
Universal Studios, 242, 254
UPN (United Paramount Network),
  232
Utley, Nancy, 104

VanCamp, Emily, 229
Vane, Dick, 121–22
Vanity Fair, 199
Vantage, 159–60
Variety, 28, 49, 169
Verhoeven, Paul, 250
Verrone, Patric, 167, 171, 187–89
Viacom, 5, 127–29, 130, 142, 154–56
video games, 60–61
video on demand (VOD), 39, 45
Voice, The, 222

Wahlberg, Mark, 138, 159
WALL-E, 262
Wanda group, 69, 71
Warner Bros.:
    and China, 70–71, 72
    and Christopher Nolan, 47, 79
    and DC catalog, 247
    decision-making in, 81–82
    and franchises, 12, 192
    and *Harry Potter,* 12, 80
    and HBO, 4
    and *Inception,* 84
    and *Matrix,* 138
    and Oscar season, 254
    Worldwide Marketing, 79–81
War of the Worlds, 143, 145
Washington, Denzel, 24, 114, 116
Wasserman, Lew, 174, 176
Watchmen, 146, 148
Wedding Crashers, The, 58–59
Weeds, 222
Weiner, Matt, 205
Weiner, Tim, 24
Weitz, Richard, 213
Welcome to the Sticks, 59
Weston, Brad, 152–53, 159–60
West Wing, 204
Whitaker, Forest, 42
White, Betty, 214
Wiatt, Jim, 137
Wiig, Kristen, 15–16, 17

Wilde, Olivia, 43
Wilkinson, Tom, 259
Will & Grace, 209, 213
Williams, Michelle, 198
Willis, Bruce, 114
Wilson, Luke, 125
Wilson, Owen, 101, 141
Winchell, Walter, 169
Winfrey, Oprah, 42
Winnie (financier), 2
Winslet, Kate, 199
Wire, The, 204, 220
Witherspoon, Reese, 133n
WME, 166, 197, 207, 210, 231, 237
Wolcott, James, 199, 215
Wolitzer, Meg, 251
Words, The, 43
World of Warcraft, 5, 61
World Trade Center, 1993 bombing,
    24, 115
World War Z, 111
Wright, Lawrence, 115
Writers Guild of America (WGA),
    162–95
Writers Guild strike (1959–60), 166,
    174
Writers Guild strike (1988), 38, 162,
    163, 166, 167, 174, 185
writers' strike (2008), 23, 109, 162–95
    aftermath of, 190–95, 200–201
    Ardent Fall, 171–76
    and author's contract not renewed,
        193–95
    and Christmas, 179–80
    and DGA, 164, 167–68, 180, 183,
        185–88
    Fading February, 180–90
    force majeure, 178–79, 193
    and Internet market, 38, 163–64,
        165, 166, 185
    and Moguls (AMPTP), 163–68,
        172, 176–79, 183–87, 190–92, 233
    narrator, 169–70

and the next one, 189–90, 233
October 2007 strike deadline,
    164–69
and Oscar deadline, 186, 190
and recession, 38
and technology, 38–39
Wu, Bruno, 69

Xbox, 234
X-Files, The, 205
Xi Jinping, 67, 72, 73–74
X-Men: First Class, 5, 8

Young, David, 171, 187
Young, Jim, 43
YouTube, 27, 45, 100, 209, 233, 239,
    261

Zelman, Daniel, 205
Zemeckis, Robert, 3, 251, 254
Zero Dark Thirty, 7, 47, 254
Ziskin, Laura, 9, 42, 123, 202
Zwick, Ed, 24, 69, 113, 114–15, 119

ABOUT THE AUTHOR

Lynda Obst, author of the bestseller *Hello, He Lied,* was an editor for *The New York Times Magazine* before entering the film industry. She has produced more than sixteen feature films, including *How to Lose a Guy in 10 Days, Contact, The Fisher King, Adventures in Babysitting, Hope Floats,* and two films with Nora Ephron, *Sleepless in Seattle* and *This Is My Life.* She is now producing television as well.